Selfishness, Altruism, and
Rationality

Selfishness, Altruism, and Rationality

A Theory of Social Choice

HOWARD MARGOLIS
Center for International Studies
Massachusetts Institute of Technology

CAMBRIDGE UNIVERSITY PRESS 1982
Cambridge
London New York New Rochelle
Melbourne Sydney

Published by the Press Syndicate of the University of Cambridge
The Pitt Building, Trumpington Street, Cambridge CB2 1RP
32 East 57th Street, New York, NY 10022, USA
296 Beaconsfield Parade, Middle Park, Melbourne 3206, Australia

First published 1982

Printed in the United States of America

Library of Congress Cataloging in Publication Data
Margolis, Howard.
Selfishness, altruism, and rationality.
Includes index.
1. Social choice. 2. Altruism. 3. Self-interest. I. Title.
HB846.8.M37   302   81-17003
ISBN 0 521 24068 9   AACR2

FOR EUGENE B. SKOLNIKOFF

Director, Center for International Studies
Massachusetts Institute of Technology

Contents

Preface

In the fall of 1974, puzzled by the results of an article on voluntary contributions to the supply of a public good,[1] I reformulated its argument and found that it led to a version of the contribution paradox discussed in Chapter 2 of this study. This in turn made me realize (although it seems obvious enough in hindsight) that the long-standing puzzle for rational choice theorists over why people bother to vote was a symptom of a deeper difficulty that can arise whenever the conventional model of rational choice is applied in the context of public goods. A note I then wrote ended with the remark that a forthcoming paper would propose a solution to this difficulty.

When I came across that note recently I was surprised by its bold ending but then remembered writing it in a "throwing your hat over the wall" spirit, without any idea of how the job could actually be done. But a couple of months later, prompted by one of those notices we all see about doing our fair share for the United Fund, I did get an idea for an allocation rule that would describe what gives a person the psychological sense that he has done his fair share in the way he has allocated his resources between spending on himself and altruistic spending. However, the social context for which I was able to work out the formal properties of the rule was very narrow, assuming a society in which there are only pure public and pure private goods, everyone has identical tastes, government spending financed by taxes is ignored, and more. Beyond all these strong simplifying assumptions a further difficulty arose, which was that I could not specify a utility function that would yield my allocation rule. Within the conventional framework, rational choice is routinely taken to mean maximizing a utility function. Hence my argument looked not only restricted in scope by the special assumptions but also intrinsically unfinished. For my part, this was unimportant compared with the fact that the rule seemed intuitively plausible and (at least within my very simple model) led to pretty results. I was perfectly willing to leave the problem of how to make it mathematically respectable to the mathematicians. But others, understandably, did not find that quite satisfactory.

I returned to the paper now and again over the next two years, revising but not essentially changing the draft. By mid-1977, though, I began working intensively on what I hoped would be a thorough treatment. The eventual result was this book. All the restrictive assumptions of the original argument have been dropped, and the whole topic is approached from a fresh point of view in terms of which the difficulty of showing how the allocation rule can be derived as maximizing a utility function simply evaporates. For in terms of the Darwinian viewpoint from which the argument now develops there is neither need nor reason to suppose that any such function exists. Oddly, given that same Darwinian point of view, one can provide a solution of sorts of the "total utility" puzzle (as shown in Appendix C). But there is no longer any reason to take the issue seriously, and that solution plays no role in the argument of the main text. On the other hand, from the Darwinian viewpoint, interesting connections are suggested between the extension of "rational choice" that arises when we allow for social as well as self-interested preferences and the old puzzle of the duality of human nature (man as private, self-seeking individual; man as citizen and social being), and with the id-superego-ego personality structure proposed by Freud.

In working all this out, I profited greatly from the comments on my drafts of George Rathjens (political science), Jerome Rothenberg (economics) and Joshua Cohen (philosophy). During this period, I was also indebted to many other people who took an interest in the work, of whom I should particularly mention Sam Beer, Amy Leiss, Lucian Pye, Ithiel Pool, and Jack Ruina. Robert Solow and Henry Brady commented on early versions of the argument. Within the economics literature, the closest analog I have run across to the kind of argument I will be making is that of Amartya Sen's "Rational Fools," which may well have influenced my own work.[2]

After the study began to circulate, I incurred a new set of debts. Particularly helpful, in one way or another, were Jack Hirshleifer, Robert Dorfman, Richard Musgrave, Joe Oppenheimer, Gordon Tullock, Russell Hardin, Martin Kessler, Nic Tideman, Marion Just, Joshua Epstein, Thomas Kuhn, E. C. Banfield, and Carl Kaysen.

I am grateful for comments on the Darwinian argument of Chapter 3 from Stephen Jay Gould, David Layzer, Charles Lumsden, Roger Masters, and Robert M. May.

Brian Barry was not only encouraging but (in his capacity as editor of *Ethics*) provided me with the occasion to write a reasonably nontechnical formulation of the main ideas (most of it now incorporated here as part of Chapter 4). Mancur Olson has been supportive of this work since its inception, and although I have not persuaded him that the departures I make from conventional utility-maximizing are as desirable as I think they are, I am much in his debt.

Almost the earliest, certainly the most detailed and helpful comments on the completed draft, and I expect also the most influential in getting others to take seriously an unconventional argument from an unestablished source, came from Tom Schelling. My own feeling that insight into social choice could be derived from rather simple abstract models itself had come substantially from Schelling's own work; so there was no one whose sympathetic interest I could have been more pleased to arouse.

I owe the most obvious sort of gratitude to the Andrew Mellon Foundation for financial support, and to the MIT Center for International Studies for a congenial professional home. Neither would have been possible without the patience and support of Gene Skolnikoff, director of the CIS, to whom this book is dedicated.

Finally, I wish to acknowledge my youngest but far from least incisive critic, Peter Margolis, and my most consistent supporter in this endeavor and closest associate, Joan Margolis.

Special notation

S = utility from the point of view of pure self-interest.

G = utility from the point of view of pure group-interest.

$S'(x)$, $G'(x)$ = marginal utility of spending on x; if no argument is given (i.e., S', G'), the spending is on whatever good will maximize marginal utility.

s = spending to maximize S-utility.

g = spending to maximize G-utility.

W = a weighting function, $W = f(g,s)$.

G'/S' = the value ratio = the ratio of marginal utilities of spending in group- versus self-interest.

C = the conventional model of choice used within economic theory.

FS = the "fair share" model of choice developed in this study.

C, FS, G, and S are used frequently to modify terms such as motivation, utility, model, and allocation. Thus G-utility is utility from the point of view of group-interest; FS-motivation is motivation as postulated by the theory developed here; S-spending is spending that maximizes S-utility (so that s, defined above, is the sum of an individual's S-spending). From these definitions, $G' = \partial G/\partial g$ (or in the notation I will often use, G_g), G'' is the rate at which G' changes with further G-spending.

Introduction

Classical economic theory always assumes that the individual will "act in his interest"; but it never examined carefully the entity to which "his" refers. Often, as when households are taken as the unit for income and consumption, it is implicitly assumed that "the family" or "the household" is this entity whose interest is being maximized. Yet this is without theoretical foundation, merely a convenient but slipshod device. In this case, as in many others (e.g., when a man is willing to contribute much, even his life, to national defense, rather than use a strategy which will push the cost onto others), men act *as if* the "his" referred to some entity larger than themselves. That is, they appear to act in terms, not of their own interest, but of the interests of a collectivity or even of another person. Indeed, if they did not do so, the basis for society could hardly exist.

Yet how can this be reconciled with the narrow premise of individual interest . . . we could simply solve the problem by fiat, letting "his" refer to whatever entity the individual appeared to act in the interest of. This obviously would make the theory trivially true, and never disconfirmable. A more adequate solution is one which states the conditions under which the entity in whose interests he acts will be something other than himself.

James S. Coleman, in Papers on Non-Market Decision-Making

. . . as regards useful acts, one might ask, useful to whom? To the individual who performs them or to society? The two utilities are only too separate and distinct, and it would seem necessary to have had very little experience of the world to maintain that an action that is useful to society is generally useful to the individual who performs it, and vice versa.

Gaetano Mosca, The Ruling Class

Although I ran across the quotations from Coleman and Mosca near the end of this effort, they sum up very happily the problem I had hoped to solve and the nature of the solution I propose.

As explained in some detail in Chapter 1, at the foundation of an empirically tenable theory of public choice, we require a model of individual choice that does not fail catastrophically in the presence of public goods. But the conventional model of choice does so fail, the most familiar illustration being its inability to account for the elementary fact that people vote.

The essential problem is to provide a model of choice capable of accounting for the observation that people make contributions to what they perceive as the public interest (as by perceiving and acting upon a duty to vote) in contexts where the return to the individual appears inconsequen-

1

tial and the effect on society is microscopic. How can this be reconciled with the notion of rational, self-interested individuals, which proves so potent in analyzing economic behavior?

Mosca gives the key to a solution: to recognize the futility of supposing that utility to society can be understood as congruent with utility to the individual. If individuals are observed to be acting in a manner that seems rational from a social but not an individual point of view, then – without prejudice yet to the conventional model of choice – we can say that they are acting *as if* they had two different utility functions.

On as small a matter as bothering to vote, or as large a matter as risking one's life in time of war, we have no difficulty seeing the behavior as a rational use of resources *if* the utility function the individual is seeking to maximize concerns group-interest rather than self-interest.

Further, such a presumption is not *necessarily* inconsistent with individual utility-maximizing. Such inconsistency would exist only if we supposed that utility to society was something determined for the individual, or given to the individual, rather than his own perception of group-interest. But if we clearly understand that the group-utility the individual seeks to maximize is his own perception of group-interest, and by no means necessarily identical to someone else's perception, then the individual is using any resources allocated to group-interest to maximize his own group-interested utility function.

So far, though, we have only reformulated the problem. Instead of a puzzle as to how an individual maximizing his own interest could use resources rationally to further group-interest, we have the puzzle of what governs the extent to which this individual uses resources to maximize his self-interested preferences, on the one hand, and his group-interested preferences, on the other. How do what we might for the moment call his "ultimate preferences" somehow reconcile his group- and self-interested preferences?

This point of view leads us to ask a question that would otherwise seem entirely bizarre. If we imagine that inside Smith there are two individuals – an *S*-Smith who values only his own self-interest, and a *G*-Smith who values only his perception of group-interest – is it possible to specify an allocation rule, or a Social Welfare Function for this two-person "society," with the property that, given this rule, Smith behaves the way we empirically observe real people to behave?[1]

I suggest a Darwinian basis for such a rule, leading to a model that is compatible with conventional economic theory in a private-goods-only context, but appears to perform splendidly in the kind of public-goods contexts in which more conventional treatments fail. Indeed, I would argue, the range of possible applications is remarkably wide.

The model turns out to have a number of interesting and some curious properties. For example, the internal G- (group-interested) and S- (self-interested) functions prove to be cardinal; but the allocation rule applied to the G- and S- functions produces a set of ultimate preferences that are defined only ordinally. So the model seen from "inside Smith" is cardinal, whereas Smith's preference structure observed from the outside appears to be only ordinal. Inside Smith, every good, public or private, is a pure public good; for G-Smith and S-Smith inhabit the same body. We require some equivalent of the referee in Samuelson's pseudomarket, which allocates Smith's income between S-Smith and G-Smith and assigns Lindahl prices for these goods.

For all this, the model remains basically very simple. Everything follows from a simple equilibrium condition. Seeing what is implied by that condition and how it might work may be difficult, but the central idea is not.

The text of this volume is intended to be accessible to a sophisticated, but not technically expert, audience. The style is informal. Technical details not essential to seeing the main line of the argument are left to the appendixes. But even a casual reader should at least look through the appendixes. For the reader with a taste for technical arguments, I have provided cross-references between the main text and the appendixes. I have tried to arrange the index to help readers who wish to review points of the argument when they are invoked elsewhere in the text.

What follows is a summary of the argument, keyed to the chapter divisions.

Chapter 1

A satisfactory theory of social choice requires a model of individual choice that is consistent with the way human beings are observed to behave. Yet, even after a generation of work on the problem of applying the economic "rational choice" perspective to social choice, often leading to striking results, this fundamental problem remains unresolved. We still lack a model that accommodates (without fudging) such obvious observations as that citizens bother to vote and do not always cheat when no one is looking. A resolution of this difficulty can be expected to require some departure from conventional assumptions.

Chapter 2

If we look at some examples of empirical situations in which the conventional model leads to paradoxical results, we can see that what is needed is a way to formulate a model that allows for three distinct components of motivation: self-interest, group-interest, and participation. Further, although this might seem easy to do offhand, for example, by summing these as three sources of utility, a little technical analysis shows that no such straightforward solution could work.

Chapter 3

From a Darwinian view, however, one can see how a mechanism for balancing the claims of self- versus group-interest might arise (trading off private versus social advantage). We are led to an equilibrium condition that turns out to incorporate the three motives developed in Chapter 2. ($W = G'/S'$, where W is the value of a weighting function governed by participation; G' and S' are marginal utilities of spending in group- versus self-interest.) Further, it turns out that this line of analysis is not very vulnerable to "selfish gene" arguments against the feasibility of such a balancing device.

Chapter 4

The same equilibrium condition can be developed in terms of an introspective argument about what gives us a sense of having done our "fair share" (that is, what gives us a psychological sense of being in equilibrium.) The two ways of reaching the equilibrium condition are complimentary. The model that results turns out to have some elegant formal properties. Several concerns and possible misperceptions that arise out of the model's departures from customary usage are discussed in detail.

Chapter 5

A further set of questions arises once we move from thinking about the model in terms of abstract choice to how it would work in real situations. Some of these issues can only be framed and approaches discussed (the dynamics of group-loyalty in complex societies, for example); some lend themselves to rather detailed solutions (how to handle choice that involves costs and benefits to both self- and group-interest, for example). Chapter 5 treats these two topics, plus satisficing, psychic income, nonrational motivation, coerced spending (taxes), and various other matters.

Chapter 6

The model turns out to have application to some matters prominent in the current economics literature: in particular, to the notion of demand-revealing mechanisms ("incentive compatibility"). This provides an opportunity to try to follow Kuhn's advice on the problem of "translating across paradigms."

Chapters 7, 8, and 9

The remaining three chapters involve no technical material beyond some equations (in Chapter 7) of the kind used by Downs in his *Economic Theory of Democracy*. However, given a model of choice that accounts in a nonvacuous way for the three components of motivation mentioned earlier, it requires no formal manipulations to see that many aspects of social behavior fit this model and that many acts often considered mutually inconsistent (and hence inconsistent with the notion of rational choice) turn out to be quite the sort of behavior the model developed here implies. Chapter 7 deals with voting; Chapter 8, with a series of topics treated by Downs and Olson in their path-breaking books; and Chapter 9 is a miscellany of further topics. These many illustrations are intended to give the reader a more concrete sense of how the model works and to suggest some areas of empirical investigation in which use of the model might prove fruitful.

The main overall result, I am inclined to argue, is how strikingly wide a range of social behavior can be comprehended in terms of what is, after all, a rather simple model. There is more "inside Smith" than S-Smith and G-Smith. But I would like to think that looking at Smith in terms of G-Smith and S-Smith is a good beginning.

CHAPTER 1

Overview

At the heart of economic theory is an abstract model of rational choice. Highly idealized actors (consumers and producers; households and firms) operate in a highly idealized setting (perfectly efficient markets) exchanging highly idealized objects (pure private goods). Each actor seeks to maximize an index known as a utility function, whose value depends on the vector (list) of goods possessed by that actor. Rationality, in the model, implies very little beyond a certain consistency of choice: if I prefer A to B and B to C, then I prefer A to C.[1]

Yet this highly artificial scheme turns out to be a powerful aid to understanding what happens in the real world, where all of its very special assumptions are at best only crude simplifications. Further, this highly idealized model provides the point of departure for more realistic analyses that relax the various "perfect" assumptions.

Since the early 1950s, there have been efforts to broaden the applicability of the scheme to include political choice as well as choices mediated through markets. However, the basic "economic man" model is unreliable in the context of public goods, which is to say, in the context of politics.[2] Here the model correctly identifies the "free-rider" problem as absolutely crucial. But it rather overkills this issue. The conventional economic model not only predicts (correctly) the existence of problems with free riders but also predicts (incorrectly) such severe problems that no society we know could function if its members actually behaved as the conventional model implies they will.

We therefore face the following puzzle: a theory of the efficient allocation of resources lies at the very core of economic reasoning. Economists – even the radical critics of conventional economics – cannot do without it. The theory involves great simplification of reality. It does not notably enhance one's ability to become a millionaire or even to be an intelligent consumer. Nevertheless, to understand economic phenomena and public policy involving the allocation of resources, you should not do without some understanding of the basic conceptual framework of economic theory, which treats the interaction of individual rational choice and social effects. This is so for essentially the same reasons that a practicing engineer finds it important to have some understanding of pure physics: in the real world there are no frictionless machines, perfect vacuums, and so on, but to deal effectively with the real world it helps to have an understanding of how things would work in the simplified world of well-chosen idealized models. In particular, the idealized models, although often unable – in engineering as well as in economics – to predict what occurs in situation A, often can say a good deal about the way outcomes will change in situation B, given a calibrating observation in situation A.

Yet the world of political behavior, like the world of economic behavior, concerns phenomena that emerge as the aggregate effects of individual choices. Further, the individuals involved need not be less rational than the individuals treated by economic theory: in fact, they are the same individuals. We are all citizens, just as we are all consumers. If it is possible to gain insight into aggregate economic phenomena by exploring models that start with idealized individual actors choosing rationally, why should not the same methods lead to fruitful results in politics?

The short answer is that it does. In fact the range of insights into social choice that have come from the economic approach is striking. A large fraction of the most interesting work on social choice (in a wide sense, which includes political choice) in recent decades has come from economists; and further contributions have come from others who approach the problems of social choice from an economic perspective.[3]

But there is disagreement on the question of how far this work can go within the conventional framework of rational choice offered by economic theory.

There is, first, the argument that, although it may not be exactly true that all human behavior can be explained in terms of narrow self-interest, that explanation is a good enough approximation on which to found the analysis of social choice.[4] A second view would allow that narrow self-interest is too narrow a basis for understanding social choice; but it supposes that, insofar as it is important to allow for social motivation, that can be done in terms of a more or less straightforward extension of the conventional theory. For there is a long tradition in economics of interpreting self-interest loosely so that self-interested behavior need not be treated as necessarily selfish behavior.[5] I will have more to say on this in Chapter 6. Here I only want to note the possibility that without departing in any radical way from what Kuhn has taught us to call the economist's "paradigm," a good deal of social motivation can be allowed for.

Third, there is the view that accounting for social choice simply requires at least two distinct modes of analysis: following Barry, the sociological and the economic modes. So one can also argue that whatever cannot be accounted for within the economic paradigm must be dealt with in terms of another, incommensurable (for now, if not necessarily forever) mode of analysis.[6]

In contrast to any of these views I will be trying to show that there is extensive, hitherto unexplored, ground where the scope of the economic model can be extended considerably – provided we do not restrict our notions of what a model of rational choice will be like to conceptions shaped by the traditional concerns, and hence also by the habits of mind, of economics. I will also try to show that in terms of the extension of the traditional model I will propose, there exist at least the foundations for a natural bridge between the economic and sociological modes of analysis.

How could it be that, even in narrowly economic contexts, a treatment in terms of rational choice could work out at all well? Any such assumption of rational choice surely involves a drastic simplification of how actual individuals behave, even in the marketplace.

But it turns out to be useful to understand how rational individuals *would* behave, in large part (though not solely) because empirically, major features of the world of economics work *as if* individuals were behaving rationally. Not only is it useful to interpret actual behavior in terms of the formal model, but where reality and the model diverge the source of the difficulty generally is not in the assumption of rational individuals but in other assumptions, such as perfectly competitive markets and complete information. Finally, the rough consistency of aggregate behavior with rational individual behavior, while perhaps greater than we could have counted on, is not astonishing despite the considerable evidence of irrationality (even in the narrowly technical sense of that term) observable in individual behavior. Real individuals, in fact, are not always rational in the sense of exhibiting internally consistent patterns of choice. But they try to be. Indeed, as the "cognitive dissonance" theorists stress, much of the irrationality (in a somewhat different and deeper sense) in actual life traces to the need people feel to make their beliefs internally consistent.[7] Thus, although individuals are not perfectly rational (even in the narrow sense of economic theory), and even though aggregate behavior may be significantly irrational (in a deeper sense), it is nevertheless comprehensible that rational (narrow sense) models turn out to work quite well over a considerable range of behavior.

However, supposing that choice might usefully be modeled using an axiom of internal consistency does not necessarily get us very far. The basic concepts of rational choice can be worked out leaving "utility" as an undefined, primitive term. But to make the theory applicable to the world we need to say something about what we suppose individual actors are being internally consistent *about*. Here it is not hard to see that some departures from conventional economic notions of utility-maximizing are likely to be required when we extend the notion of rational choice from markets to politics. For supposing the reader will grant that it might be possible to apply some kind of rational choice (i.e., internally consistent) model of individual choice to politics, he may very reasonably doubt that one can get very far simply by imposing on politics the classical economic model of choice. This classical model is profoundly shaped by its root concern with the problems of the marketplace. But in politics we are dealing with goods allocated largely through some coercive process, not through voluntary market transactions; and political "goods" (such as justice) are often inherently unmarketable. Nonmarket effects (externalities) which are aberrations – market failures, which one seeks to correct – for most economists are the central feature of political life for political scientists.

We can expect that Samuelson's notion of public goods (which can be best understood as a generalization of the notion of externalities) would play a central role in any viable formal theory of politics, and indeed that is the case. It is not too strong a statement to say that societies, and hence politics, exist because public goods exist. Further, one can expect, as is the case, a growing overlap between the interests of economists and political scientists, even though the central orientation of the two disciplines remains distinct. The correction of market failures typically requires changes in social arrangements that can only be brought about through political action; changes in regulation, taxes, government investment (for example, research and development), and so on. However, government action taken in response to market failures may or may not yield net social benefits. (Correcting one problem may create others.) Hence even that rarity, the humble economist, is easily drawn into what Tullock once called "the poorly defended provinces of political science."[8] Economists have always been interested in public policy, but the extent to which their work is focused on what government might (wisely or not) do or fail to do has increased enormously in the past generation. On the other hand, political scientists are drawn to the work on market failures and public goods, not only because it deals with important political issues, but (for the theorist, at any rate) because the work in fact has – in contrast to the study of pure private goods – much of the look and feel of politics.

It is, in short, quite natural that the increasing interest among economists in the problem of market failures should coincide with the rise of interest in developing formal theories of politics on economic lines. (The essentially independent development of game theory was another important stimulus; but it plays a minor role in this study.)

An objection sometimes raised to this sort of argument claims that economic theory deals only with prices and quantities of things observable in the marketplace. Politics, and social choice generally (beyond those choices mediated through markets), lack this character of concreteness and unambiguous quantifiability; thus the supposition that the economic point of view can be fruitfully extended to nonmarket behavior can appear unrealistic on its face.

Stated this bluntly, the objection is easily answered. For a long time (implicitly, at least, even since the beginning) economists have treated their field as the science that studies the efficient use of scarce resources. The most obvious application of this work is to market-related behavior, and, as I have already had occasion to stress, the economic paradigm has been deeply influenced by that primary focus. Nevertheless, important areas of economics do not have any simple relation to the empirical study of prices and quantities in markets, and among these are a number of topics (welfare economics, decision theory, public goods) with obvious relevance to broader questions of social choice.

A more promising attack (one that a number of first-class economists would support) could be mounted on narrower grounds allowing that, although the economic approach might in principle be applicable beyond the range of market phenomena, it seems unrealistic to suppose that it can be fruitfully extended as far as the general study of social and political behavior. But that is an argument that depends on results. In principle, even in terms of possibilities for strictly quantitative predictions, social choice offers a great deal in the way of measurable observations with which to work. Voting behavior, opinion polls, government budgets, and so on are obvious examples. And the history of every science has been that many of the most important measurable quantities are discerned only *after* a theory that can "see" their role has developed: energy and temperature in physics, velocity of money and elasticities in economics are examples.

This leads to a more fundamental point. The history of science is very clear in showing theory's powerful role in organizing understanding, generally well before it has reached the stage where it establishes itself on the basis of providing indisputably powerful quantitative predictions. Copernicus and Darwin provide the most famous examples. Copernicus offered only a very marginal improvement in quantitative power over the Ptolemaic system, and the historical importance of his book comes from what Kepler and Galileo did once seized by a conviction of the qualitative superiority of the Copernican view as a description of how the world worked.[9] Darwin's theory did not begin to be the basis of quantitative work until the twentieth century, and its original power lay wholly in its effectiveness as a way of comprehending a wide range of qualitative observations. Indeed, Adam Smith's *Wealth of Nations* contains almost nothing of the detailed study of prices and quantities in markets, being once again an example of work that owes its initial impact to its usefulness as a way of seeing how things fit together qualitatively.

In short, quantitive prediction is entirely reasonable as the goal of a science. But neither logic nor history allows that goal to be set up as the test of a newly proposed theory.

Altruism and persuasion

In a model of rational choice in which public goods obviously must play a major role, two changes in the traditional economic model become especially important. The first involves what might variously be called *altruism,* or the sense of social responsibility, or the sense of community, and which will appear in the model to be developed here as "group-interest." The second concerns the role of *persuasion.*

Almost no economist would deny the possibility of altruism in rational choice. Indeed, in recent years, efforts to incorporate altruistic preferences within the conventional framework have become fairly common.[10] This does not imply, however, that any serious effort has been made to integrate explicit treatment of altruism into the main body of economic theory. Rather, as we will see in more detail in Chapter 6, it remains a special topic very generally ignored in the literature. And in the classical domain of economic theory, there are very good reasons for that treatment.

The actors in economic theory are *necessarily* self-interested only in the technical, and in fact redundant, sense that each seeks to maximize his own preferences. But if we are concerned only with private goods, it will generally be possible to bypass the question of Smith's *motivation.* If Smith is a saint, he still maximizes what we will for the moment call his "total utility," although we may suppose he gives great weight in this total utility function to the preferences he has for the well-being of others. But as long as we are concerned with market equilibria for private goods, we can simplify the analysis by ignoring any specific taste Smith has for helping others. To the extent that Smith's altruism takes the form of giving money to the poor, this transaction does not go through the market. Rather, the now somewhat enriched recipient enters the market, and it is his preferences that are of interest. If Saint Smith gives bread to the poor, then the benefited poor do not enter the market, but Smith's preference map incorporates the demand for bread to give to the poor. We have no more need to distinguish between the bread Smith buys to give to the poor and that which he buys for his own consumption, than to distinguish his neighbor's demand for sugar to make cookies from his demand for sugar to make gin in the cellar.

Of course, none of this implies that either Smith's generosity or his neighbor's illicit gin lack either normative or descriptive interest, but traditional economic theory does not claim to deal with all questions of interest to mankind. For its own purposes, it is ordinarily both convenient and reasonable for economics to start from a distribution of income, *after* any public or private redistribution, and treat the individual as satisfying his preferences without dealing explicitly with the possibility that his preferences include a taste for helping other people.

It would be surprising, though, if this simplification remained harmless once we are much concerned with public goods, where what Smith spends provides something that is available not just to Smith or some other private individual he gives it to but also to the community at large. Now many benefit from Smith's generosity. One might suppose that cases would arise in which an individual spends on goods of a public character under circumstances when the private value (to himself or any other single individual) is quite obviously inadequate to justify the spending. In fact, we have no trouble at all identifying such cases. If Smith contributes $25 to public television, no sensible observer will suppose that he does so expecting this will lead to $25 worth of improvement in his private viewing of television, or indeed that his contribution will have any perceptible effect at all. Such behavior looks extremely puzzling in terms of a nontautological interpretation of self-interest.

To go directly to a political matter, the much debated "paradox of rational voting" turns on the implausibility of supposing that a rational man will find that his personal utility gain from bothering to vote in an election with millions of other voters justifies any significant effort.

The particular importance of the paradox of rational voting is that it provides a splendid test case for any rational theory of politics. For until we have a theory that is consistent with the elementary observation that most citizens bother to vote, we can hardly expect to have much confidence in the ability of rational choice theory to get very far in probing subtler aspects of political behavior.[11]

Of course, one can "account for" giving to public television by assuming that the individual has a taste for giving to public television; account for bothering to vote by assuming the individual has a taste for voting; and so on. This kind of theorizing is able to explain everything but predict nothing. Substituting "duty to" in place of "taste for" changes nothing essential. A nontrivial theory will have to say something about what governs the taste for or duty to perform altruistic acts. No topic is more fundamental to the study of politics and (more generally) social choice. As Coleman notes, no society could exist in the absence of such social motivation. And no science of society is likely to get very far without some conceptual understanding of what shapes the propensity and directions of social motivation.

As the title of this book indicates, the problem of how to handle altruism within the rational choice framework will be the major concern of this study. Persuasion will have to await another occasion for detailed treatment. A brief comment is in order here, however.

In conventional economic models, tastes are generally taken as given. Since Veblen, at least, there has been criticism from within the profession on this point. No one doubts that custom, fashion, and so on make the tastes of individuals in a society depend on as well as influence the social environment. Further, oligopolists explicitly try to influence the preferences of consumers; even in industries that approximate the purely competitive ideal, one of the functions of trade associations is typically to mount publicity and advertising campaigns intended to persuade consumers to want more of the product. But the role of persuasion is far more important in politics, for reasons that are easy to understand.

If I like Scotch better than bourbon, or ice cream better than cake, the finest efforts of Madison Avenue are unlikely to persuade me to order my preferences otherwise. But in politics persuasion has a great role to play. Even if I am narrowly self-interested, it is often not easy to judge how various policies affect my interests. If my behavior is tinged with altruism, it becomes relevant to make judgments on others' deservingness of my altruistic interest. (We all indulge our follies to some degree, but even the most generous among us are reluctant to indulge someone else's follies.) Hence it is not surprising to note that politically active people devote a large portion of their time and political resources to efforts at what may generally be termed *persuasion*: efforts to influence others' patterns of preferences by means of arguments, manipulation of symbols, dissemination of information, and so on. Thus, although one may be able to go far in economics with models that ignore persuasion, it seems implausible that political theory can go far without explicitly incorporating the role of persuasion in the formal structure of the theory.

To sum up, we have good reason to expect that a viable formal theory of politics will need to extend the traditional model of rational choice in at least three ways: provision of a central role for public goods; explicit treatment of altruistic motivation; and explicit treatment of the role of persuasion. Public goods is already a familiar aspect of formal theory. Persuasion was given great emphasis by Downs, but twenty years later not very much has been added.[12] Despite the concern with altruism that has begun to emerge in recent years, this topic remains by and large neglected in the public choice literature, to the point where Dennis Mueller's well-regarded recent survey could *define* the field as the application of the axiom of egoistic utility-maximizing to political behavior.[13] Finally (a topic which I have not discussed), the integration into empirical theory of the work on aggregation of preferences (Arrow's theorem and related matters) has scarcely begun.[14]

Eventually, I believe, all these matters will be dealt with in a way that begins to look satisfactory. Out of these diverse strands will come a new kind of political theory – for which the work we have presently available will provide a point of entry – in which a novel kind of theory of coalitions will play the same central role that the analysis of market equilibria plays in economic theory. Of this ambitious menu, little will be attempted in this study beyond the construction of a new model of individual choice, where the crucial test of the model will be its ability to deal in an empirically tenable way with the presence of public goods.

Notes on terminology

At one point Pareto explains that he introduced the term *ophelimity* "for the sole purpose of avoiding the battle of words to which the ideas suggested by *utility, scarcity*, etc. have only too frequently given rise... From the rigorously scientific point of view all these terminological questions do not have the slightest importance."[15]

Some readers may be troubled by my usage of the terms *utility* or *rationality* or *altruism*. Even readers who see nothing unusual about the way I use them may be helped by some explicit statements.

To begin with, the reader should understand that *rationality, altruism,* and *utility* are used throughout in a deliberately narrow technical sense; as I will try to make clear in the next few paragraphs, no ethical or normative content whatever should be read into any of these terms. I mentioned earlier that the main content of the term *rationality* is to imply a certain consistency in individual behavior. This leaves open the possibility that an individual who behaves in a way that reasonable observers would judge harmful to both himself and others may nevertheless be behaving rationally (in the technical sense just stressed). This usage is, in fact, the prevailing one among economists, which may seem perverse; and indeed it is perverse, leading to useless battles over words of the kind Pareto hoped to avoid. The difficulty of changing usage, though, is illustrated by the failure of Pareto's "ophelimity" to supplant the term (*utility*) whose shades of meaning he wanted to avoid. (The commonest interpretation today seems to be that ophelimity comes from the Italian for utility.)

There is nothing unusual in all this. Words, especially words conveying abstract ideas, invariably acquire varying shades of meaning; and it is the shared responsibility of both reader and writer to avoid interpreting them in a sense foreign to the context in which they are being used. The context of this study is the presentation of a formal theory, and in that context customary usage gives such terms as *rationality* narrowly technical meanings.

This narrow and artificial usage hardly implies that normative judgments are unimportant. Our judgment about the desirability of democratic government will certainly depend a great deal on our judgment of whether voters behave in a way that we judge normatively rational (e.g., sensible and morally acceptable). But for the context at hand, rationality is used only in the special sense described.

In much the same spirit, I now stress the absence of any normative content in the terms *altruism* or *group-interest* as used in this study. Indeed, there is no doubt that there will be aspects of "altruistic" behavior that every reader will find repugnant. We have no great trouble identifying examples of "other-regarding" behavior that none of us would care to have directed our way. As Sam Beer likes to say, there is such a thing as "altruism with teeth." What we mean by altruism in the technical sense used here is that the individual's allocation of resources is influenced not only by the bundle of goods he obtains for himself but also by the effect of his choice on others or on his society, qualified only by the condition that the *actor* (not necessarily the recipients) regards this behavior as benign. An altruistic act *need not* have negative or zero value to the actor. What defines altruistic behavior is that the actor could have done better for himself had he chosen to ignore the effect of his choice on others.

However, questions about words arise not only if nontechnical usage is read into technical terms but also if technical terms take on a new or extended meaning in the context of a new theory. This matter will be taken up in detail in Chapter 6. But you already know from the introduction that the "choosers" in the theory I will be developing will be, not directly Smith, but S-Smith and G-Smith operating subject to an allocation rule "inside Smith." These metaphorical actors are rational utility-maximizers in the conventional sense. That is a very important technical aspect of the theory.

However, Smith is not. We can make him so by giving a novel definition of what is meant by a utility function, or by saying that Smith maximizes utility subject to a constraint that governs the share of his resources allocated to satisfy G- versus S-preferences. But the latter course scarcely helps a reader accustomed to the conventional model because the constraint here is "inside Smith"; and the former, although more congenial to people accustomed to the conventional model, turns out to be clumsy and misleading.

Is this, then, really a model of rational choice? Should we choose some novel term for the model, say, "dual-rationality"? My own view is that any such special term is unnecessary and unwise. Rationality has been defined by the conventional theory only for the case of self-interested motivation. But what if it turns out, as indeed it does, that rationality defined in this narrow way cannot describe the way human beings we regard as reasonable (such as you or I) behave in the context of social choice? Then unless you are prepared to argue that, by definition, social motivation must be irrational unless it can be formulated in terms of self-interest, there appears to be something wrong with the conventional definition: it is too narrow to account for actual behavior. One of the few leading economists to address this problem explicitly (Amartya Sen) was able to sum up his message in a two-word title: "Rational Fools."

The essential problem is to discover what we can understand rationality to mean when we allow, as empirically we must, for social as well as self-interested motivation. We can, however, insist that a proper definition must be such that, for the special case where only self-interested motivation need be considered, the expanded definition reduces to the conventional one. As will be seen, rationality as defined under the model to be developed here meets this test, as well as some more stringent tests to be explored in Chapter 6.

In the strictest technical sense, there is not even a serious matter for discussion in all this. The utility function that economic man maximizes has been drained of any necessary empirical content. As understood by contemporary economic theory, the statement that the utility of A is greater than the utility of B ordinarily means nothing more than A is preferred to B. Since numbers are themselves transitive (if $A > B > C$, then $A > C$), a preference pattern that is transitive (consistent, rational) can be described by a utility function; similarly, assuming that an actor is maximizing a utility function builds rationality into our model. Using a utility function is not the only way to do that (Arrow's famous work on social choice uses none). So utility has been reduced to a convenient device, a kind of mathematical trick, drained of all the substantive content it so unquestionably held in the nineteenth century and still holds in contemporary use in fields such as philosophy. [16]

Now, under the model I will develop, choice is in fact consistent. If Smith prefers A to B and B to C, he will prefer A to C. But it happens to be inconvenient to treat his overall preference pattern as maximizing a utility function. The trick is still available, but because it is no longer convenient we have no reason to use it. It is hard for most economists to accept that, or to avoid a powerful intuitive conviction that saying such a thing must be unsound. I will take considerable pains to deal with this matter as we proceed through the study.

CHAPTER 2

Paradoxes

In the presence of public goods, the behavior of a self-interested "economic man" conflicts with everyday observation. Indeed, it is positively bizarre. I begin this chapter with several illustrations of this point. It will be obvious that the paradoxes can be exorcized if we allow for behavior that is not narrowly self-interested. But the problem of reconciling two qualitatively different kinds of altruistic propensity, each with a compelling claim to validity, is not so simple.

At the conclusion of the chapter, I give a formal statement of the technical problem that must somehow be resolved if we are to reconcile the conflicting notions of altruistic motivation, which I label "goods altruism" and "participation altruism."

Of the three paradoxes I will now introduce, the first two are familiar, so that the briefest account should be adequate. The third, although empirically of utmost significance, has been ignored (entirely so, as far as I have found) in the literature. I therefore treat it in more detail.

Paradox of rational voting

Why should a rational citizen bother to vote in an election with millions of other voters? Why should the voter accept anything more than trivial inconvenience to vote when, even in a very close election, the chance that his particular vote would make a difference in the outcome is itself trivial: even Kennedy won by over 100,000 votes. Yet most people do vote, and in general the propensity to vote increases with education. Thus the voters more likely to be aware of the argument that voting is not rational are in fact particularly likely to vote. Further, the voter turnout in U.S. presidential elections that are regarded almost universally as forgone conclusions (Johnson–Goldwater, Nixon–McGovern) tends to be only slightly smaller than that in close elections. [1]

Prisoner's dilemma

Two examples of this familiar paradigm for an important class of situations are shown in Figure 2.1. [2] The first number in each box is the payoff to

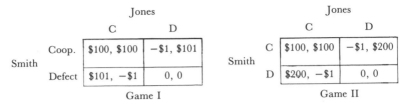

Figure 2.1. Payoff matrixes for Game I and Game II.

Smith; the second is the payoff to Jones. So, for example, in Game I, if Smith chooses D (defect) and Jones chooses C (cooperate), the payoff is $101 to Smith and −$1 to Jones. The only rules of the games are that the players are not allowed to communicate, so that they have no opportunity to agree on how they will play, and that the two players choose simultaneously. (Smith cannot have an agreement with Jones, or an arrangement to divide their joint winnings after the game, or wait to choose his move until after Jones has chosen.)

In Game I, you can see that the temptation to choose D is slight (even if the game is to be played just once). Each player can improve his outcome by defecting (choose D), no matter which choice the other player makes. But the gain is only $1. In Game II, the temptation to defect is strong. We will want to consider these games under the alternative conditions that either game is to be played exactly once or exactly 100 times.

What makes the 100-plays context especially interesting is that if the players are perfectly self-interested, the standard rational choice analysis says that they will choose strategy D not only in both Game I and Game II if played once, but also on *each* of the 100 plays if either game is to be repeated 100 times. The 100-plays argument is that rational, self-interested players will certainly defect on the hundredth play because there is no longer any way that their opponent could punish them for defecting. But if both Smith and Jones will defect on play 100, then neither has any reason not to defect on play 99. However, if both will defect on play 99, neither has any reason not to defect on play 98. And so on. Hence, a strictly self-interested and rational player, opposed by another player also known to be strictly rational and self-interested, will be led to defect on every play of a series of known, finite length. So Smith and Jones, if rational, need not bother to play if offered the opportunity to play Game I 100 times. For they would foresee only defections and no payoff. However, if Smith and Jones were so irrational as to choose C (cooperate) on each play, then each would win $10,000.

Even as enthusiastic expositors of the theory as Luce and Raiffa find this result unpalatable.[3] They retreat from formal rationality on this point, suggesting that perhaps it would be better strategy to cooperate as long as the other player does so, until some point very close to the end of the series (say until play 95 of the 100). Empirically, though, we find that real players do not even approximate the behavior implied by the theory of rational choice. In particular, they frequently "lock in" on the cooperative strategy, and when they do they are unlikely to defect on the last several plays, even when it is a sure thing that they will gain by doing so.[4]

We will consequently want to consider amendments to the hypothesis of narrowly self-interested behavior that account – in a manner consistent with our resolution of the other paradoxes – for the failure to defect at the end of the 100-play series. We also need to account for why we can expect players to be more prone to defect on a single iteration of Game II than on a single iteration of Game I. Here, however, the answer seems obvious: it costs less to depart from purely self-interested behavior in Game I. But we will want to see how this "costs less" resolution can be defined in a way that can be consistently applied across the paradoxes.

Public goods paradox

Suppose we consider some everyday approximation of a pure public good that is supported by voluntary contributions: for example, a listener-supported radio station. Empirically, there is no question that the amount of money that can be raised from listeners will depend strongly on the number of listeners. The paradox is that it can be "proved" (in terms of the usual model of rational choice) that the amount of money that can be raised will be very nearly independent of the number of listeners: the station should be able to raise about as much money if it had five listeners as if it had 50,000.[5] Or, to put the same paradox another way, because a station could not raise significantly more money from 50,000 listeners than it could from 5, and because 5 listeners would not contribute enough to keep the station on the air, then we deduce that listener-supported radio stations cannot exist. But they do.

It is an interesting comment on the state of the field that when journal articles appeared carrying this implication – one by a political scientist, another by an economist – neither the authors nor, apparently, anyone else was moved to remark that there was something bizarre about such results.[6]

Here (informally) is how the argument goes:

Imagine our rational guinea pig (Smith, once again) as he hears the station's first announcement of a fund-raising drive. So far no one has contributed a cent. Smith decides to give $10 and goes to the phone to call in his pledge. Under the conventional model, this reflects Smith's feeling that $10 is a worthwhile way to spend his money, but not $11. (Why not? Because if

Smith thought $11 was worthwhile, he rationally should have given $11. But he didn't.)

However, before he is able to complete his call, the station announces that someone else has phoned in with the first pledge, which happens to be for $10. As a rational man, the conventional model says that Smith reacts in the following way. Because the radio station's output is a public good, available to all, this other person's $10 contribution makes the situation Smith faces exactly the same as if he in fact had contributed the $10, but had simultaneously become $10 richer. If Smith did not think that an eleventh dollar was justified when he was spending his own money, why should he think so now? Why should he not abandon his plan to make a $10 contribution? The reader not familiar with economic models of rational choice will regard this as a rather crazy way to think. But the reader familiar with such models will (at least, once he gets over any feeling of surprise) recognize that this is just the way the conventional model supposes the individual will behave.

Under the usual form of the economic model of rational choice, the $10 contribution for Person 2 is indeed exactly equivalent to a $10 increment in income to Smith which he has then donated to the station. The funds to the radio station are the same as they were before Person 2 contributed, and Smith reconsidered, his contribution; but now Smith still has the $10 in his pocket. Since he is, effectively, a bit richer than before, Smith may want to buy a bit more of the public good supplied by the radio station. Maybe he now thinks it worthwhile to spend an eleventh dollar. (This is a strong assumption: it means that Smith's marginal propensity to contribute to the station is such that he would spend 10 percent of an increase in income on this particular good, although the percentage of his income he had been willing to contribute to that point was tiny.) Under this generous assumption, the station now gets, from Smith and Person 2 together, a total of $11: $10 from Person 2, plus $1 from Smith.

Following through this logic, we find that the total amount likely to be raised from an arbitrarily large number of listeners, taking account of feedback effects (technically, under a Cournot equilibrium), will never reach twice the amount that the most generous single listener alone would contribute.

Equally curious, suppose we now turn this situation around, so that Smith is the last, rather than the first, listener to contribute, some thousands of others having already done so.

Apparently he still finds the marginal utility of $10 given to the station higher than using the $10 for private consumption; and, as before, taking an eleventh dollar from its alternative use (private consumption) apparently does not meet this condition. This is plausible enough in terms of the conventional theory, it being customary and plausible to assume diminishing marginal utility. Hence each dollar added to private consumption yields less utility, and, the reverse, so that each dollar taken away from private consumption to give to the station "costs" more (in utility) than the previous dollar.

We will assume that diminishing marginal utility also applies to the value of adding another dollar to the station's budget. However, here Smith's contribution is microscopic compared to the total that everyone contributes. So we cannot expect to see any *perceptible* difference in marginal utility between the tenth and eleventh dollar, or for that matter between the first and the hundredth dollar.

Now, imagine that instead of hearing that someone else has contributed $10, as before, Smith now finds he is $10 richer than he thought. If marginal utility from spending on the radio station in fact changes only negligibly with shifts in the station budget on the scale of what a contributor like Smith gives, then the logic of the conventional model now tells us that Smith will give all of his $10 increase in wealth to the station!

It does no good to answer that in fact, we must suppose that there is *some* decrease in marginal utility for additional dollars in the radio station budget. For suppose the change in marginal utility were *not* negligibly small with respect to shifts in the total amount contributed on the scale of Smith's own contribution. Then Smith's own contribution would vary crazily with the precise amount contributed by all others. For fractionally tiny shifts in that total will easily be huge compared with Smith's own contribution when he is one among thousands (sometimes millions) of contributors. On the other hand, if the change in marginal utility *is* negligible, then we are led to the absurd result that, if Smith contributes at all, he would contribute all of an increase in his wealth. (The situation can be seen best in terms of the shape of Smith's income-spending path, as shown in Appendix A.)

It is not at all hard to resolve these paradoxes by allowing sufficient scope for altruistic motivation. However, it is not as simple to do so in a way that produces a model with much analytical power.

We can define two qualitatively different conceptions of altruistic motivation. In the first, which I will label "participation altruism," our sample individual (Smith) gains utility from giving resources away for the benefit of others. He has a taste for participation in social acts. In the second, which I will label "goods altruism," Smith gains utility from an increase in the goods available to others: his utility function incorporates a taste for having other people better off. You will not, I think, be surprised to hear that we will reach the conclusion that it is necessary, somehow, to incorporate both these notions if we are to obtain a viable model of choice.

In the participation conception, giving resources away is another of

Smith's tastes, not necessarily different in character from a taste for fancy motor cars or dollar cigars.

Formally,

$$U^* = U^*(x,y) \qquad\qquad 2.1$$

where U^* is the utility function of Smith the participation altruist; where $x = (x_1, x_2, \ldots)$ is the vector of goods for Smith's own use, such as food and motor cars; and y is the value of resources Smith gives away.

In contrast, we have the utility function, U^{**}, for Smith as a pure goods altruist:

$$U^{**} = U^{**}(x, z) \qquad\qquad 2.2$$

where x is as defined for Equation 2.1, and $z = (z_1, z_2, \ldots)$ is the vector of bundles of goods available to other entities in which Smith has an altruistic interest.

Thus the altruistic component of U^* turns on what Smith gives; the altruistic component of U^{**} turns on what other people have. A \$5 donation from Smith to the Red Cross would affect the value of both U^* and U^{**}, but not in the same way. It would appear as a \$5 increment to y in U^*; whereas in U^{**} it would appear as a \$5 increment to the total amount of money raised by the Red Cross.

A \$5 donation by *Jones* to the Red Cross would not enter U^* at all (because the altruistic argument in U^* refers only to Smith's participation); but a \$5 donation by Jones would have exactly the same effect in U^{**} as a \$5 increase in his own income for Smith that Smith had then donated to the Red Cross. Almost all the models of altruism in the economic literature are goods models.[7]

It will seem natural to write:

$$U = f(U^*, U^{**}) = U(x,y,z) \qquad\qquad 2.3$$

as the utility function for Smith if his motivation turns on both participation and goods altruism. As far as I have found, there has been no serious effort in the literature to develop such a model.[8]

To return to the three paradoxes described earlier. Note that the first and third paradoxes may be interpreted as prisoner's dilemma (PD) situations generalized to more than two people. In both, the structure of payoffs is such that, if everyone in a group behaves selfishly, the outcome is worse for everyone than if everyone behaved cooperatively. But the incentive to each individual actor, if he maximizes his strict self-interest, is not to cooperate (to be a free rider). The essential difference between the voting paradox and the voluntary contribution paradox is that, in the former, Smith faces a dichotomous choice (do or don't vote), whereas in the latter he faces a continuous choice (contribute $x, x \geq 0$). In the two-person PD we must introduce constraints to create the dilemma: if Smith and Jones are allowed to bargain, they are unlikely to have any difficulty agreeing to cooperate. But in the n-person case (increasingly so as n grows large) the costs of bargaining and of enforcing agreements create the dilemma even when there are no explicit constraints forbidding bargaining.

The voting paradox could be resolved in terms of either participation altruism alone or goods altruism alone. In the former, which is the usual explanation for voting in political science or sociology, Smith gets satisfaction from the act of voting (doing his duty, or some equivalent formulation). In the latter, Smith considers the benefit to society from the election of what he deems to be the better candidate, and he considers the benefit to society from the sheer fact that citizens take an interest in politics and bother to vote (see Chapter 7).

The two-person PD (the second paradox) could also be dealt with under either a pure goods or a pure participation formulation. But now only the participation formulation seems plausible. In the participation formulation, Smith gets satisfaction from helping others, and it seems plausible to assume that he gets particular satisfaction from helping people whom he expects would help him had they the opportunity. But the cost of helping is higher in Game II than in Game I (see Figure 2.1). So it could be consistent for Smith to cooperate on a single play of Game I even if he would defect on a single play of Game II. But at the end of a long series of cooperative plays, the satisfaction from helping one's playing partner (given the prior mutual helping) will have increased. Thus there would be nothing paradoxical should Smith cooperate on the last play of a Game II series, even though he would not have done so on a single play.

This is particularly the case because, at the end of a long series of cooperative plays, Smith is richer than he was before and can afford to "buy" more participation. But it would require stringent assumptions to use this "Smith is richer" argument to account for cooperating at the end of a series in terms of pure goods altruism. For although Smith is indeed richer, so also is Jones. If the cost (in utility) to Smith of cooperating has declined, so presumably has the value (altruistically shared by Smith) of helping Jones. Consequently, it could be consistent with a pure goods model for Smith to be *less* likely to cooperate on the last of a 100-play series (cooperative to that point) than on a single play. Whereas the voting paradox might be resolved in terms of either participation or goods altruism, the PD paradox can be handled in terms of pure participation but not plausibly in terms of pure goods altruism.

The same conclusion holds even more strikingly in the voluntary contribution paradox. If a pure goods model holds, then the conditions that created the paradox will hold, as you can see by reviewing the argument, and we are stuck with an absurd result. To avoid the paradox, it is essential that the model of choice incorporate the participation motive so that the contribution of Person 2 is *not* completely equivalent, in its effect on Smith's utility, to a contribution from Smith himself.

On the other hand, a pure participation model, although it can let us resolve the three paradoxes discussed, would not be satisfactory. A realistic model must allow for the observation that Smith's propensity to participate in supporting a cause is somehow contingent on his perception of how good a cause it is, and (more particularly) on his perception of the value of the contribution at the margin he might make. If Smith learns that his station has already raised much more money than a station in another city offering comparable service, we would expect that to affect his propensity to contribute. Such reactions are easy to account for in terms of a goods model, but would be missed by a pure participation model.

A more fundamental problem is this: If we could imagine the share of Smith's resources allocated to unselfish uses (given his income) as *fixed,* then we could combine the goods and participation motives in the following simple way. Let Smith's utility function be *lexical,* in the following sense: first Smith chooses an allocation to unselfish spending, reflecting his taste for participation; then Smith allocates this fixed bundle of resources where he thinks it will do the most good, so that goods altruism governs the use of the participation resources.

Empirically, however, we can see that propensities to participation are not fixed. The portion of an individual's resources and time spent on "participation" can be observed to depend partly on the individual's sense of the opportunities for socially useful participation. Indeed, in time of war, revolution, natural disaster, and so on, the propensities not only of individuals but of whole segments of a society, and sometimes the entire society, can change dramatically. Goods altruism interacts with participation.

Thus the hope that we could deal separately with participation and goods altruism turns out to be quite as forlorn as the hope that either participation or goods altruism alone could provide an empirically viable model.

Yet it is likely to seem intuitively obvious to many readers that there must be some simple way of combining the Equations 2.1 and 2.2 to get something on the nature of Equation 2.3.

However, the problem is trickier than it may seem. For example, consider Smith's contribution to the radio station. Where does it go in Equation 2.3? It goes into x, unless Smith himself is not a listener to the station. It goes into z, because Smith is certainly not the only listener. It goes into y, because it is Smith's own contribution. So if we ask about the marginal utility to Smith from that dollar, it must be some function of U_x, U_y, and U_z all at once.

In general, complications arise in part because the model has to handle simultaneously: (1) goods paid for *by* Smith and goods *for* Smith but not necessarily paid for by Smith; (2) goods for Smith and goods for others; and (3) goods available to many people (often, although not necessarily, supplied by the government, and if so partly paid for by Smith's taxes) and goods available to Smith alone (or others alone). Thanks especially to Samuelson, the conventional model has been extended in an elegant way to handle the third factor. As noted earlier, various ways of incorporating the second have been explored; however, as you will see in Chapter 6, the conventional analysis offers no satisfactory way of handling the second and third together. Yet what is really required, we have now seen, is a way to handle all three at once.

There are further problems. In a conventional economic model one routinely takes "tastes as given." But in the context of social choice we require – for reasons outlined in Chapter 1 – a model that can allow for the three complications above and at the same time be capable of handling changes in perceived spending opportunities and the perceived value of those opportunities (due to changes in social situation, changes in public sentiment, crises, dramatic news events, and so on). In the context of social choice, taking preferences as fixed would be as crippling as if in an economics context our model were unable to deal with changes in prices.

Finally, the model must be capable of handling the reality that goods in the real world are rarely pure public or pure private goods; that spending is not always purely self-interested or purely altruistic; and that participation in the real world is not always a matter of pure choice, social pressure and more direct means (taxes) being obviously significant.

CHAPTER 3

A Darwinian argument

Darwin devoted several chapters of the *Descent of Man* to the influence of natural selection on animal behavior, and in particular to the influence of selection on human behavior and morals. Exploration of this theme has become the focus of much new controversy since the publication of E. O. Wilson's *Sociobiology*. [1] But the general notion that there are some connections between man's evolutionary history and his behavior implies no special commitment (whether philosophical, political, or scientific) that a sophisticated critic of sociobiology could not accept. If you will accept that, the basic argument I want to make here is quite simple, although it leads to a puzzle.

An immediate consequence of the Darwinian analysis is that self-interested creatures, other things being equal, will be able to leave more descendants carrying their genes than would non–self-interested creatures. Hence natural selection will favor self-interest. (As always in a Darwinian context, "self-interest" must be understood to include kin-altruism, where the helping behavior yields direct advantage in terms of inclusive fitness. This usage is not, in fact, very far from that ordinarily seen in economics. [2])

On the other hand, in competition *among* breeding groups, within some of which individuals are endowed with a propensity to act in the interest of the group (rather than solely in self-interest), the groups whose members have a propensity to act in group-interest will have a selection advantage over the groups deficient in that propensity.

So we can imagine another kind of competition, between self-interest and group-interest, as the propensity that will be most favored by natural selection. Within a group, self-interest will be favored; among groups, group-interest. The possibility then arises that the outcome might be a compromise of some kind, especially in species in which there is great potential advantage to groups that are able to sustain a high level of cooperative behavior beyond the level of small kin-groups. In particular, much human behavior seems to involve some such compromise.

Yet there is a strong case against significant group-selection pressure, particularly due to the fact that selection among groups would be rarer than the selection among individuals, which must go on continually; consequently, even a modest input of selfish genes (by mutation or recombination of genes or through gene flow) would seem to counteract the effect of group-selection. On the other hand, if a measure of group-selection (or some functional equivalent of group-selection) will never be significant, then some observed animal behavior and a good deal of observed human behavior must be explained in ways that seem on their face about as hard to make plausible as group-selection. Either way, there is a puzzle. What I will suggest is a possible connection between this puzzle and the participation versus goods altruism dichotomy developed in Chapter 2.

A key notion in recent work on the evolution of social behavior is that of an "evolutionarily stable strategy" (ESS).[3] Interpreted to suit our context, and whether we regard group-interest as real or only "as if," what an ESS requires is that group-interested behavior be tempered in such a way that the selection advantage of self-interest is kept under control. An obvious example would be if some mechanism evolved that would allow free-riders (nonhelpers) to be identified and punished by helpers. But the mechanism would have to take account of the selection pressure on free-riders to mimic helpers sufficiently well to avoid ready detection.

What I will now try to show is how the combination of goods and participation altruism we were led to invoke in resolving the paradoxes of Chapter 2 happen to provide a plausible basis for an ESS favorable to the survival of a measure of group-interested motivation. This will suggest how these qualitatively very different kinds of altruism (one based on internal psychic benefits from the sheer fact of participation, the other based on externally observable benefits) turn out to be interpretable as different aspects of the natural selection pressures on which I would like to ground the theory of choice developed in the balance of the study.

The simplest way to develop the argument is to start from consideration of what would happen if initially individuals were perfectly group-interested and see what sort of mechanism might prevent this perfectly group-interested society from being invaded and finally overwhelmed by the selection advantages of selfishness.

Even if everyone were perfectly group-interested, individuals would not be indifferent to their own self-interest. For each individual is himself a member of the group so that *complete* neglect of his self-interest would be inconsistent with his commitment to group-interest.

Let me give a concrete illustration. Is it in the group-interest for an individual member of some species to alert his fellows of the approach of a predator? This kind of behavior is commonly found in animals, and it ordinarily involves some risk to the animal who gives the alert, for in the process he also draws the attention of the predator to himself. Giving the alert will be in the group-interest only if the alert is more likely to save a member of the group than to cost the life of a member. If the only animal close enough to the predator to be seriously at risk is the one who could give the alert, then it may well be that the most likely affect of giving the alert is to cost the life of him who gave it. And our perfectly group-interested animal, were he discriminating enough to make this calculation, might find it in the group-interest (but purely incidentally, self-interest being absent, by assumption, from his motivation) to act in a way that happens to be just what would serve his self-interest: namely, not to give the alert.

In general, if we let G' be the marginal utility of allocating a bit of resources in whatever way best serves the group, and S' the marginal utility of using the bit of resources in whatever way best serves the individual's self-interest, then even for our for our perfectly group-interested creature there could be situations in which $S' = G'$. The predator warning example just given is one illustration. Another would be if G' would be maximized by using the bit of resources to help the neediest member of the group and the chooser himself happened to be the neediest member.

However, this kind of perfectly group-interested rule would not provide as ESS. Perfectly group-interested individuals would be vulnerable to exploitation by individuals who gave special weight to themselves so that they acted in self-interest not only if $S' = G'$, but whenever $WS' > G'$, with $W > 1$. In the extreme, letting W grow, the individual always acts in self-interest and acts consistent with group-interest only in the special situations when $S' = G'$. To restate this in a more convenient form; perfectly group-interested individuals (for whom, by definition, $W = 1$) would be vulnerable to exploitation by individuals who acted in self-interest whenever $W > G'/S'$, with $W > 1$. Let $\hat{W}$ be the average value of W for the group. We can imagine $\hat{W}$ gradually growing (in our hypothetical initially perfectly group-interested population). If no mechanism exists that gives some protection to less selfish individuals, group-interested motivation would be eliminated because within-group selection would always favor individuals for whom $W > \hat{W}$.[4]

However, the presence of competing groups changes the dynamics of the situation. Within a group, individuals for whom $W > \hat{W}$ would have an advantage, other things equal. However, among competing groups, the group that has the lower value of $\hat{W}$ will have an advantage because members will be less prone to sacrifice group-interest to self-interest. So there would be a group-selection advantage for genetic mechanisms that serve to limit the vulnerability of individuals for whom W is relatively small to exploitation by individuals for whom W is large.

There is no reason to suppose that some single mechanism serves this function, although behavior inconsistent with genetic self-interest is common enough in human societies that it seems that some repertoire of protective devices does exist. Indeed, as will be discussed in the second half of this chapter, a considerable repertoire of such mechanisms can be gleaned from the literature. Here I want to discuss a further device that suggests itself in the light of the discussion of Chapter 2.

Note first that the ratio, G'/S', is related to the notion we have labeled "goods altruism" (see Chapter 2). An efficient strategy, one would suppose, would always increase the propensity to group-interested allocations as that ratio increases. The problem cannot be solved by removing goods altruism: in fact, the problem can be defined as that of finding some mechanism(s) that makes it possible to sustain a measure of goods altruism in the face of the selection advantage of selfishness.

The notion of "participation altruism" suggests a solution, or at least a component of a solution. One way in which relatively unselfish members of the group might be protected from exploitation by consistently selfish individuals is if these relatively unselfish members had a propensity to limit their willingness to act in group-interest to the extent that they have already so acted. In other words, let us suppose that W is not a constant for each individual but varies in such a way that, *the less the individual has already allocated to the group, the more the individual wishes to participate (other things equal); and vice versa.*

In a sense this is a simple, even obvious modification of the specification which says that the individual acts in self-interest whenever $W > G'/S'$. The same statement continues to hold, but we drop the assumption that W is a constant. Then if we think of how W might vary in a way that would reduce vulnerability to exploitation by more selfish individuals, the most obvious specification would be that W increases (i.e., more weight is given to self-interest) as the effort the individual has already expended in group-interest increases.

Even with W constant, there is some protection against exploitation; other things being equal, diminishing marginal utility will cause G'/S' to decrease with the share of resources given to group-interest. But making W variable in the manner described would increase this protection, allowing a lower *sustainable* value of $\hat{W}$ for the group as a whole. Insofar as a propensity for group-interested behavior provided a between-group selection advantage, we may expect that a breeding group endowed with the mechanism described would have an advantage over a competing group lacking it.

Further, the importance of this limiting mechanism would vary with the situation of the individual. If he were very well off, he could afford to allow himself to be exploited (allow the risk of being exploited) more than a less well-off individual. Thus the mechanism could be made still more effective if the propensity for self-interested allocation not only increased (i.e., W increases) with the amount of resources allocated to group-interest, but also decreased (i.e., W decreases) with the amount of resources already allocated to self-interest. Mathematically, this amounts to postulating (with s = resources allocated to self-interest, g = resources allocated to group-interest):

$$W = f(g, s); \partial W/\partial s < 0, \partial W/\partial g > 0 \qquad\qquad 3.1$$

with the individual in equilibrium when $W = G'/S'$.

The simplest form for a model satisfying Equation 3.1 would make the W-function depend only on the ratio, g/s. But using that particularly simple form would also enhance the plausibility of the model as consistent with ESS. For between-group competition will be most severe in bad times (drought, and so on) and least severe in good times. A formulation in terms of the ratio, g/s, allows a W-function that would do better (versus groups not so endowed) in bad times without making group-interested behavior excessively vulnerable to within-group competition in good times.[5]

We are consequently led to take as our working hypothesis this simplest specification, where the individual is in equilibrium when:

$$W = G'/S' \qquad\qquad 3.2$$

where

$$W = f(g/s); W' > 0. \qquad\qquad 3.3$$

This is the model we will be exploring in the balance of the study.

We have no reason or need to suppose that the mechanism defined by these equations alone accounts for the possibility of sustaining a measure of group-interested motivation. Rather, the argument is that, given whatever devices exist (evolve) to allow a species to maintain a measure of group-interested behavior, the effect would be enhanced by the device defined by Equations 3.2 and 3.3. Thus we are interested in seeing whether the recent literature on evolution provides any plausible basis for postulating some further repertoire of devices that could serve to sustain a measure of group-motivation. In what follows I survey some possibilities. Throughout, you should be aware that analysis of this topic – whether sympathetic or opposed to the view I am taking – is inherently tentative. The processes by which evolution moves are still poorly understood, even with respect to such gross features of life as the predominance of sexual reproduction.[6] A useful antidote to the illusion that evolutionary theory is a completed area of inquiry (like, say, geometric optics) rather than a field that is exciting just because we know there are surprising new things to be learned, is given by John Maynard-Smith (himself one of the most frequently cited theorists in the selfish gene literature) in his contribution to a volume called *The Encyclopedia of Ignorance.*

Proponents of the selfish gene view, in accounting for human social behavior, stress the argument that, to the extent such behavior is genetically influenced, it must reflect the conditions of hunter-gatherer life. For, under conventional assumptions about the pace of evolution, the human gene pool could change very little over the short period (in evolutionary terms) during which human aggregates larger than small tribes have existed. In the hunter-gatherer context, though, still following the usual selfish gene argument, there would be selection pressures on the one hand to punish individuals who were found to have sacrificed the interest of the group to self-interest, and, at the same time, there would be selection pressures for individuals to in fact sacrifice group-interest to (genetic, inclusive) self-interest whenever possible. (The best situation for selfish Smith is that everyone acts in group-interest, except Smith. A bad situation for selfish Smith is that everyone cheats uninhibitedly.) But punishing others can be dangerous because the defendent might defend himself too well, and it can become ineffectual if the criteria for assuming a violation are too loose, so that such punishment as occurred was too random to maintain a clear deterrent value.

From such considerations, one can construct an argument that says:

1. Be increasingly harsh (quick to accuse, nasty in punishment) as the violation of group-interest is clearer.
2. Take account of the record of the suspected offender, being less quick or less nasty to an actor who has done much for the group than to an actor who has rarely been observed acting for the group.
3. In the role as cheater, take account of the above, being aware that risks increase as – to use now the notation of this study – G'/S' increases, but decrease as W increases.

This leads, or at least can be led, to the same equilibrium condition given by Equations 3.2 and 3.3. Consequently, one way to reconcile the emergence of the allocation rule of Equations 3.2 and 3.3 with the selfish gene argument is to treat group-motivation as a purely "as if" phenomenon that in fact reflects only self-interested motivation.

It is at least questionable, however, that strict selfish gene arguments are an adequate basis for observed social behavior (quite aside from any relation to the argument of this chapter). On the selfish gene view, if Smith acts in a way that serves his notion of group-interest at the expense of self-interest (for example, sends a contribution to the public television station), this is to be understood as a kind of triple-cross. Smith tells himself he is acting in a socially responsible way; actually he is deceiving himself because he is following an allocation rule that was shaped by a tendency to cheat on socially responsible actions as much as possible. However, his self-deceptively altruistic, actually selfishly motivated, act turns out to be unselfish after all. But this is only by the accident that human society changed faster than his genes so that, in a large modern society, with many opportunities for anonymous behavior, Smith still acts substantially as if living in a small hunter-gatherer group, where his every act might possibly be observed by someone who knew and would judge him.

But it is not clear how this "genetic inertia" line of argument could be made plausible other than in a context in which there is also a measure of direct or indirect group-selection able to shape the selfish gene pressures postulated here. This is not because the selfish gene argument can never explain self-sacrifice (for we can suppose that society could make up for that by taking very good care of the families of its heroes). Rather, it is because it is hard to see why purely selfish gene motivation does not lead to behavioral rules such as "always cheat if no one is looking."

Absent a measure of group-selection pressure, the way the genetic inertia argument comes out looks convenient rather than persuasive. Indeed, given only the selfish gene argument, together with the capacity for discrimination and subtlety in human intelligence, it is hard to see how human society grows beyond small kin-groups. Hobbes's war of all against all seems the likeliest outcome.

On the other hand, to the extent that proponents of the selfish gene view find themselves relying on genetic inertia arguments, it becomes arbitrary to shut the door entirely on a measure of group-selection. Suppose, as seems entirely reasonable, that at a sufficiently early period in human (or humanoid) history we would find such small bands of hunter-gatherers, closely related, that inclusive selfishness (aside from any prospect of reciprocity or vengeance) would alone support a measure of commitment to group-interest. One can then argue that some tendency to group-interested motivation survives as a kind of fossil kin-altruism (genetic inertia carried one step further); *or* that the sort of selfish gene rule discussed a moment ago (mimicking group-selection) took hold under the influence of such fossil kin-altruism; *or* (a direct group-selection argument) that what led to man, while other humanoid species went extinct, was the emergence in one of these humanoid species (namely ourselves) of some mechanism or combination of mechanisms that made it very difficult for this species to lose completely its propensity (from fossil kin-altruism) for group-interested behavior. The last of these possibilities is the most interesting, and what follows is a brief sketch of some possible mechanisms for it.

First, writers such as David Layzer and Stephen Jay Gould have stressed that genetic variation (the raw material on which selection acts) is not simply random.[7] Although variation is blind, its pace and direction are not "white noise" but show definite propensities. There are known to be genes whose function is to control the behavior of other genes – the tendency to mutate, reassort, and so on. There are complicated and important relations among genes (gene redundancy, gene linkages, gene synergies, and so on). Nevertheless, for analytical convenience, and because too little is known to formulate a generally agreed alternative, most mathematical modeling assumes a single gene for each character. Even, as in our context, such a complex character as propensity to act in group-interest is ordinarily treated as due to a single gene, which varies randomly and independently from all other genes. No one argues that this model is adequate. On the other hand, Dawkins and various other defenders of the selfish gene approach are certainly correct to argue that it is not as completely vulnerable to objections as critics sometimes assert. The situation seems mainly characterized by the need to avoid dogmatism. No one is quite sure, or even reasonably sure, of how far from adequate the simple model really is and, in particular, in what contexts it can or cannot be used as a reasonable approximation. The kinds of arguments developed by Layzer, Gould, and others at a minimum serve as a reminder of that.

To give a crude example, if a mutation that increases the propensity toward selfish behavior also increases the propensity toward feeble-mindedness, then selfishness will hardly have a within-group advantage. Yet the link itself would be only weakly susceptible to within-group selfish gene pressures, there being a selfish advantage to losing the link only in later generations. The longer run the selfish gene advantage, though, the more vulnerable it would be to a group-selection advantage to keeping the link. A more deeply embedded linkage (even less susceptible to short-run within-group advantages) might then make the loss of the first link disadvantageous.

Of course, any particular hypothesis about such mechanisms will seem – and in fact will be – intrinsically highly improbable. But much of what we see in the world around us is highly improbable. Nature has had a long time to work the problem; many variant arrangements might work; and the advantage to an evolutionary line which finally stumbled on some mechanism that served to protect the propensity to social behavior would have enormous evolutionary advantage against competing lines.

To turn to the second possibility, there are a number of proposed mechanisms (not necessarily explicitly associated with group-selection) that turn on special circumstances which would allow an increase, or avoid pressure for a decrease, in genetic propensity to a measure of unselfish behavior. In the direct class are models of the kind discussed by R. M. May,

R. M. Gilpin, and D. S. Sloan, for example, where the ratio of social to selfish genes increases in a population due to differential survival of temporary groups (hunting packs, seasonal settlements, and so on). Axelrod and Hamilton give a related model, as do Boorman and Leavitt.[8]

In the indirect class is the "punctuated evolution" theory of Gould and Eldredge. Here evolution is rapid, following abrupt speciation events, so that selection pressure between new and old species plays a much larger role than in more conventional views. Gene flow, by definition, is foreclosed in this model, except within the new species. And the species that emerges from such an evolutionary event, if successful, is likely to be quite stable against further change.[9] Another indirect model is Layzer's, in which the controller genes give a propensity to variation in certain directions, some of which involve cooperative behavior, which in turn can favor (in later generations, under appropriate circumstances) individuals carrying the cooperative-disposing controller genes.[10]

Third, it is not at all uncommon for adherents of the selfish gene view, when considering human behavior, to resort to arguments that assume explicitly or implicitly the influence of cultural influences shaped substantially by group-interest.[11] Of course, one can turn this kind of view upside down, seeing the human propensity to follow cultural norms as the device by which a measure of group-interested motivation is sustained. More promising, I think, is to take the propensity for culture building and for following cultural norms as interdependent with a propensity for group-interested motivation. Here I note a conjecture that Layzer attributes to a former student, J. D. Kelly, which suggests that the evolution of intelligence and social behavior are tightly linked. Layzer points out the limited utility of intelligence (versus programmed instinct) in a context in which the results of previous applications of intelligence (culture) cannot be drawn upon and the results of an individual's own applications have no "future." This seems to apply particularly to the tendency to experiment, to make records, and to conceptualize experience in lore, myths and (much later) science.

A mathematical theory recently worked out by C. J. Lumsden and E. O. Wilson implies that the interaction between culture and genes can greatly speed up the evolution of behavioral propensities in a way that would increase the compatibility of cultural and genetic influences on behavior.[12] Because cultural norms, even under a strictly selfish gene view, will tend to favor group-interested behavior, the Lumsden–Wilson argument, which is controversial, seems to imply that within-group advantage to more selfish behavior will be diminished by a culture–gene linkage disadvantageous to genetic propensities that violate cultural norms. Because the essential argument against a significant role for group-selection turns on the speed with which the rival selection pressures act, any such argument that increases the efficiency with which group-oriented propensities can be made genetically adaptive, or decreases the efficiency with which more selfish propensities can be introduced, would help sustain the equilibrium rule of this chapter. Contrarywise, that rule (by providing protection against exploitation) makes any of the mechanisms we have been considering easier to sustain. In turn, a synergy favorable to a measure of social motivation, such as could emerge from the range of possibilities we have been sketching, makes the human societies we actually observe a less mystifying outcome of the evolutionary process.

In all of this, my purpose is the modest one of explaining why I do not regard the selfish gene arguments as a serious problem for the Darwinian argument developed in the first half of the chapter. However, the more I have looked into the evolutionary arguments and talked with the theorists (in contrast to various interpreters of the theory among social scientists, who often have far fewer doubts about the adequacy of simple selfish gene arguments than do the biologists), the more it seems to me that the kind of equilibrium rule developed in the first half of this chapter can fit very comfortably with what is in fact known about the evolution of social behavior.

The strict selfish gene argument turns on an application of Occam's razor, not a proof of its validity, as the leading selfish gene theorists have themselves often pointed out. Which way that razor cuts depends a good deal on whether you are studying human beings or something else. [13]

CHAPTER 4

A new model

The same equilibrium condition reached through a Darwinian argument in Chapter 3 can be obtained by a very different line of reasoning, this time based on intuitive perceptions of what it is that gives a human being the psychological sense of having done his or her "fair share". The chapter goes on to develop the basic properties of this equilibrium and then comments on the dual-utilities character of the resulting model and the role of the Darwinian argument in the light of the alternative "fair share" derivation. The last section gives a comparison of the model developed here with the well-known Harsanyi dual-preferences formulation.

The FS allocation rule

There is nothing about the intuitive "fair-share" (FS) argument to follow that is incompatible with the Darwinian argument of Chapter 3. The two arguments illustrate the characteristic complementary relation between deductive and inductive ways of proceeding. The Darwinian argument of Chapter 3 considered what sort of model we would be led to if we allowed for some measure of group-selection (or "as if" group-selection); the FS argument here considers what sort of allocation rule we might guess from our intuitive sense of what gives a human being the feeling of psychological equilibrium associated with the fair-share notion. Work from both points of view proceeds more or less simultaneously; and it is only after the fact that we can separate them out and construct distinct, self-contained arguments.

The inductive argument goes this way. Suppose we try to think of what it is that seems to give a person (such as yourself) a sense of having done his or her "fair share" in allocating resources (time, money) between private values and social values. A rule that seems to capture the essentials of this sense is this:

> The larger the share of my resources I have spent unselfishly, the more weight I give to my selfish interests in allocating marginal resources. On the other hand, the larger benefit I can confer on the group compared with the benefit from spending marginal resources on myself, the more I will tend to act unselfishly.

36

Note well that this FS principle (or pair of principles) does not purport to say how a person *ought* to behave. The reasonableness of the principle as an empirical hypothesis turns only on how well it accounts for the way people are observed to behave. The rule has a certain interest if viewed as an ethical proposition, but that aspect is not dealt with here. Note also that the two components of the principle are independent, with the first related to the notion of participation and the second related to the notion of goods altruism. I hope you will watch carefully to see that, within the formalism of the model, two distinct motivating forces are indeed at play.

Suppose that Smith has been contributing to some activity that he takes to be socially valuable, say, the Red Cross, a political campaign, or an arts organization. We make the usual assumption of diminishing marginal utility for all goods. (As shown in Appendix B, this is not an essential feature of the model, but it is convenient and harmless here.) Further, we will suppose here that, as is very often although not necessarily the case, Smith's own social contribution (to the Red Cross, or whatever) is but a microscopic fraction of the whole effort. Thus the marginal social value of another dollar will not be perceptibly affected by any contribution of the magnitude that an ordinary citizen such as Smith might make. The ratio of marginal utilities from group- versus self-interested spending will define what we will call the "value ratio" of Smith's spending opportunities.

Suppose now that Smith donates an additional $100 to the activity but simultaneously receives a $100 increment to his wealth. His participation has changed: both the magnitude of his total contribution and the fraction of his wealth contributed have increased. But there has been no change in the marginal utility from private spending and no perceptible change in the marginal utility from social spending. Therefore, although participation has changed, there is no (perceptible) change in Smith's value ratio.

Alternatively, an emergency (for example, a flood in the next county) can create an abrupt shift in Smith's perception of the marginal utility of a contribution; while a fire in Smith's own house would create a corresponding shift for Smith's spending on himself. Now participation has not changed, but (in either version of this illustration) the value ratio has changed.

Ordinarily these two components would be mixed together because if we imagine how Smith allocates a *fixed* bundle of resources, then necessarily a little more spent on social goals means a little less spent on private goals. Hence, a shift in participation will ordinarily be accompanied by a shift in the value ratio. However, as has just been illustrated, it is easy to define situations in which participation changes but not the value ratio, or vice versa. The two notions are conceptually distinct, and the model is driven by the interaction between these two motives.

Let G and S be Smith's utility from the point of view of perfectly group-interested G-Smith and perfectly self-interested S-Smith, respectively. For any given situation, let G' and S', then, be the corresponding marginal utilities of a dollar spent to maximize utility to G-Smith and S-Smith, respectively. Thus the ratio, G'/S', is the value ratio already introduced. For this ratio to be well defined, G- and S-utility must be measured on some common scale. But the internal logic of the model provides that. See the discussion at the end of this chapter and in Appendix B. Smith himself is one member of the group: hence G-utility "includes" S-utility. (This does not mean that Smith will see value to aiding the blind, for example, only if he himself is blind; but the blind who are helped must be part of a larger entity of which Smith feels he is a part.)

Now G-utility evaluates Smith's perception of the situation of society as a whole (not excluding Smith, but giving no special weight to Smith); and S-utility evaluates Smith's own situation. Neither depends on any necessary relation to Smith's own resources. It is easiest to see this in connection with public goods. For S-utility will depend substantially on the supply of public goods in Smith's society, which will be essentially independent of Smith's own wealth or spending; and G-utility will ordinarily be almost entirely independent of Smith's own wealth or spending. Hence the value ratio, although defined in terms of Smith's own values, is not defined in terms of Smith's own resources. There is no necessary connection between the value ratio and Smith's own participation in the provision of goods either to himself or to society at large.

Smith's participation, on the other hand, depends only on how large a share of Smith's resources have been devoted to group-interest, not at all on his judgment of the value of the spending (or of the value of the resources he has devoted to self-interest). If Smith contributes to a charity he later discovers to be fraudulent, his judgment of the value of his contribution changes drastically, but there is no change in the extent to which he has participated.

Let g be the total amount that has been allocated to G-Smith (which by definition will have been spent to maximize G-utility); and let s be the total amount that has been allocated to S-Smith (which by definition will have been spent to maximize S-utility). The ratio, g/s, which we will call the "participation ratio," gives the ratio in which Smith has allocated his resources between spending to maximize G- versus S-utility. Finally, let W be the *weight* that Smith gives to S-utility in choosing whether to allocate a marginal dollar to S-Smith or G-Smith. (Actually, it is better not to say "Smith gives" but perhaps "the referee inside Smith gives" because we are not postulating a rule Smith consciously follows but rather an internal mechanism of which Smith may be quite unconscious.) In sum what the FS principle requires is that:

1. The larger the value ratio, G'/S', the greater the tendency must be for Smith to allocate a marginal dollar to G- rather than S-Smith.
2. The weighting function, W, must vary positively with the participation ratio, g/s, because the likelihood that Smith will allocate a marginal dollar to S- rather than G-Smith must increase with increases in the participation ratio.
3. Smith will be in equilibrium when the propensity to favor self-interest balances the propensity to act in group-interest.

Casting this in mathematical terms, all of the preceding discussion can be summarized very neatly by defining the FS equilibrium condition as follows:

FS equilibrium holds *if and only if*:

$$W = G'/S' \qquad\qquad 4.1$$

where

$$W = f(g/s); \; W^0 \geq 1; \; W' > 0. \qquad\qquad 4.2$$

What Equation 4.2 says is that, until Smith has spent *something* in group-interest (i.e., as long as $g = 0$), then $W = W^0$. In the simplest case, setting $W^0 = 1$, he gives no more weight to his self-interest than he does to his perception of group-interest. However, any increase in the participation ratio, g/s, increases W. Hence $W' \equiv dW/d(g/s) > 0$.

As long as the ordinarily reasonable assumption of diminishing marginal utility holds, then if Smith is out of equilibrium with $W > G'/S'$ he will move closer to equilibrium by shifting resources from group-interest to self-interest (decreasing g, increasing s); and the reverse holds if he is out of equilibrium with $W < G'/S'$. Shifting resources from g to s decreases the ratio g/s, hence decreasing W, and simultaneously increases G'/S'; the reverse is true if the shift is from s to g.

Figure 4.1 illustrates this equilibrium notion. The dashed line slanting upward to the right shows W increasing (Equation 4.2) as the share of Smith's income allocated to group-interest (g) increases from 0 to his whole income, I, along the horizontal axis.

The solid line slanting down from the left in Figure 4.1 gives the value ratio, G'/S', which (provided that $S'' < 0$, $G'' \leq 0$) will have a negative slope, as shown, yielding the unique equilibrium allocation at E.

Figure 4.2 illustrates a fundamental property of Smith's equilibrium income-spending path (the set of equilibrium allocations as Smith's income increases) for the important special case in which Smith is an ordinary

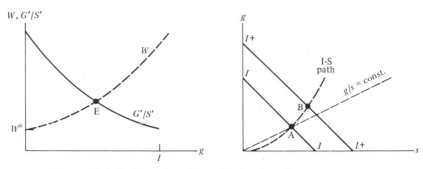

Figure 4.1 (left). The unique FS equilibrium is at E.

Figure 4.2 (right). The dashed line through points A and B gives the equilibrium income-spending path.

citizen in a large society and faces stable spending opportunities. For this case (which has already been mentioned in introducing the model), G' will not be affected by Smith's own allocation, which will be microscopic compared with the spending of all members of society on outlets for group-interested spending.

In Figure 4.2, Smith's allocation to G-Smith (g) is now shown on the *vertical* axis, and his allocation to S-Smith (s) is shown on the horizontal axis. Together, $g + s =$ Smith's income, I. Possible allocations Smith might make, subject to his income constraint, are given by the $-45°$ line labeled II. As we move northwest along II (equivalent to moving to the right in Figure 4.1), W increases, while G'/S' decreases. Somewhere along this line there will be a unique equilibrium point (recall Figure 4.1) such that $W = G'/S'$. In Figure 4.2 this is point A.

We now draw a vector (the straight line in Figure 4.2) from the origin through point A. This will be the locus of all points such that the participation ratio, g/s, hence also W, will be the same as at A. However, as we move out along this constant-W vector, the value ratio, G'/S', must increase (for S' is decreasing, but G' is remaining constant). So A must be the *only* point on that line at which Smith could be in equilibrium, as well as the only such point along the income constraint line, II. At points along the constant-W line closer to the origin than A, we must find $W > G'/S'$ (G' would be the same as at A, as is W; but S' must be greater, hence the value ratio would be reduced); and vice versa at points on the constant-W line, but further from the origin than A. This means that if Smith's income is less than I (the income constraint lies closer to the origin than II), the equilibrium point must lie southeast of the constant-W line; and for incomes greater than I the equilibrium point will lie northwest of the constant-W line.

This argument can be applied to any equilibrium point. Therefore Smith's equilibrium income-spending path must have the upward-bending shape sketched by the curved dotted line in Figure 4.2. For example, at income $I+$, Smith's equilibrium allocation must lie at a point, such as B, northwest of the intersection of the constant-W line and the enlarged income constraint, $I+I+$. At a still higher income level, the new equilibrium would lie northwest of a line drawn from the origin through B. And so on.

So it turns out, given some rather innocuous-seeming assumptions, that the allocation rule implies that spending in group-interest will be a superior good: as income increases, the fraction of resources allocated to G-Smith increases, even though (in a sense) Smith is becoming more selfish (W is increasing).

However, one or more of the assumptions on which this result depends (such as "fixed spending opportunities") will be violated in many practical contexts. Although the upward-bending income-spending path illustrated in Figure 4.2 is a very important property of the model, with many empirical implications, other situations arise in which allocations shift even though income has not; where relatively poor individuals are moved to great efforts in what they deem to be group-interest; where individuals face unstable spending opportunities so that the assumption that G' can be taken as constant with respect to Smith's own spending does not hold; and so on. Thus it is by no means the case that all the behavior implied by the model follows from or is contingent upon the validity of the superior good result. The result is important, but not universal.

In general, what I have developed here are the salient points of the FS model – sufficient to allow a reader who wishes to bypass details to proceed through the balance of the study. But I would urge even such readers to look through Appendixes B and C, where the formal properties of the model are treated in much greater detail.

The dual-utilities

We come now to a particularly controversial issue. If you compare either the Darwinian argument of Chapter 3 or the fair-share argument just concluded with the discussion of goods versus participation altruism in Chapter 2, you will see that we have not explicitly addressed the formal problem posed in that chapter. That is, we have not postulated a utility function for Smith based on self-interest plus participation altruism (Equation 2.1) and another based on self-interest plus goods altruism (Equation 2.2) and then sought a way of combining these into some specification of total utility incorporating both (Equation 2.3). In fact, we have no total utility function, only a rule allocating between Smith's distinct G- and S-preferences.

Nevertheless, the W-function of Equations 4.1 and 4.2 captures an intuitive sense of participation altruism (or, we might say, participation selfishness, since the greater the participation ratio the more weight Smith then gives to self-interest at the margin). And the value ratio, G'/S', captures an intuitive sense of goods altruism. But we have defined no grand utility function *from* which we could then derive the FS allocation rule as the first order condition which maximizes that function. Rather, in either the Darwinian or fair-share formulation, the FS allocation rule comes directly from an argument about what form a rule might take that governed allocation of resources between the rival claims of group-interest and self-interest.

However, the W-function in Equation 4.2 *could* be interpreted as akin to the familiar economists' notion of diminishing marginal rate of substitution (MRS): here, diminishing MRS between spending in group-interest and spending in self-interest. Further, the absence of a total utility function, of which the G- and S-functions would be components, seems strange or even palpably wrong to most economists. A happy solution would be available if we could define some reasonably neat total utility function, whose first order maximizing condition was given by Equation 4.1 and where the W-function appeared in the form of diminishing MRS.

Now, at least for the special case of voluntary spending by a typical citizen facing fixed spending opportunities (meaning that the value ratio, G'/S', can be treated as a function of Smith's spending only, with everything else taken as given), it is possible to do all that, as shown in Appendix C.

Nevertheless, as I stress in Appendix C, nothing essential to the argument of this study turns on this matter. (Recall the discussion at the end of Chapter 1.) We have no reason to limit the model to those situations for which it happens to be possible to define a neat total utility function, or, alternatively, to burden the analysis with a clumsy total utility function when the special conditions do not hold. To the contrary, on the internal logic of the FS model, it would be quite artificial and in fact misleading to handle the model in that way, even if it were practical to do so.

The following economic analog may be helpful.

Imagine a country that desires to hold down investment overseas, but not forgo it entirely, and that also does not wish to allow a few firms to monopolize the resources permitted for overseas investment. Specifically, suppose this country adopts the following principle:

> Other things equal, the higher the ratio of rate of return (ROR) overseas compared with home, the more a firm can invest overseas. On the other hand, the more a firm has already invested abroad, the higher the ROR ratio must be to permit a further addition to overseas investment.

Now let g be dollars invested overseas by a firm; and let s be dollars invested at home. Let $G' = ROR$ overseas; and let $S' = ROR$ at home. Then the government's policy is to make investment overseas (increments to g) contingent on the ROR value ratio, G'/S', and also on the overseas participation ratio, g/s. Specifically, the more the firm has already invested overseas (the higher g/s), the higher G'/S' for that firm must be to allow an incremental dollar to be invested overseas. The rule is: a firm invests overseas only if $W < G'/S'$, where $W = W(g/s)$; $W(0) \geq 1$; $W' > 0$. So an individual firm will be in equilibrium if and only if $W = G'/S'$.

This makes the equilibrium condition for our economic analog identical to the FS condition; hence, whatever total utility function could be imputed to Smith would also serve as a total utility function for the firms in our hypothetical country.

For the economic analog, however, no one would think of the firm as maximizing any such total utility function. We know that the allocation rule was chosen as a compromise between the rival claims of maximizing return and restraining overseas investment in a politically acceptable way. To base a theory of how firms in this country are behaving on a total utility function the firm seeks to maximize would only obscure the true situation, which is that the allocation rule was there before the utility function. It is hard to imagine a clearer case for the application of Occam's razor.

Yet, under FS, as in the economic analog, the individual actor (person or firm, respectively) has an equilibrium allocation rule that arises directly from the competing influences on the class of actors studied (natural selection or political, respectively). In terms of the Darwinian argument, the U-function of Appendix C is just as much an artifact for FS as it would be for the economic analog, even though customary practice in economics leads one to think instinctively that what a rational actor does is maximize a utility function.

A famous situation that is at least roughly akin to the one here is this. Tycho Brahe never believed that the drastic departure from received views Copernicus proposed was needed to obtain the Copernican results. He pointed out that, mathematically, the Copernican system was identical to a system in which all planets *except* the earth went around the sun, while the sun went around the stationary earth. Technically, Brahe was correct, as on the humbler matter at hand it is technically correct that the FS model can be framed in terms of a sufficiently complicated U-function. But mathematical equivalence is not the same as cognitive equivalence. Brahe's model led to pseudo problems and dead ends; it was the more radical but simpler view that led to modern science.

On the issue at hand, as long as you "see" the model in terms of a U-function, I believe it will be very difficult indeed to grasp the full role that the Darwinian view plays in the analysis to come. On the other hand, once you find that you are seeing the model in terms of the Darwinian argument of Chapter 3, I think you will find many other points in the argument relatively easy to grasp.

For examples, from the Darwinian viewpoint, it is obvious why Smith's allocation is between group-interest, which includes Smith as well as others, and self-interest, which includes only Smith, *instead of* Smith's altruistic interest in others versus self-interest. The Darwinian argument accounts for the two distinct components of altruistic motivation (participation and the value ratio). It tells us why the G- and S-functions are defined in terms of Smith's and the group's well-being in the world rather than in terms of this well-being plus various kinds of psychic goods, such as the satisfaction of doing one's duty. It sheds some light on the difficult problem of defining group-loyalty. It lets us see how cultural rules of thumb could be a significant component of motivation without making the theory so loose as to be analytically useless (since we can see how the rules of thumb are ultimately constrained by the underlying FS structure). Finally, it helps us clear up a number of puzzles related to the fact that, in the real world, Smith's spending opportunities are much richer than the abstract "spending in self-interest" and "spending in group-interest" considered to this point. All of these matters are discussed in Chapter 5 and in Appendixes D and E.

In sum, there is a powerful advantage to "seeing" the argument from the Darwinian view. But it is precisely from that Darwinian viewpoint that focusing attention on a total utility function is unessential, unnecessarily complicated, and in fact misleading.

Comparison of FS and Harsanyi

The notion that human beings might possess the kind of dual preference structure posited by this study is very old, going back at least to Plato's distinction between man as a private individual and man as citizen.[1] I will not try to survey or comment on that literature in general, but a brief discussion of treatments within economics may help clarify some things about the formulation here. In the early 1950s two of the best-known economic theorists touched on this topic: Arrow in his distinction between a person's tastes and his values; Buchanan in his suggestion that the preference structure of a citizen when he is voting may be different from his preference structure when he is acting as a private individual. But neither said much more on the subject than I have just repeated. However, about the same time a third economist, John Harsanyi, developed a treatment in some detail that is still widely cited and that therefore may provide a good basis for bringing out, through parallels and contrasts, some aspects of the FS structure.[2]

Harsanyi proposed that each individual possess both the set of personal preferences ordinarily assumed by economists plus an additional set of preferences that concern not himself but his judgment about social welfare. Harsanyi calls this second set of preferences the individual's social welfare function (*SWF*). The following remarks compare the Harsanyi dual preferences with the FS group-interested *G*-preferences and self-interested *S*-preferences.

First, the FS *G*-function, like Harsanyi's *SWF*, expresses "what this individual prefers. . .on the basis of impersonal social considerations alone."[3] Also, in FS, as in Harsanyi, the individual simultaneously has a second set of preferences. Harsanyi calls this the "utility function," which expresses "what he actually prefers."

However, Harsanyi's *SWF* is subordinate to his "utility function" in the sense that the Harsanyi *SWF* "will, by definition, express what he prefers only in those possibly rare moments when he forces a special impartial and impersonal attitude upon himself." In contrast Harsanyi's "utility function" will "express his preferences in the full sense of the word as they actually are, showing an egoistic attitude in the case of an egoist and an altruistic attitude in the case of an altruist."[4]

The relationships are quite different in FS. The FS *S*-function is, by definition, perfectly egoistic; and the *G*-function is not something that appears in "possibly rare moments": it is just as much an expression of "what the individual actually prefers" as is the *S*-function. In the context of the most concern to economics (the marketplace), an analysis in terms of the *S*-function alone ordinarily will give an adequate approximation of individual behavior. Even in the marketplace, though, the *G*-function is operating, and (as illustrated in Chapter 9) its influence on behavior can be observed. Harsanyi gives no specification of the extent to which an individual would use resources to further his *SWF* as opposed to his "actual" preferences. In contrast, the FS model turns on an allocation rule for dividing resources between *S*- and *G*-Smiths.

We might sum up as follows: the Harsanyi *SWF* is almost (see below) equivalent to the FS *G*-function; and his utility function is equivalent to the FS *U*-function of Appendix C. It is the FS *S*-function that is missing from Harsanyi's formulation, except of course for the special case in which an individual actually is a perfect egoist, so that (in FS terms) his *S*-function and *U*-function are identical.

Because the Harsanyi formulation gives no allocation rule, it leads to no empirically testable inferences. (Nor does Harsanyi imply that it does; see below.) If an individual behaves in a manner inconsistent with his personal preferences, it is apparently one of the "rare occasions"; however, since the individual's personal preferences may be altruistic, we cannot predict that he will exhibit altruistic behavior *only* on rare occasions.

On a more narrowly technical point, Harsanyi provides an argument (based on the von Neumann–Morgenstern (NM) axioms) that the *SWF* (and also the utility function) is cardinal in the NM sense. It turns out, as shown in Appendix B and C, that the internal *G*- and *S*-functions of FS are also cardinal. But there is no relation between these results, and the meaning of "cardinality" is different in the two contexts. (See the technical discussion in Appendixes B and C.)

Next, Harsanyi's discussion is normative, defining how ethical individuals *ought* to specify their *SWF*. But the FS model claims only to be descriptive and does not contain various normative judgments used implicitly or explicitly by Harsanyi. In particular, and in contrast to Harsanyi, there is no reason to stipulate in FS that the individual gives equal weight to everyone in the *G*-function, (although he gives not special weight to himself) and no presumption that the individual attempts to estimate other people's preferences and employ them as arguments in his *G*-function. In particular, *G*-Smith's view of the marginal utility of more bread or more gin to Jones represents Smith's preference on this matter given his perception of group-interest. There is no presumption that it coincides with Jones's preference.

However, there is an important exception to this last remark. Although we by no means suppose (the Darwinian argument in no way leads us to suppose) that Smith's judgment of what is good for Jones is identical to Jones's, we have every reason to suppose that *G*-Smith's judgment of what is good for Smith is the same as *S*-Smith's; similarly, *S*-Smith's judgment of what is good for Smith's society is ordinarily the same as *G*-Smith's.

Thus, when I speak of *S*-Smith and *G*-Smith "inside Smith," obviously you should not think of a pair of unrelated homunculi dividing up a pie (Smith's resources) in some backroom of Smith's mind. Although I think the *G*-Smith–*S*-Smith metaphor is helpful, the model could just as well be discussed in terms of Smith's social and private preferences (*G*- and *S*-preferences), both of which he values and between which he must somehow allocate his resources. The allocation that satisfies him best is the one defined by the FS principle introduced at the opening of this chapter. When formulated in mathematical language this takes the form of Equations 4.1 and 4.2. From the Darwinian viewpoint developed in Chapter 3 and earlier in this chapter, we can understand how it comes about that Smith has both social concerns (*G*-preferences) as well as private concerns (*S*-preferences) and why the allocation principle which describes the allocation that gives him a sense of equilibrium happens to take the form given. However, from the Darwinian view, it would be only in pathological cases that Smith could be thought of as schizophrenic, with *S*- and *G*-preferences incompatible.

CHAPTER 5

Applying the FS model

The argument of the previous two chapters leads to a set of further issues that arise when we begin to think about applications. As you will see, on the matter of handling the "group" to which "group-interest" refers I mainly identify a complex problem which the present study barely addresses. With respect to the balance of the material, I elaborate on the model as presented thus far in several ways that involve primarily an unfolding of what is already implicitly there. Following comments on the group-identity issue, I discuss the role of "satisficing" and customary behavior. Then the handling of "mixed" and "coerced" spending is developed. I next define the notions of FS static, comparative static, and dynamic analysis. Finally, I comment on nonrational aspects of motivation and on some points related to the notion of "psychic income."

Group-loyalties

To this point, I have simply taken the notion of group-interest as something that could be discussed in the usual way, as we talk of "social values," "the public interest," and so on. However, with any of these terms – no more, I think, with the notion of group-interest here, but also no less – it turns out to be quite difficult to be precise about exactly what we mean. One of the merits of formal theory is that it makes us recognize the imprecision of everyday language. But facing the problem does not resolve it. I will have almost nothing to say in this study, that is, nothing precise enough to become part of the formal theory, on the question of defining group-loyalty. Rather, I will use the term pretty much in the rough but intuitively useful way that is common not only in informal discourse but also in most scholarly work.

In that spirit, what can we say about the nature of the group whose group-interest G-Smith seeks to advance?

In terms of the Darwinian argument this is not a salient problem. For a very long time, the group to which a human being belonged was obvious. But as human societies come to be organized on a larger scale, the problem of group-identity becomes more and more complicated. In the modern world it is very complicated indeed, involving a very rich mixing of affiliations based on locality, kinship, common traditions, religion, cooperative interactions, and so on. If we wish to move ahead with work using the FS model, we will be quickly drawn into what are generally recognized as the central issues of sociology. I will argue, however, that we are not talking here about a weakness of the FS model. In contrast to the conventional rational choice model, in terms of FS it is possible to begin to address the crucial sociological puzzle of the nature and determinants of group-identity.

Furthermore, as Sam Beer has pointed out to me, the situation is hardly worse – indeed it is not essentially different – from that under the standard rational choice analysis. The theory of rational choice does not allow us to deduce an individual's tastes. Rather, given those tastes, the theory tells us something about how he can use his resources as efficiently as feasible. Here we have group-interested as well as self-interested preferences. As under the standard analysis, we must look to psychology and sociology to understand how those preferences are determined.

The Darwinian point of view gives us some insight into how to proceed on such an enterprise. Specifically, we would expect that the cognitive cues that identify group-interest would have evolved from cues that originally developed as means of identifying kin (people with whom one interacts closely, people who seem like oneself in various ways); or cues that served to identify individuals with whom a reciprocity relation exists. For we would suppose that group-commitments arise when evolutionary conditions are such (by some set of mechanisms along the lines of those discussed in Chapter 3) that propensities that have their roots in strictly "selfish gene" motivation are perpetuated beyond the conditions in which they arose.[1] One would have to be cautious even about this much. Although it is easiest to imagine altruism as having its deepest roots in kin altruism, with reciprocal altruism probably coming next, and group-altruism probably last, there seems to be no strong reason to suppose that evolution proceeded in a single cycle, rather than in some much more complicated way.

A crude but I think useful first cut, sufficient to let us get on with a beginning discussion of empirical applications of FS, is to suppose just two levels of loyalty: say, national and local. In other words, we will set aside the undoubted fact that Smith is likely to have subnational (and even transnational) loyalties of many kinds (local, professional, religious, and so on). G-Smith, we will suppose, will never willfully use his resources to advance local interests at the expense of national interests; however, as among alternative ways to contribute to national interest, he will particularly favor those uses of resources which favor local interests.[2]

In a perfectly homogeneous world in which there also was perfect information, this interpretation of group-interest might have no strong implications; cases in which local interests served to discriminate among equally attractive ways to advance national interests could be regarded as not very important empirically. But in a heterogeneous world with vastly imperfect information there is no reason for G-Smith to believe that all local interests (his and Jones's and Green's) are equally important to the national interest. Grossly imperfect information leaves G-Smith quite uncertain about just how effective various ways of using resources in group-interest might be. However, Smith will naturally be much better informed on his own local interests than on those of Jones or Green. Even this modest beginning to the problem of formalizing the notion of group-loyalty leads to empirical inferences that seem to me of some interest, as will be discussed in Chapters 8 and 9.

A more elaborate attack on the problem will certainly draw much insight from the extensive sociological literature on the matter of group-loyalty. It also will, I think, turn out to draw significantly on the now very lively research going on under the general heading of cognitive studies. Having to draw a line somewhere, however, I have not tried to add sociology and cognitive psychology to the economics and evolutionary biology that is used in the theory as presented in this study.

"Satisficing" and the role of culture

In the sort of abstract analysis that will be carried out in Chapter 6, as in most "theory" papers in the conventional literature, we bypass various practical problems, implicitly supposing that individuals can somehow or other carry out whatever elegant optimizing routines may be desired to suit the convenience of the analysis. For empirical applications, though, we need some understanding of how things would work for real Smiths, not idealized Smiths.

A literature that bears directly on the formal issues that then arise is that on portfolio selection, particularly that which incorporates Herbert Simon's "satisficing" notion. We will have no occasion, at the level of detail in the applications here, to draw explicitly on that literature. But if you keep the portfolio analogy in mind, I think you will have no difficulty in understanding why a real Smith would ordinarily "spread his money around," choosing some safe ways to spend G-resources (give to the Community Chest) but with only modest expected return, and take some flyers on high risk, possibly high return uses of G-resources. He would not, as a literal interpretation of the model might suggest, survey all possibilities with infinite refinement and put all his G-resources into the single outlet that yields the highest expected utility. (There is a further cause of the "spreading" effect having to do with the role of S-resources, as will be discussed later.) Further, we can expect that, as one of Simon's satisficers, Smith will make a good deal of use of "rules of thumb" to simplify his decision making.

A certain class of rules of thumb is of special importance, namely those rules of thumb which are embodied in the culture of Smith's society so that they influence not only some individual, such as Smith, but large numbers of individuals. We will call these social rules of thumb (to extend the notion to rules reflecting fashion, professional usage, and so on). A social rule of thumb will have some influence merely by identifying a usual behavior, quite aside from any role it may play as a rational guide.

Circumstances will certainly arise in which Smith finds that, given his particular situation, following customary behavior would be an inefficient use of G-resources (Smith would have to make an expensive trip in order to vote; or Smith thinks the political system so corrupt that voting is socially pointless.) Nevertheless, that certain activities are customary in Smith's society gives a certain salience to such activities. Smith may or may not find these activities attractive outlets for his own G-resources, but the mere fact that Smith will be aware of these activities gives them an advantage over outlets for G-resources that Smith may never have heard of. Further, to the extent that failing to conform to customary usage is regarded as anti-social behavior by Smith's fellows, which might incur costs to Smith personally, then Smith will be subject to an incentive to conform, and this will influence his behavior in a way that will be developed in the next section of this chapter.

Most important of all, because it would be irrational for Smith to devote any substantial fraction of his G-resources to trying to choose the very best way to use G-resources (as he would not rationally use a substantial fraction of S-resources to look for the very best way to use S-resources), Smith will often judge it prudent to accept customary usage in his society as a guide to his own judgment.

In sum, questions of the general form, "what would someone in my position usually do" and rules of thumb reflecting socially prevalent answers to such questions are likely to be important for the kinds of reasons that apply in general to "satisficing" behavior. We can distinguish several ways in which such rules of thumb play a role: giving salience to certain ways of using G-resources; as a source of pressure to conform; as a reflection of prevailing judgment in this society, which Smith might reasonably accord some weight (as he might be careful about going swimming right after a big meal even though he has no personal basis for judging that imprudent).

With respect to the last, Smith should not be thought of as (always) merely following prevailing social rules. On occasion, and at least in part, he may make his own judgment, using a question of the form, "what if

everybody in my position . . ." as an aid to "seeing" what a reasonable estimate of G' might be.

In other words, Smith may use a judgment framed in terms of the group
(what could be called a Kantian judgment) as a way of estimating G' for
various outlets for G-resources. In a large society, both Smith's spending
and the benefits from that spending will be microscopically small from a
social point of view. It will often be hard, therefore, for Smith to "see" the
ratio of benefit to cost directly in terms of his own act. However, it may be
quite easy to estimate this ratio (in particular to compare this ratio across
alternative ways of using G-resources) in terms of a judgment about the
ratio of aggregate benefits and cost of everyone in Smith's position behaving in a certain way.

But to the extent that Smith, Jones, Miller, and so forth all are led to
similar judgments about a situation, then that judgment will become a cultural (or, for more ephemeral matters, perhaps only a fashionable) rule of
thumb in Smith's society. Williams, who has never himself made a judgment on the issue is aware that everybody knows . . .

Thus social standards (culture) and individual preferences are interdependent, although if we look at any one individual we naturally find that the culture of his society exerts far more influence over his preferences than he does
over the culture. On the other hand, looking at aggregates of individuals
over long periods of time (looking historically) we can expect to see culture
itself change to come more nearly (leaving some scope for cultural inertia) into
line with plausible individual judgments about the rational use of resources.

None of this, I should perhaps say again, involves an alternative to or a
change from the FS model as developed in Chapters 3 and 4. Rather, all of
the behavior discussed here involves what we can expect to observe given
the FS model of motivation and Simon's observations about rational
behavior in the face of limited information and limited information-
processing capability.

Finally, as shown in Appendix C, in addition to externally observable
rules of thumb that Smith may consciously or implicitly use, the mathematical structure of the model turns out to suggest a simple internal rule of
thumb for choosing an equilibrium allocation. I attach no great significance to that particular rule, but it is a useful reminder that various internal
(subconscious) rules of thumb could exist, as indeed they obviously do exist
in other areas of human cognition.

Detailed allocations "inside Smith"

The model as discussed in Chapter 4 dealt only with simple choices between
spending in group-interest and spending in self-interest. But empirically it

is obviously essential that we be able to handle "mixed spending" (spending that elicits a significant willingness to pay (wtp) from both S- and G-Smith) and "coerced spending" (mainly tax-supported government spending). The model, in fact, must be able to handle not only mixed and coerced spending but also all the combinations: purely S- and G- voluntary spending: mixed voluntary spending; pure S- and G- coerced spending; mixed coerced spending; and variants of all these involving goods that are public, private, or in-between in Smith's external society.

The Darwinian argument of Chapter 3 gives us a guiding principle by which to approach this set of issues. In terms of the Darwinian argument, G-Smith is just as authentically Smith as S-Smith. Whatever rule governs allocation between the two, we are led to suppose that the way the allocation rule operates in the more complicated contexts we are now considering should be consistent with the basic evolutionary outcome and not subversive of that outcome. Therefore, our basic requirement in thinking about how the "inside Smith" process might work will be that the process must be (to choose a label) "nonsubversive." S-Smith cannot be allowed to exploit G-Smith, and vice versa; nor can the control arrangement favor one over the other.

Further, the Darwinian point of view leads us to postulate that the allocation mechanism will be not only nonsubversive (analogous to the equity, or fairness, requirement in a conventional social welfare analysis), but also efficient. For, among variant outcomes, selection will favor the most efficient scheme.

The key to seeing what form this mechanism will take is to notice that, because S-Smith and G-Smith inhabit the same body, all goods (whether purely public, purely private, or in-between in the external world) are public goods "inside" Smith. S-Smith cannot have a drink without G-Smith also having a drink; G-Smith cannot risk his life for God and country without S-Smith running precisely the same risk.

Further, in what turns out to be the sense we require, self-interested behavior holds for our "inside Smith" society. This point can be made fully explicit only in Appendix D. But notice that it would be redundant to suppose that G-Smith has some extra concern for S-Smith beyond what is already incorporated in the G-function. The same applies, more obviously, to S-Smith's preferences: to the extent that utility to G-Smith is valued by S-Smith, that utility is already incorporated into the S-function (specifically, just so much as serves Smith's pure self-interest.)

Consequently, *inside* Smith, the conventional analysis of efficient social choice in a society of self-interested individuals works just fine, even though the starting point for the study is the observation that that analysis works quite badly if we use it to judge how Smith behaves in the external society. In particular, we can apply the analytics of Samuelson's "pseudo-market" to define efficient choice and allocation of costs for the two-person society inside Smith.[3]

Because it would be incongruous to imagine that a revelation of preference problem exists "inside Smith," a scheme which Samuelson treated as unimplementable in practice and hence limited to normative applications, turns out to have an interesting positive application, though in an unexpected domain. Yet, given the marvelous efficiency of nature's "designs" (evolutionary outcomes), I do not think it unreasonable to suppose that nature managed to stumble on a process that Samuelson was shrewd enough to conceive. After all, nature managed to stumble on the process that produced Samuelson.

It is convenient to postulate an entity that governs this "inside Smith" arrangement (the analog here of the omniscient referee in Samuelson's pseudomarket). Thus, in addition to G- and S-Smith, we may imagine a third metaphorical entity, U-Smith. The FS model is then that U-Smith allocates Smith's income between G-Smith and S-Smith so as to maintain (or come as close as is feasible to maintaining) the equilibrium condition, $W = G'/S'$.

Let S-wtp and G-wtp represent S- and G-Smith's willingness to pay for a marginal unit of the good at issue, yielding S-wtp and G-wtp schedules analogous to the marginal wtp (marginal demand) schedules in a conventional model. Then (as worked out in Appendix E) Smith's demand for voluntary goods (i.e., those for which Smith is at liberty to spend as much or as little as he cares) will be determined by the Lindahl–Samuelson logic, given the formal equivalence of the "inside Smith" society and the self-interested society of the conventional model. This means that Smith spends such that the summed marginal wtp just equals the marginal cost (S-wtp + G-wtp = MC), where the allocation of cost inside Smith (tax prices), as in the Samuelson or the earlier Lindahl scheme are equal to marginal wtp (i.e., S-wtp for S-Smith, G-wtp for G-Smith).

Mathematically, this is the only scheme that will be feasible (S-wtp + G-wtp = price); efficient (pareto-optimal "inside Smith"); and fair (non-subversive). The scheme applies to all voluntary spending, (whether on goods that are public, private, or in-between in Smith's external society). However, except for goods that are pure public goods in the external society, goods with different uses (for example, bread for Smith to eat; bread for Smith to give to the poor) must be treated as distinct goods because G- and S-wtp schedules will ordinarily be different for different uses of the good.

However, for coerced goods that situation is less simple; only after we have completed the analysis of the next chapter will I be able to explain (in Appendix E) the basis for the following rule for coerced goods:

> Divide the assigned tax price to Smith such that the unit cost "inside Smith" which is charged to S-Smith is S-Smith's "Lindahl" price, and assign any balance of cost to G-Smith.

Finally, note that the process of allocation inside Smith (between S- and G-Smiths) of Smith's income (analog of the distribution of income in a real society) must be interdependent with the pseudomarket process because nonsubversiveness plus efficiency requires that (analogous again to the Samuelson scheme) after the fact both the FS rule and the Lindahl conditions are fulfilled. In our metaphor, the outcome must be simultaneously efficient from all three points of view: U-, G-, and S-Smiths's.

This last remark is in fact merely a more explicit statement of the "nonsubversiveness" requirement developed earlier in this section. If in fact an allocation of costs "inside Smith" is nonsubversive – neither S-Smith nor G-Smith is being exploited – then each must be doing as well as he could do if it were possible for him to act as a separate entity, given the allocation of Smith's income according to the FS rule.

We can now hardly avoid observing the following curiosity. We have "inside Smith" a G-Smith that seems to have properties rather like those of Freud's supergo, an S-Smith that looks rather like Freud's id, and a third entity, U-Smith, that mediates between these two and that appears to have the integrating function so essential to the Freudian notion of the ego. I certainly do not want to claim that the FS scheme is just what Freud had in mind, or that it is what he should have had in mind. However, given the explicitly speculative tone of Freud's own treatment, I doubt that it can be fairly argued that the FS trichotomy is fatally inconsistent with Freud's insight on this matter. After this aspect of the model turned up, I was struck especially to come across the following remark by Freud: "Man is not only far more immoral than he believes but also far more moral than he knows... Human nature has a far greater extent, both for good and for evil, than it thinks it has – i.e., than its ego is aware of through conscious perception."[4]

Summing this up, the Samuelson "pseudomarket" analysis (showing how efficient allocations to public goods would be made if, contrary to fact, there could be an omniscient referee for society) finds a kind of real existence in the FS model, made necessary by the internal logic of the model and made possible by the fact that the revelation of preferences issue does not arise if the revelation need go no further than to some other entity "inside Smith." This scheme allows the model to handle cases of mixed

		Private goods	Public goods	
			Tax-supported	Voluntary
Mainly charge to*	S-Smith	Bread for Smith to eat	Cancer research	
	G-Smith	Bread for Smith to give to the poor	Braille books for public libraries	Cancer research Braille books

Figure 5.1. Allocations "inside Smith" by type of good. *Assumes that Smith is well off and has no blind dependents.

motivation in the use of resources (self-interest and group-interest are both involved). This is an important feature of the model because mixed goods are obviously very important empirically. It also allows the model to handle allocations (between g and s) of coerced spending, mainly taxes for public goods, which obviously is also very important empirically. In turn, this leads to a trichotomous structure inside Smith that looks rather like the kind of structure that Freud intuited. Figure 5.1 illustrates the allocations we would expect.

What can we say about U-Smith? Very little. Yet we are no more in the dark here than in explaining any other sophisticated function of the brain. We observe that a certain function is performed (here, that human beings appear to have some internal mechanism which tells them if they are in equilibrium with respect to doing their "fair share"), and so we postulate the existence of a mechanism that does this job. This brazen procedure frequently turns out to be useful, as the postulating of atoms and genes was useful during the decades in which chemistry and later genetics managed to make some progress although no chemist or geneticist had the slightest idea of what (physically) an atom or a gene might be or how it might perform its postulated function.

In the case at hand, it would be quite astonishing if the scheme described – built up purely out of the internal logic of the FS model and its Darwinian viewpoint combined with Samuelson's abstract analysis of public goods – should turn out to be just right empirically. Nevertheless, it seems to me promising that the logic of the model leads to such an elegant conceptual solution to the problems of mixed and coerced goods.

Static versus dynamic FS analysis

In applications of FS, it will often be possible to simplify the discussion by taking the allocation between S-Smith and G-Smith as given. Or, somewhat more complicated, we sometimes need to consider a change in Smith's allocation (the simplest case here is when spending opportunities are unchanged but Smith's income increases), following which we again can consider only how this new allocation is used. Finally, there are situations in which Smith's spending opportunities or his circumstances are such that his equilibrium condition is unstable and his use of resources must be studied in terms of dynamic interaction with his internal allocation.

I will label these situations the (1) static; (2) comparative static; and (3) dynamic contexts, where "static" and "dynamic" refer to the FS allocation inside Smith, not (as in ordinary usage in economics) to whether time is a dimension in the analysis. To avoid confusion with the more usual usage, I will insert the label "FS" whenever there is any reasonable risk of ambiguity. Similarly, wherever necessary I will write "FS allocation" to refer to the allocation (in ordinary economic usage "distribution") of Smith's resources between S- and G-Smith. G- and S-Smith then allocate G- and S-resources, respectively, over various spending opportunities, in the usual usage of "allocation."

As in the discussion of rules of thumb, there is nothing in the notion of FS static analysis that involves any change in, or alternative to, the model developed in Chapter 4. All inferences from the model must be defensible in terms of a dynamic FS analysis (context 3). However, it often happens that we can see that a significant change in the FS allocation would not occur, or would not effect the results in a certain discussion (context 1), or that we need consider only a one-time change in allocation (context 2). Spelling this out in a bit more detail, we have the following.

FS static analysis

As long as Smith is an ordinary individual facing stable opportunities (life is going along as usual), we can suppose that an all-at-once FS allocation has been made between G- and S-Smiths such that $W = G'/S'$. Smith then has bundles of resources, g and s, which are to be used in whatever way would maximize G- and S-utility, respectively. In the language of Chapter 2, we need only consider self-interest (governing S-resources) and goods altruism (governing G-resources), participation having been resolved prior to the analysis.

However, in many situations (for example, the outbreak of war or the appointment of Smith to high office, or indeed various less spectacular occurrences), the nature of Smith's spending opportunities will shift substantially. In the static context, we need take account only of how Smith will be observed to behave, given the internal allocation between S- and G-Smiths, with each using his share of Smith's income to maximize, respectively, S- and G-utility. However, if Smith's spending opportunities change so that there is a change in his value ratio, G'/S', there must follow a change in the allocation of resources between S- and G-Smiths. Smith would find himself out of equilibrium, and he would respond accordingly. This could involve either a one-time readjustment, analogous to a comparative statics problem in ordinary economic usage; or it could involve continuing readjustments.

FS comparative statics

If Smith's opportunities change (his situation in life changes; the world around him changes) but the new "menu" of opportunities is stable, then there is a one-time reallocation to meet the changed conditions (such that $W = G'/S'$ in the new context). Smith then uses his G- and S-resources as in context 1.

In the language of Chapter 2, we can treat Smith as if a lexical utility function is sufficient to describe his behavior: an allocation is chosen between S- and G-Smiths (participation is decided), and we then proceed as in the static context. What is of interest is how Smith's behavior changes between two situations that lead to different FS allocations (FS comparative statics).

FS dynamics

Finally, there is the situation of unstable opportunities. For an ordinary citizen such a situation is likely to represent a time of special crisis – natural or personal disaster; front-line service in wartime; and so on. But for political leaders, such unstable opportunities may be the norm. In these contexts we would need to look at what is happening at the margin, thinking less in terms of a one-time allocation between G- and S-Smiths, and much more in terms of resources – often perishable resources – coming to hand and being allocated at the margin between G- and S-spending. The equilibrium condition remains the same: Smith tries to use the resources to keep himself (comes as close as feasible to keeping himself) in an equilibrium situation, with $W = G'/S'$. But we have to think of the FS condition as governing a dynamic rather than static equilibrium.

Nonrational behavior and FS

Because there is undoubtedly more "inside Smith" than S-Smith and G-Smith, a comment on the relationship between the FS model and other aspects of human choice may be useful. In particular, I want to say something about how the FS structure might relate to those aspects of behavior which seem least amenable to treatment in terms of rational choice.

Almost all of us are aware of aspects of our own behavior that we would

		Schelling	
		Programmed	Calculated
FS	G-Smith	E.g., mob behavior	E.g., picketing
	S-Smith	E.g., overeating	E.g., dieting

Figure 5.2. Relation between Schelling's struggle and the S-Smith–G-Smith dichotomy.

prefer to be without: eating, smoking, or drinking too much and losing tempers are obvious examples. Schelling has recently given an account of this kind of phenomena.[5] I provide some comments on this in Appendix E, giving a particular interpretation to Schelling's "inner struggle."

The simplest relation between Schelling's struggle and the S-Smith–G-Smith dichotomy is illustrated by the two-by-two matrix in Figure 5.2. Smith has a rational, calculating side and an instinctive, programmed-rule side. Sometimes the two come into conflict. Smith also has the G-Smith, S-Smith dichotomy, which is the focus of our interest in this study. Because S- and G-values may vary, depending on the state of Schelling's internal struggle, marginal allocations (either between G- and S-Smiths or in the way in which G- and S-resources are used given an allocation) will be subject to the effects of this variation in control. How this would work will certainly be tied (at least) to the "cognition" issues noted earlier in this chapter and set aside as beyond the scope of the present work. But the interactions between the FS scheme and Schelling's internal struggle, treated as two dimensions of motivation, suggest what might prove to be a promising line of inquiry. The conceptual framework of Figure 5.2 is rich enough (taking account of variations in side conditions) to account for a wide range of behavior by a single individual, and even for striking differences in patterns of behavior across individuals or across cultures. If we are fortunate, we may find that scheme the basis for a simpler theory of behavior than many students of the subject have believed possible.

Note, however, even the illustrative behavior mentioned in Figure 5.2 would need to be looked at in context: for example, it is easy to think of special situations in which overeating serves some calculated purpose. More important still, calculated and programmed behavior are often mixed closely together, and often are reinforcing. (It is not ordinarily the case that programmed responses are inconsistent with what the individual would want himself to do). Thus I am not suggesting that the categorization of Figure 5.2 can be construed as doing more than what has been said, that is, suggesting the possibility for a theory that is simpler than many people have supposed possible. There is no suggestion that such a "simpler" theory would be easy to work out.

The role of "fair share" in the FS model

What is often called "psychic income" concerns utility due to the fact that Smith feels better about himself by behaving in a certain way, for example, the sense of well-being that accompanies satisfaction of one's sense of duty, or doing one's fair share. The public choice literature is ambiguous on this matter, with some writers seeming to have no qualms about invoking psychic income to explain behavior that seems irrational in terms of the more usual components of an economic utility calculus (for examples, Mueller and Riker and Ordeshook), whereas others (for example, Barry) treat psychic income as mere ad hocery that explains nothing at all in terms of rational choice.[6] This latter view does not necessarily deny that doing one's duty, or fair share, means *something* real in human motivation, but it does insist that simply invoking the words "psychic income" or something equivalent does not tell us anything more than we already know, namely, that there is apparently something which does not fit in a conventional utility calculus that accounts for the observed behavior. This issue will be taken up in the concrete context of the analysis of voting in Chapter 7. A more general argument follows here.

As far as I have been able to find, there is no generally understood sense of just what "psychic income" means, or of how it is to be treated in an analysis (i.e., under what conditions it is to appear as an explicit argument in an individual's utility function, and when not). This is the situation we could expect to hold if in fact the notion were only a device for papering over difficulties. It is not always the case that psychic income is understood as limited to serving social or moral goals. For example, conspicuous consumption intended to elicit admiration or envy of others may be lumped together with satisfaction from doing one's duty as psychic income. In what follows, though (and in the continuation in Chapter 7), I will be considering mainly what might be termed "moral" income. (A comment on conspicuous consumption is given later, in Chapter 9.)

Reviewing the Darwinian argument in Chapter 3, you will see that G- and S-utility must reflect Smith's perception of external reality (fitness being a property of the external world and not a psychological state). So, under FS, we can never say that Smith does something to obtain psychic income, as distinct from its anticipated effect on the external world. That is why, in the formal definitions of Appendix B, G- and S-utility are defined as functions of the state of the world, not as functions of the state of the world plus Smith's (and/or others') internal state of mind.

Therefore psychic income (or variants of that notion) under FS must be understood as the conscious correlate of the motivation to seek FS equilibrium and to use resources efficiently. Naturally, we expect to find analogous correlates with respect to S-spending. However, since S-spending directly relates to Smith's personal situation, there is less occasion (in a conventional analysis) to say that Smith is acting to gain psychic income that accrues with his expenditure, than to say that Smith is acting to obtain the good. In contrast, when the good is imperceptibly small (the effect of one vote in an election, one contribution to a large charity, and so on), it becomes tempting (in a conventional analysis) to "explain" the behavior by recourse to psychic income.

From the FS point of view, however, G-resources are not spent to benefit Smith personally, and no special puzzle arises when they do not do so. Rather, the relation of the conscious correlate of this spending to the underlying model is precisely that of love, anger, and so on in a Darwinian account of animal behavior: it is not an additional motivation outside the maximizing behavior oriented to the external world. We would no more say that Smith votes because it is a reasonable use of a bit of G-resources, and in addition he gets satisfaction from doing his duty, than a biologist would say that the lioness maximizes inclusive fitness by caring for her cubs, and, in addition, she loves them.

Through their relation to the kinds of rule-following behavior discussed earlier in this chapter, these correlates are more than artifacts. They can influence behavior rather than merely mirror it. Nevertheless, you would have the matter backwards if you supposed that Smith chooses an equilibrium allocation (such that $W = G'/S'$) in order to do his fair share, or do his duty, or gain psychic income. Rather it is essential to understand that the opposite is the case. Given an equilibrium allocation, Smith has a sense of having done his fair share. (So it would be utterly meaningless, for example, to make a normative judgment that Equation 4.1 does not define the notion of "fair share" correctly. Equation 4.1 could prove to be empirically unsound. But it cannot be presumed to be wrong because it fails to accord with some normative argument about how a person ought to behave. Nor could we say that the FS equilibrium ought to be ethically appealing merely because (or if) we believe it to be empirically plausible.)

The role of psychic income under FS, in sum, is what we expect of psychic or emotional sources of motivation from a Darwinian viewpoint. The conscious satisfactions of doing one's duty or one's fair share are no less real and no less natural than the emotional states connected with narrowly self-interested behavior or genetically self-interested behavior. However, these emotional states are not the primitive notions of the theory. Both the emotions and the behavior associated with or prompted by the emotions are things which the theory must account for: we are never permitted to "explain" behavior merely by pointing to its emotional correlate.

CHAPTER 6

Translating across paradigms

The balance of the study deals with results from the FS model. These fall into two classes: applications to empirical issues; and applications to conceptual issues that arise when the conventional economic framework is extended to allow for public goods. The last three chapters will deal with empirical applications. The present chapter deals with conceptual applications. Although even here I have tried to keep the formal apparatus to a minimum (with technical detail left mainly to Appendixes D and E), the argument is not always an easy one. But I hope that at least a sense of the way the argument goes will come through even to readers with little background in economics.

In a certain way the FS proposal has a conservative character. The economic man analysis was shaped by its concern with what we now call "private goods." With the extension of this analysis to public goods, serious anomalies arise. With rare exceptions, however (for example, Amartya Sen's "Rational Fools"[1]) the anomalies have been allowed to lie dormant.

The FS proposal is conservative in the sense that one can deduce that the conventional model will work in the case of impersonal exchanges of private goods in the market (see Chapter 9). Consequently, the core of neoclassical economic theory is left essentially intact. Yet certain anomalies that arise in the context of public goods disappear.

What we are considering, then, is a way of generalizing the notion of rational choice so that some serious difficulties are remedied, but without requiring any great change in what Kuhn would call the central "exemplars" of the existing theory.

The chapter was stimulated by the discussion in Kuhn's "postscript" associating the difficulty of communicating across paradigms with the shift in the "tacit" meaning of terms that inevitably occurs.[2] Kuhn is hardly optimistic about the chances of persuading committed adherents of the older view. But he does offer a suggestion. The problem might be eased by carefully worked out examples of the application of the new view and the older view to concrete problems, taking special care to explicate subtle shifts in the meanings of words. I will try to do that.

The result of this exercise seems to me to illustrate how a new point of view can open up neglected issues and show how they can be resolved. The original purpose of the chapter was merely to illustrate how FS could be applied to "demand-revealing" (DR), a salient topic in the recent economics literature. However, as you will see, we are led into the deeper issue of defining efficient choice when individuals may be motivated (in part) by social concerns, and when public goods are present.

Demand-revealing (DR)

Demand-revealing is intended to provide a solution to the "free-rider" problem in social choice.[3] Crudely, if you have a good that is simultaneously available to everyone (such as national defense or clean air), the amount society as a whole should buy can be construed as the level of supply such that the sum of what everyone in the society is "willing to pay" (*wtp*) for one additional unit (say, the next $1 million worth) just equals the required cost (here $1 million). (In the preceding sentence and in what follows, quotes around the first use of various terms will alert the reader to terms that we will find require "translation across paradigms." For the moment, however, we will proceed as if there were no problem in extending the use of terms developed in the context of private transactions in the market to the context of social choice.)

Let Q be the budget level under consideration, and suppose we have gotten everyone to reveal honestly his *wtp* schedule, or marginal "demand" schedule, which shows what an incremental million dollars in the budget is worth to the individual as a function of Q. If we make the usually reasonable assumption that *wtp* declines with the number of units, Smith (our sample citizen) will then have a higher *wtp* for the first $1 million budgeted for defense or cleaning the air than for the hundredth; a higher *wtp* for the hundredth than for the thousandth; and so on. If Q^* is the budget level at which the sum of everyone's *wtp* for another $1 million just equals $1 million, then Q^* is, on this scheme, the right social choice: society has a *wtp* greater than the cost for units up to Q^*, and they should be bought; and social *wtp* for units beyond Q^* does not cover the cost, and they are not worth buying.

The problem is, how do we get citizens, such as Smith, to reveal their *wtp* schedules?

Suppose we have assigned "tax prices": the amount – based perhaps on income or whatever other tax scheme is judged fair – that Smith pays per $1 million in the budget. We then ask Smith for his *wtp* schedule, with the understanding that his response will have *no* effect on his tax price. What we want, of course, is his "true" *wtp* schedule. However, because Smith can give us any answer he pleases with no effect on his own tax price, he has an incentive to vote strategically, choosing the *wtp* schedule he reports for the effect it will have on the outcome. For values of Q less than he judges desirable, he might as well exaggerate his own *wtp*. This will make the sum across voters (the social *wtp*) higher than it would have been if he revealed his true *wtp*, hence the social choice will increase (Q^* will be larger), and at no cost to Smith beyond his preassigned tax price applied to the increment. For values of Q higher than he thinks desirable, he has a similar reason to understate his true *wtp*. Thus, simply asking people to reveal their true *wtp* schedules would give voters an incentive to do otherwise.

Suppose then that we use Smith's reported *wtp* schedule to set his tax price. As before, the social choice, Q^*, is to be where the summed *wtp*s of all voters just balances the cost of another unit of the good. However, now Smith's tax price is not preassigned, but will be set to equal his self-reported *wtp* at Q^*. Were Smith and all others in fact to reveal their true *wtp* schedules, then we would have a truly elegant solution to the problem of social choice. Q^* would be that level of supply at which not only will the summed individual *wtp*s just equal the cost of the last unit bought, and the sum of the taxes across all individuals just equal the total budget, but also each individual, given his tax price, would "prefer" that same social choice, Q^*. This is known as the Lindahl–Samuelson (LS) equilibrium. [4]

However, as Samuelson stressed when he presented the first really clear formulation of these ideas, each individual will be motivated to understate his true *wtp* schedule if that schedule will be used to set his tax price. For the response of any single individual in a large society will have only a microscopic effect on the social outcome. Therefore, if tax prices were based on voluntarily revealed *wtp* schedules, each individual could lower his own tax price without noticeably lowering the supply of the public good by claiming a minimal *wtp*. Since everyone is given this same pernicious incentive, the aggregate result would be an inadequate supply of the good. Hence, Samuelson concluded, the need for some political process to choose the level of supply.

What DR proponents think they have found is a way of getting around Samuelson's result: a way of giving voters just the right incentive to reveal their true *wtp* schedules. This would create a kind of quasi market for public goods such that individuals acting to promote their own interests will miraculously produce a social outcome which serves everyone's interests as nearly as possible. [5] That this miracle will actually occur in the case of perfectly competitive markets for private goods is the central proposition of conventional economic theory. DR purports to show that, in principle, it is possible to extend this result even to a situation far removed from perfectly competitive markets, the case of pure public goods.

Understandably, this development has generated a good deal of interest. It is as if physicists had discovered an approach to energy conversion that appeared, in principle at least, to get around the Carnot limits on efficiency. Everyone involved agrees that there are a great many obstacles to implementation of DR: some political, some technical, some having to do with the ethical judgments that may be implicit in the scheme. So there is a great deal of skepticism that a version of the scheme can be worked out that handles enough of the objections to make DR practical. The result, however, is still astonishing. Waiving all second-order objections, no one working within the paradigm has questioned that in principle DR is capable of solving the famous "free-rider" problem. Given the fundamental assumptions of economic theory, in particular given the basic assumptions about choice by rational, utility-maximizing individuals, DR in principle solves what might be claimed to be the most fundamental problem of social choice.

How does it work? We may pass over details here, dealing only with a fairly simple point that is the key to the whole analysis.[6] You will recall from the previous discussion that *either* if Smith's tax price is unaffected by his revealed *wtp* schedule, *or* if tax prices are completely set by revealed *wtp*s, voters (such as Smith) will have an incentive to vote strategically and not reveal their true schedules. Suppose, however, voters pay a preassigned tax price on all units of the good *except* the few units at the margin that are affected by their own vote. Now Smith will have no incentive to falsify his *wtp* for units that will either be bought or not bought regardless of what response he reveals: neither his tax price nor the social choice with respect to such units will be affected. On the few units that Smith's vote does effect (around one-millionth of the total if Smith is a typical voter in a society of 1 million voters), Smith is charged at a rate that approaches (but never exceeds) whatever *wtp* he has revealed at the point of his demand schedule that turns out to coincide with Q^*. Here again he has no disincentive against revealing his true *wtp*. For Smith only hurts his own interest if a unit at the margin is not bought because he revealed a lower *wtp* than he was truly willing to pay; the reverse is true if a unit at the margin is bought because Smith said he was willing to pay (and therefore, under this scheme will have to pay) more than his true *wtp*.

An immediate objection is that, if Smith's "vote" will have but a microscopic effect (Q^* will look very much the same no matter what he does, even if he does not bother to vote at all), then why should Smith bother to vote at all? The conventional theory has no answer here: it observes that the same problem arises in the context of ordinary voting and that empirically, although for reasons beyond the scope of "economic man," citizens by and large do vote. Thus the conventional theory takes the fact that Smith votes as beyond the scope of the analysis, but it assumes that we can analyze *how* Smith votes, given that he votes, "as if" he were simply conventional economic man. We should not be terribly surprised if this presumption leads to difficulties.

The FS model vs. the conventional model

What I will be trying to show is that (1) the economic man paradigm does no better at predicting how citizens vote than in accounting for why they vote; (2) once you notice how citizens are likely to vote under DR, a serious question arises about the Samuelson public goods analysis; and (3) in contrast FS correctly predicts how citizens are likely to respond to DR incentives and resolves the puzzle about the status of the Samuelson analysis.

We will use some simple notation and special terms:

Let C-Smith be "conventional Smith" – the self-interested economic man of the conventional theory.

Let FS-Smith be the Smith of the model I am proposing.

And from earlier chapters, let G-Smith be Smith to the extent he behaves as a perfectly group-interested individual, and let S-Smith be Smith to the extent that he behaves as a perfectly selfish individual.

All of these Smiths can be treated as rational utility maximizers. But each has a different sort of utility function, which he may be thought of as maximizing.[7] Consequently, each will have a different sort of *wtp* schedule, showing *C-wtp*, *G-wtp*, and so forth.

When we speak simply of "Smith" (without a prefix), we mean none of these theoretical constructs but rather a typical individual as empirically observed: in fact, you may think of Smith as yourself. When we discuss how Smith might behave in certain situations, ask yourself how you would behave.

I will now say a few things about C-Smith, trying to follow Kuhn's advice about paying special attention to the tacit penumbra that concepts acquire in use by leading writers and in widely cited papers. For, if Kuhn is correct, the difficulties in translation we are trying to overcome derive less from C-Smith's "official" character than from what workers within the paradigm tacitly assume about C-Smith as indicated by the way he is handled in Kuhn's "exemplars" of the conventional paradigm.

The first issue concerns just what is understood (within the paradigm) by the term *self-interest*. This term illustrates very well the sort of problem I take it Kuhn has in mind in talking about the tacit commitments within a paradigm. For although every beginning student of economics learns that economic man (C-Smith) is self-interested, there is no standard definition of what this term means. In the overwhelming bulk of the economics literature, C-Smith is simply S-Smith. C-utility depends only on the goods affecting C-Smith personally and not at all on goods affecting only others. Yet, in a small but significant (i.e., widely read, cited, and discussed) subset of literature, C-Smith has a utility function that does include goods available to other people. His "interest" is interpreted to include a taste for the well-being of other people. *Self-interest* then means only that C-Smith chooses in terms of his own preferences, without implying that C-Smith's own preferences are necessarily selfish. In this looser sense of self-interest, G-Smith is just as self-interested as S-Smith or C-Smith.

It would not be misleading, I think, to say that within the paradigm altruistic motivation – cases in which C-Smith is not simply S-Smith – is a tolerated anomaly. Invocation of altruism is, in principle, welcome. But if you look at the literature it seems that altruism is tolerated only to the extent that the usage is treated as a special case, which mainstream economics can ignore by and large.

Perhaps the clearest indication of this tacit understanding of how self-interest is to be handled within the paradigm is that even writers who have used the wider notion of self-interest somewhere in their work – and this includes at least Samuelson and Arrow among the Nobel Prize winners – unquestioningly use the narrower sense (C-Smith as S-Smith) in the great bulk of their work, apparently "seeing" no need to reconcile the inconsistent usage.

The other tacit commitments I will next describe are related to the first in the following way: As long as C-Smith is treated as if he were an S-Smith, questions relating to these commitments cannot arise. In the presence of altruism, they easily become important. However, given the attitude toward altruism already described, it is not surprising that workers within the paradigm tend to assume tacitly that one can add a bit of altruism (see Equation 6.1) without changing the character of the model in any other way. A little crudely, one can say that C-Smith in special situations may value goods affecting others as well as goods affecting only himself, but aside from this one anomaly he "wouldn't do anything that S-Smith wouldn't do."

Consequently, if you examine work incorporating altruism that could plausibly be classed as a Kuhnian exemplar for the field (all papers incorporating altruism that have probably been at least looked at by most economists and are routinely assigned to students, such as those of Becker, Harsanyi, and Hochman and Rogers),[8] then I know of no exception to the following statement: C-Smith's utility function is (not by definition, but de facto) always what I will term a "goods function."

Formally, what this means is that we can write C-Smith's utility function in the following form:

$$C\text{-utility} = U[(X_1, X_2, \ldots X(\text{Smith}), \ldots X_n]$$ 6.1

where X_1, X_2, ... X_n are the bundles of goods available to Citizen 1, Citizen 2, ... Citizen Smith ... Citizen n. Public goods of course appear in many different – for a pure public good, all – bundles of goods simultaneously. If C-Smith is narrowly self-interested, the only bundle that "counts" is $X(\text{Smith})$; Smith's own bundle of goods.

Although every good economist is aware of ambiguities in the way self-interest is interpreted within the paradigm, it is not clear that many economists are aware in the same way of the commitment to goods functions. My impression is that if we say that Equation 6.1 and its subsequent explication contains a strong and highly debatable *empirical* premise (beyond rationality), then most economists will be puzzled and will wonder what we could be talking about.

The debatable premise is this. A goods utility function has the impersonal character that utility depends only on the bundles of goods available to various individuals. It does not depend on whose actions provided the goods. For example, in a goods function it can make no difference (the marginal utility of spending an incremental dollar in various ways would be the same) if a given scale and distribution of goods were attained with C-Smith as a bystander, looking out solely for his own personal interests, or with C-Smith performing some heroic social role that contributed greatly to the scale and distribution of goods.

In other words, the tacit commitment to goods functions leaves out the possibility that whatever incentive Smith has to act in ways that are more than narrowly self-interested may depend not only on "goods altruism" but also on some notion of "participation."

Bear in mind that I am not claiming that workers within the conventional paradigm would explicitly deny that participation as well as goods altruism might be important in a model that goes beyond narrow self-interest. I do not think that is the case. But in terms of the understanding by doing that comes from working over the exemplars of the field, if you are in the habit of treating Smith as C-Smith you may have difficulty "seeing" that an important empirical assumption is built into all the well-known altruistic models in the economics literature, or that in all the widely cited discussions of "utility" the only formulations considered are examples of goods functions. Indeed, even to talk about this point it was necessary to invent a term: goods functions.[9] Within the paradigm, no well-established term exists, there being so little occasion to use it. As already noted, the vast bulk of the literature concerns analysis in which actors are either self-interested in the narrow sense, or might as well be so because, even if altruism is allowed for in principle, it plays no explicit role in the analysis and alters no results. The tacit commitment to goods function becomes interesting only in the context of explicitly altruistic motivation, so the occasions are rare when an economist or his students might be led to notice, much less ponder or question, this tacit premise.

Much the same comment applies to the next point. With respect to private goods, it is tautological in the conventional paradigm that social demand is simply the summed demand of all individuals. As a technical definition this is unproblematic, although on both normative and scientific grounds one would want to be careful to understand that other concepts might be labeled "social demand."

Samuelson showed more clearly than earlier writers how the notion of social demand, in the technical sense used here, might be extended to the case of public goods (by summing demand curves "vertically" rather than "horizontally"). Here, though, a problem arises in the event that citizens are not narrowly self-interested, although again it is hard to "see" the problem from within the paradigm.

Start with a pure private good, such as sugar. Here there is no problem in seeing that social demand (say at a price of $1 per pound) is just the sum of the demand of all consumers at that price. Further, *if* citizens are narrowly self-interested, then we have the Lindahl–Samuelson extension of the notion of demand to cover the case of public goods. No one cares about costs or benefits to anyone but himself, and the social demand can be taken to be (as described earlier) the amount at which the summed *wtp*s of all consumers just equals the marginal cost, with demand treated "as if" each individual could buy a quantity of the public good for himself alone. But if citizens might not be acting purely out of narrow self-interest, then it is not clear what demand for public good means.

Suppose that within a family a good available to all (say, a new television) is worth – the members are willing to pay – $100 for the father alone, $100 for the mother alone, and $50 each for the two children. The television is apparently worth $300 to the family. However, if we ask the father and the mother separately what each is willing to pay for the television, each may say $300. These are "true" *wtp*s: neither parent is falsifying his demand, but since each has already given full weight to the other's preferences, as well as the children's, we have gotten "true" *wtp*s that cannot be added: they are not "summable" to produce an LS equilibrium. You can see, though, that if each answers just in terms of his or her own demand, because the demand of others is taken account of elsewhere in the process, the answer will come out right. So it is tempting to say that, in the broader social context, if it is understood that the aggregation process takes into account the preferences of everyone, then each individual's "summable" *wtp* will be just his self-interested *wtp*.

There are problems here. For example, if the children have no money, their *wtp* must be zero. But would that be fair? The paradigm deals with this sort of difficulty by noting that fairness as well as efficiency counts: although the formalism of the theory focuses mainly on efficiency questions, efficiency alone does not provide a sufficient basis for choice. (Samuelson himself has been a particularly vigorous exponent of this point.)

Nevertheless, for purposes of formal analysis, it is almost always assumed within the paradigm that the principle of "consumer sovereignty" governs so that the value of a unit of a public good is just the sum of what all citizens are willing to pay for that unit.

Within the paradigm, as self-interest is sometimes understood loosely but almost always treated strictly, so the definition just given is sometimes interpreted loosely, to take account of the fact that it really deals only with technical efficiency, neglecting fairness. But that qualification is itself commonly neglected. Further – and this is the point I want to stress – this criterion for (efficient) social choice tends to be extended into an assumption about rational individual choice.

As with the tacit commitment to goods function, workers within the paradigm generally use this assumption implicitly, quite unaware that they have made an assumption at all. However, as with goods functions, there is a real question as to whether this describes the way real Smiths will behave. It is certainly not obvious that citizens in general, or even trained economists (in their role as citizens), would feel that their rational input to a fair process of social choice must consider only what the choice is worth to themselves as individuals. This would follow only if, for example, a rational individual can reasonably be defined as someone who acts "as if" the socially best level of defense spending, or spending for publicly financed abortions, is necessarily simply the point at which the summed personal *wtp*s of all citizens equals the cost of an incremental unit.

To this point we have three tacit commitments:

T1.   *C*-Smith can be treated as narrowly self-interested.
T2.   *C*-Smith's utility function is a goods function.
T3.   *C*-Smith chooses in conformity with the principle of consumer sovereignty.

And to these we must add the most deep-seated of all:

T4.   *C*-Smith has one utility function.

Under FS, however, the G-function violates T1 and T3 (for G-Smith acts in group-interest; and his sense of group-interest is his own sense of group-interest, not a summation of everybody's sense of self-interest). And the FS allocation rule (see the discussion introducing Equations 4.1 and 4.2) implies that a total FS utility function would violate T2, because the W-function turns strictly on participation and not on goods. Of course, such a FS utility function would also violate T1 and T3 because it must incorporate G- as well as S-utility. However, we have no occasion to work with any such total FS-function, as already stressed in Chapter 4. Therefore, under FS, we abandon all four tacit commitments. Of these, we will not find a competent economist who would say explicitly that T1 is a requirement inherent in a reasonable notion of rational choice; and the same would, presumably, hold for T2. Many economists feel attached to T3 (violations of consumer sovereignty are customarily labeled "paternalism"), but few would argue that choice consistent with T3 is a necessary condition for rationality. Nevertheless, simultaneous violation of all three of these conditions poses difficulties for someone accustomed to the conventional model. Even after allowing that the violations are quite all right, it remains easy to slip back (tacitly, of course) into more familiar assumptions. Violation of T1, T2, and T3 in the context of a model that then violates T4 as well naturally poses much greater difficulties.

Nevertheless, almost everyone will now agree that "paradigms" shape our ability to understand things in the world, so in principle we will almost all allow that what seems difficult or intuitively wrong in a novel theory may be only a reflection of our own habits of mind, not of some intrinsic flaw in the theory. Having come to understand that paradigms are essential features of human cognitive processes, we understand why in areas of human knowledge undergoing development, the problem of paradigm shift arises.

What was highly fruitful becomes, gradually, something of a handicap. If it is never changed, the field involved will stagnate. On the other hand, a paradigm is most unlikely to become unproductive everywhere at once; and there is a strong tendency to perceive the boundaries of what might profitably be studied as the boundaries of what can be studied within the traditional framework. In any event, the people inside a field that is close to stagnating may be the last to notice: they are busy as ever, as long as there remain puzzles to work at.

Yet a paradigm is not something you can try on, like a jacket, and set aside if you decide it does nothing for you. Kuhn compares a shift to a religious conversion. Further, he is surely correct to deny that any objective rules can identify the right moment for a paradigm shift. But it is certainly also true (and made explicit particularly in Kuhn's "postscript") that reasoned arguments can be brought to bear on the question of how the existing paradigm is doing and how it compares with an alternative way of looking at things.

A reasonable indicator of when a paradigm is starting to become an intellectual handicap might be when things that are obvious and obviously important can be seen more easily by a naive observer than by specialists who turn out to be armed with a theoretical perspective that blinds them to the obvious. Consider, then, what has happened with respect to DR, the scheme for efficient social choice discussed earlier in this chapter.

A thought experiment

Under all versions of DR, there would be two kinds of cost for public goods.[10] First, every voter would have to pay his regular "tax price." For a typical voter in a society of 100 million taxpayers, this will be $1 per $100 million of spending if the sum of the tax prices across all citizens is to just equal the required $100 million. If the total budget for this good is $1 billion (10 × $100 million), our typical voter would therefore pay a total tax of $10 as his share of the cost of this item.

Second, but only if he so chooses, under DR a citizen may pay an additional tax, based on what I call his "DR price." It turns out (the details are not essential to the argument here) that the DR tax is just half the DR price applied to the *change* (up or down) in the social choice due to the individual's vote. The more the individual is willing to pay to change the outcome (the bigger in absolute value the DR price he volunteers), the more effect he has on the outcome and hence the more he pays as a DR tax. The conventional analysis then proves that the "Lindahl" (summable) *wtp* described above will be just the sum of the individual's assigned *tax price* plus the voluntary *DR price*. In effect, then, the voter is offered an opportunity to buy a shift in the social outcome by reporting a nonzero DR price. On the logic of the conventional model, the desired pareto-optimal budget, Q^*, will then be determined as the point where the sum of the DR prices (some positive, some negative) across all voters just equals zero.[11]

If the logic of the DR argument is correct, the DR price revealed near Q^* by reasonably typical voters cannot vary greatly from the average tax price.[12] This has allowed proponents of DR to calculate how much of a DR tax such a typical voter might be expected to incur. Scaled to a $1 billion budget item ($Q^* = $1 billion), this turns out to be a *very* tiny sum: about one-hundred thousandth of a penny in a large society.[13]

For comparison, Table 6.1 gives this choice, together with some other choices a voter could make. This first column shows various ratios between the DR price the voter could report and the average tax price. The second

Table 6.1. *Some choices open to a voter under DR*

Ratio of DR price to average tax price	Effect on outcome	Cost to voter
±1	$20	$0.0000001
±100	$2000	$0.001
±310	$6200	$0.01
±1000	$20,000	$0.10

"Lindahl" outcome = approx. $1 billion
Social elasticity = 2

column shows the effect of the possible choices in column 1 on the social outcome (increasing the budget if the DR price of column 1 is positive, decreasing it if the DR price is negative). Column 3 then shows the corresponding DR tax. Thus, column 3 gives the cost of "buying" the budget shift in column 2, which occurs if the voter reports the DR price in column 1.[14]

For the reason given in note 12, if the conventional model is even crudely correct, then a typical voter would rarely have an effect much larger than $20 on the outcome and would rarely incur a tax much larger than one-hundred thousandth of a penny.

The voter's "consumer surplus" on this transaction (as mentioned earlier, his DR tax comes to just half his reported DR price applied to the shift his vote buys) will be the same as his tax: again, about one-hundred thousandth of a penny. A naive observer might ask how it could be rational for someone to take the trouble to cast a vote that he values at one-hundred thousandth of a penny.

Again, a naive observer might suppose that, given whatever it is that moves a person to bother to vote at all, it is possible that this same motivation would lead him to spend, let us say, a penny, so that the effect of his vote (looking at line 3 in Table 6.1) would be over $6000 instead of just $20. And, in fact, the numbers in Table 6.1 make it obvious that the conventional model's inferences about how voters would respond to the DR incentive must ordinarily be in error by several orders of magnitude.

However, once you allow that real voters, if faced with the DR incentive, can be expected to "spend the penny," a deeper problem emerges. The conventional theory "proves" that DR will elicit Lindahl (i.e., summable) *wtp* schedules. But consider a good (such as pollution control) for which we can assume that everyone would prefer more if the cost were low enough. By assumption, then, at Q^*, or even at twice Q^*, every individual in the society will have a positive *wtp* for this good; it follows, therefore, that the social *wtp* for this good cannot be negative. Now consider what happens with respect to such a good under DR.

Empirically, for the reason already given, we expect people motivated to vote at all to be motivated to reveal DR prices (positive if they prefer a larger budget, negative if not) that are typically enormous compared to their tax prices. They will spend (at least) the penny. Consequently, the absolute values of the individual DR prices will ordinarily be enormous compared to the individual tax prices; hence the same will also be true for the sum of these absolute prices across all individuals. However, the algebraic sum (positive DR prices canceling negative) need not be large. In fact, as we increase the budget we must find a point where the positive and negative DR prices just balance to zero. This is the point the conventional model claims to be the pareto-optimal budget choice. However, as we move to higher budget levels we will have more and more voters who "spend the penny" to reduce the budget as opposed to fewer and fewer wishing to increase the budget. Thus, the algebraic sum of the DR prices across all voters will be increasingly negative. Eventually we must find a budget level – indeed, for plausible elasticity, a budget level only slightly larger than the purported optimum – at which this negative algebraic sum of all voters' DR prices is (absolutely) larger than the sum of the tax prices. The sum of these sums (tax prices plus DR prices), which the logic of the conventional model requires *must* be the social *wtp*, will then be negative. But the social *wtp* for a universally valued good cannot be negative. Therefore, the conventional model proves that the summed DR responses must represent social *wtp*. But the thought experiment, which is only open to doubt if you doubt that voters would spend the penny, demonstrates the contrary.

Interpretation of the thought experiment

We want to begin by considering the result in the light of the responses commonly offered when an inference from the conventional model is shown to be inconsistent with empirically plausible behavior.

Two of these customary arguments have already been mentioned in another context (see Chapter 1). They deal with the role of self-interest in the theory. One says that, although human beings may not be perfectly self-interested (in the narrow sense), they are sufficiently so to make analysis in terms of self-interest a good approximation of reality. However, this defense fails in the DR context because the DR outcome will be dominated by DR prices, which vary enormously (and often even have the wrong sign) from plausible DR prices for strictly self-interested actors.

A second version says that self-interest means only whatever interests the individual values, not necessarily only selfish interests. Tacitly, this response assumes that "interests" have a form that can be accommodated within the conventional analysis (for, without some such restriction, the statement has no content).[15] If the response were tenable, though, then DR would evoke the summable *wtp* schedules, as the conventional theory says it must. But we have seen that this cannot be true.

Another more desperate kind of argument says that the thought experiment is irrelevant because economic theory is properly to be regarded not necessarily as a theory about human behavior but rather a theory of idealized choice. If human beings do not behave the way the theory says a rational individual will behave, that is no criticism of the theory. On this defense, economic theory ceases to be a scientific theory. It can be interpreted either as a branch of pure mathematics, where it is irrelevant whether there actually exist real choosers whose motivation is adequately approximated by the theory, or as a branch of moral philosophy concerned with the appropriate norms of behavior for a society of rational egoists. But very few economists would care to endorse such a retreat of economic theory from reality. In any event, it would be irrelevant to our purpose here, which is to explore how the conventional theory might be enlarged to make it more useful in social science.

Finally, there is the defense which says that economic theory, like most scientific theories, has only a limited domain of applicability; therefore one can dismiss certain anomalies – such as the inability to account for the fact that citizens bother to vote – as beyond the scope of the theory. But the issue at hand (DR) is the creation of economists, not an anomaly discovered empirically and thrown up as a conundrum for the conventional theory. The two best-known articles were published as lead articles in two of the most prestigious journals in economics. On at least two occasions, entire issues of journals have been devoted to this one topic. In the four years since the leading DR articles were published, two book-length expositions have appeared, plus several compendia of papers.[16] So it would be rather late to discover that DR is not within the scope of economic theory after all. Furthermore, serious questions would arise about how one could dismiss DR as dealing with something that turns out to be beyond the scope of economic theory and yet continue to claim that the analysis of choice in the context of public goods, of which DR after all is an example, is within the domain of economic theory.

In fact, there seems to be no plausible way of avoiding the conceptual dilemma. What causes the contradiction we have been exploring is that real people turn out to violate T1 and T3. But the Lindahl–Samuelson notion of a public goods equilibrium cannot tolerate that. The standard mathematical formalism defining social demand for public goods falls apart in the event that citizens have what are usually labeled "paternalistic" preferences: that is, if they violate T1 and T3.[17] Consequently, what the thought experiment here amounts to is a demonstration that the behavioral model on which the Samuelson analysis of public goods relies – and that analysis is so prominent in the economics literature that it could serve as virtually an exemplar for what Kuhn means by an exemplar – leads to empirically bizarre inferences about social preferences. One can "rule out" this possibility by asserting that (in terms of FS) only S-preferences, not G-preferences (only Smith's private preferences, not his social preferences) are to be counted in analyzing efficient social choice. But even if endorsed by the very best economists, no such dictum would change human nature to accord with the model of choice that economists have found analytically convenient. Although (as you will see) a normative argument of some interest might be constructed that bears a relation to such a dictum, in order to discuss what such a judgment might involve, and what its merits might be, we still need an enlarged version of Lindahl–Samuelson, which allows for the preferences that real human beings actually exhibit.

The heart of the problem, as I have mentioned, is that real human beings freely violate the tacit assumptions of the conventional model, and (what is critical to the DR issue we are examining and to Lindahl–Samuelson) they violate T1 and T3. Economic analysis of public choice issues has gotten around this problem (when it has not been simply ignored or "ruled out") by resort to Musgrave's notion of "merit goods." A merit good, in effect, is any item of public expenditure that seems socially reasonable but cannot be accounted for within the ordinary economic theory of demand. It is a kind of formalized escape clause, playing very much the role at the level of social choice that psychic income plays in dealing with apparent violations of rational choice at the individual level (see below in this chapter and Chapter 7).

Musgrave's idea is nevertheless a considerable improvement over the ignoring or ruling-out tactic: at least it allows for the preferences human beings actually exhibit, as psychic income at least allows for people to behave (vote, donate to charity, and so on) the way they actually behave. But it is not the sort of solution anyone could realistically imagine provides real scope for growth of a scientific field. The DR work we have been examining raises some question about the prudence of continuing to paper over these difficulties. Could any scientific discipline that was not moribund simply ignore the fact that one of the mainstays of its intellectual armory (here the Lindahl–Samuelson analysis of public goods) leads to a perfectly crazy result: namely, that given DR incentives voters would fail to "spend the penny."

Let me now try to state the technical problem precisely. The thought experiment tells us that, at the DR outcome, many individual voters will be reporting negative willingness to pay for an incremental unit of the good: they will be reporting DR prices that are "more negative" than their tax prices; they will spend the penny to reduce the budget; and they will do so even when, as we have assumed here, the good is positively valued by each individual in the society. Furthermore, for budget levels somewhat larger than the claimed optimal choice, we will find that the social *wtp* is negative: although by assumption every citizen values the good positively, society as a whole values it negatively.

But this is a strict impossibility (like proving that a circle is square), and therefore it follows strictly that something must be wrong (empirically) with the assumptions underlying the conventional model. As I have already stressed, what is wrong is that human beings freely violate T1 and T3.

What we would like, therefore, is to find a way to extend the Samuelson analysis to situations in which T1 and T3 are violated, because empirically (as reflected by the thought experiment and much other evidence) that is the situation that obtains. If we can define an extension of Samuelson analysis in terms of FS, however, we will have what we want. For under FS, violations of T1 and T3 are permitted (in fact, expected). Furthermore, we will also have an explanation of why this problem has not been solved within the paradigm. If FS is empirically valid (if it is more than a curious coincidence that FS seems to work), then because FS violates not only T1 and T3 but T2 and T4 as well, it is understandable that workers trying to resolve the problem only by relaxing T1 and T3 failed to find a solution. Finally, the extension would have the highly desirable "correspondence" property so that for the case where behavior can be approximated as purely self-interested (in FS terms, where only *S*-behavior need be considered), the analysis reduces to the conventional formulation. In a context in which it is reasonable to treat Smith "as if" he were concerned only with self-interest, then we would have the limiting case of FS in which nothing is allocated to *G*-Smith. Here the FS analysis would reduce to the conventional analysis, because *S*-Smith's behavior is consistent with all the conventional assumptions.

To construct this FS extension of Lindahl–Samuelson, however, we must be able to answer the following rather complicated-sounding question: How would it be possible, conceptually, to choose a social outcome and a set of tax prices assigned to FS-Smith, FS-Jones, FS-Miller, and so on such that the budget is covered and (in terms of our "inside Smith" metaphor) *S*-Smith and *G*-Smith (hence FS-Smith), and simultaneously *S*-Jones, *G*-Jones; *S*-Miller, *G*-Miller, and so on are *all* in equilibrium? In contrast to the problem of seeking to extend Samuelson within the conventional framework we require that not only Smith and Jones but distinct entities "inside Smith," "inside Jones," and so forth be in equilibrium and that this be so even though in principle these internal entities cannot be assigned a tax price by any external agent.

FS extension of Lindahl–Samuelson

As in Samuelson's "pseudomarket," we are concerned with the conceptual problem of what efficient social outcomes would be like if we had available an omniscient observer who could look into each citizen's heart, know their preferences completely, and on this basis specify a social choice, Q^*, and a set of tax prices for each citizen such that all are in equilibrium. Although we expect the results eventually to prove useful in the study of actual social choice processes, we are not here trying to solve any *practical* problem. On the contrary, as in the Samuelson analysis, we are abstracting from all the complications of the real world. Citizens are assumed to have precisely definable preferences; there are no politics; there is a well-defined set of goods; and there is Samuelson's demon, who will tell us whatever we wish to know about the preferences of individuals within the society.

An analogy may help the reader to follow the argument. Although within the grasp of high school students today, square roots of negative numbers – "imaginary" roots, a term that certainly would not be adopted anew – were once a great mystery to even the best mathematicians. The mathematician could reach certain results if he assumed the existence of imaginary roots. But it seemed impossible to understand what such roots "really" were, or how such an apparent absurdity could be of any use. And, as long as thinking was tied to the one-dimensional notion of the number line, the concept of imaginary roots was bound to remain a mystery. Only with the notion that "number" might be understood to have a second dimension, so that a number could be a point in the complex plane (with a "real" and an "imaginary" axis) was it possible to *see* how it could be meaningful – in fact physically meaningful – to say that a negative number can have a square root.

This extension could never have been achieved without a certain loos-ening of the conventional meanings of "number," "addition," and "multi-plication." Here, as in many other examples in science, one could not expect that familiar notions would have *exactly* the same content in the enlarged domain. That is why thinking, however hard and ingeniously, about how to interpret imaginary roots within the original framework could never reach a clear resolution. But the reverse held: it was easy, from the enlarged point of view, to see why the enlarged notions continued to have their familiar character for the special cases where only the original, narrower domain needed consideration. What I will be trying to show is how a suitably enlarged notion of Samuelson's "pseudomarket" leads to a resolution of the problem of defining a Lindahl–Samuelson equilibrium in the enlarged domain of rational choice that allows for group-interested as well as self-interested (social as well as private) motivation.

In particular, in the conventional analysis, the appropriate *wtp* schedule' for constructing choices for public goods gives the prices at which *C*-Smith would be in equilibrium if he were choosing the budget for himself alone. In other words, for each possible budget choice, Q, the schedule shows that value of *C-wtp* which would lead *C*-Smith to choose Q for himself if he were assigned *C-wtp* as his tax price.

This is an artificial notion, because of course Smith does not face any such choice. If he did, his choice, by the nature of a public good, would be a choice not just for himself but for all of society. However, if Smith obeys T1, this creates no problem because then his preferences will not be affected by effects on other people. He does not care about other people, and for the purpose of devising a summable *wtp* for *C*-Smith, he can be treated as if he were making a decision for himself alone. For the subtler reason discussed in the beginning of the chapter, this artificial notion will also yield the desired summable *wtp* even if Smith is not narrowly self-interested (he violates T1), as long as he obeys T3.

S-Smith obeys all the assumptions of the conventional analysis (specifically obeys T1 through T4), so this *C-wtp* construction works also for *S-wtp*. But there is no reason to suppose that this same construction would work for *G*-Smith, who acts purely in (his perception of) group-interest, violating T1 and T3. If we treated *G*-Smith as if these essential differences could be ignored, we would not get the required summable schedule, for the same kind of reason as came up in the discussion of the mother's and father's responses earlier in this chapter. Rather, the equivalent notion for *G*-Smith (see Appendix D) is that *G*-Smith's *wtp* schedule reflects his willingness to *donate* to the supply of the public good at issue. The logic of the situation can then be summed up as follows.

G-Smith acts in Smith's perception of group-interest and only incidentally to benefit Smith. In contrast, *S*-Smith acts in Smith's narrow self-interest, and only incidentally to benefit society.

Parallel to this basic dichotomy (making *G*-Smith's motivation just the reverse of *S*-Smith's), when we extend the notion of preferences with respect to public goods to FS-Smith, the definition of an equilibrium tax price, p_g, for *G*-Smith is (subject to a qualification) just the reverse of the definition for p_s, *S*-Smith's equilibrium tax price. Specifically, given a social choice, Q:

For *S*-Smith (as for *C*-Smith) the equilibrium tax price is p_s such that, given p_s, *S*-Smith would voluntarily choose Q as his preferred outcome.

For G-Smith, however, the equilibrium tax price is p_g such that, given Q, G-Smith would voluntarily choose p_g as his preferred tax price.

If, given Q, G-Smith would wish to donate q dollars, then his equilibrium tax price, p_g, will be just q/Q, so that the cost to G-Smith is just the amount he would voluntarily donate. But it would be false to suppose that G-Smith prefers Q as the social outcome. His preferred social outcome will almost always differ from Q, as the equilibrium tax price to S-Smith will almost always differ from the tax price he would truly prefer: namely, zero.

The problem of tax prices "inside Smith" then takes a very simple form for the idealized special case we have been considering, in which the social choice is exactly that of the extended Lindahl–Samuelson equilibrium. For if S- and G-Smith separately would be in equilibrium if assigned the tax prices, p_s and p_g, respectively, then if Smith is assigned the tax price $p = p_s + p_g$ the only internal allocation which would not upset the equilibrium would charge G-Smith p_g and S-Smith p_s. Hence this internal allocation must hold; any other would violate the principle of nonsubversiveness developed in Chapter 5. So although no outside agent could assign tax prices "inside Smith," the logic of the situation is such that, if we assume Smith's preferences are known to the outside agent, the agent could assign an appropriate tax price to Smith, and the internal allocation would take care of itself. (See Appendixes D and E.)

The qualification noted just above turns on the fact that what has been defined so far gives a strictly voluntary outcome for G-people, plus the conventional (imposed) fully cooperative outcome for S-people. However, as shown in Appendix D, we need to allow for a G-analog of the free-rider problem. This implies some departure from voluntary G-preferences. In contrast to the self-interested context (the conventional model or the FS analysis with respect to S-preferences only), the outcome for G-people under uncoordinated choice may not be grossly pareto-inferior to a fully cooperative outcome. But it is significant enough to require attention.

Proceeding again with the main argument, the FS extension of Lindahl–Samuelson (with or without the qualification just discussed), in contrast to the conventional Lindahl–Samuelson equilibrium, will define social preferences with respect to all goods, including goods (merit goods) of which little or none might be bought in terms of a scheme that assumes each actor is motivated solely by self-interest: for example, aid to the indigent and expenditures to benefit remote future generations.

In addition, other familiar issues that we can readily recognize as political in character arise from this abstract analysis of public goods. In the conventional analysis, we can see that there is a role for organized social choice, but it is hard to see how social behavior would arise, or what forms it might take. The same free-rider problem that leads us to expect gross undersupply of public goods from uncoordinated individual choice suggests that social activity will itself be undersupplied to the point where politics of the kind that characterizes actual human societies could not be sustained.

Under FS, several additional functions for political activity appear, for example, brokering among varying views of group-interest, seeking to reduce unexploited gains from trade at the uncoordinated (Nash) G-equilibrium, and attempting to gain leverage or control over whatever social processes govern choices in a real society.

Under FS, however, there is not only an enlarged function for organized social choice but also a source of resources for organizing interest groups, coalitions, governments, and oppositions to governments. For a particularly obvious way in which resources might be used in one's perception of group-interest is to seek to shape the way that social forces, including but not limited to the coercive power of government, shape social outcomes.

Thus, although we started by assuming a highly abstract context explicitly devoid of politics, politics arises from the FS analysis as naturally and inevitably as such things as banking and insurance arise from the conventional economic model. The remaining chapters will survey some of the consequences.

I should note that the various equilibrium notions developed here do not tell us just what government should do. In particular, normative questions come up about what the basis would be for the use of coercion with respect to G-spending; to the extent that individuals allocate resources to group-interest, those resources can simply be donated to favored causes. (Aside from the more practical considerations noted below, I think that a plausible justification can be offered, although I will not try to do that here.)[18]

In practice, empirical considerations could certainly be important to a normative judgment: the extent to which, in fact, there were likely to exist gains from trade at the G-Nash equilibrium; the extent to which whatever governmental process is used could in fact be taken to be an improvement over uncoerced G-choices; and the extent to which all of this is complicated by revelation-of-preferences problems, which (for the reason noted in Appendix D) can arise even with respect to G-preferences.

There also of course arises another class of questions. Given whatever normative arguments about the conditions that justify coerced spending are put forth (conflicting arguments, no doubt) and in view of the issues mentioned in the previous paragraph, how should we expect real citizens to behave with respect to coerced spending that would elicit very little voluntary willingness to pay from S-resources (such as aid to the indigent). Even without detailed answers to the earlier questions, something can be said about how this issue looks in terms of FS, as is discussed in Chapter 9.

Return now to the DR thought experiment. The DR incentive offers Smith an opportunity to buy a shift in the social outcome. This will have only microscopic interest for S-Smith, for the reason considered in the thought experiment. Consequently, the DR response will for practical purposes be a G-response, reflecting what G-Smith is willing to pay to buy a social shift, with the numbers in Table 6.1 illustrating some choices he might make. This will reflect not his sense of any private consumer surplus from the shift he buys but his sense of the social surplus (benefits to society net of costs to society).

Consequently, what would result from a DR vote is some loose approximation of average social judgment, not at all the summation of individual preferences that the logic of the conventional model leads us to expect. We have no obvious reasons to attach any special significance to this outcome, and in particular there is no apparent reason to regard this outcome as better than the outcome of more familiar ways of making a social choice.

Finally, the results of the thought experiment, so obviously inconsistent with the conventional analysis, are just what we would expect in the event that FS, rather than the conventional model, is a more nearly adequate model of actual human motivation.

Quirk and Saposnik make explicit the common view among mathematical economists when they note that selfish preferences (T1 here) are "virtually impossible to avoid if any interesting theorems concerning the operation of the economy are to be formulated." Under FS some theorems of the conventional theory are therefore lost, for example, those proving that DR will lead to pareto-efficient choices with respect to public goods. However, in the case of DR at least, the thought experiment has shown us that what was lost was a scientific gain, since empirically we can see that DR would, in fact, elicit responses grossly inconsistent with the inferences of the conventional theory. In general though, the theorems of the conventional theory would continue to hold under FS with only some mild reformulation or qualification, for reasons I have tried to show in various discussions of correspondence between the FS- and C-theories. This raises the following question: Can a theorem be found such that (a) the theorem is true under C-motivation, false under FS-motivation, and subject (like DR) to a clear empirical test; but (b) the empirical test supports the conventional theory?

CHAPTER 7

Voting behavior

The puzzle of how to account for voting in terms of rational choice has generated a large literature in economics, sociology, and philosophy, in addition to political science. The topic is one in which every reader will have some first-hand experience. And because voting involves only a tiny fraction of an individual's resources, it also provides an example of a topic that can ordinarily be dealt with in terms of a static FS analysis. Thus it lends itself to a simple, essentially nontechnical treatment.

For the most part, we will simply be considering what voting opportunities look like once we take the view that Smith's resources should be thought of as allocated between a G-Smith and an S-Smith. Given that some of Smith's resources are to be spent (are allocated to G-Smith who will spend them) to maximize what he takes to be social values, or group-interest, how should we expect Smith to respond when given the opportunity to vote?

From this point of view, there is no paradox of rational voting because, as mentioned at the very outset of the study, virtually no one supposes that resources used for voting are used irrationally from a *social* point of view. But this raises the question of why anything like FS is required to deal with a problem that seems trivial once you allow that a person might use – might prefer to use – some portion of his resources to further his conception of social values. On the other hand, there must be some difficulty in this simple explanation; otherwise the issue would not have been a puzzle for the conventional theory of rational choice for the past twenty-five years, as it has been.[1] It is worth going through a rather detailed argument to see exactly why that is so.

Rationality and the observation that most people vote

Under any model invoking formal rationality, including FS, an individual votes only if he values voting at least as highly as he values any alternative use he could make of the resources required (for voting, always time and sometimes various material costs, such as gasoline). In the notation I will be using, this essential condition says that Smith will vote if:

$$wtp \equiv \max[wtp(i)] \geq C. \qquad\qquad 7.1$$

This means that, if we examine the various ways Smith might use his vote (with i varying over the possibilities: vote for X, vote for Y, etc.) finding the most valuable way, then Smith votes if this value – his willingness to pay (wtp) for voting – exceeds the (opportunity) cost of voting.

The benefits Smith might see in voting, which can contribute to wtp, fall into two categories. First, we can imagine that the election actually is decided by one vote, so that Smith's vote (or Smith's abstention) could change the outcome. We will label Smith's judgment of the value of his vote in this special contingency as V_{xy}, where the subscripts refer to candidates X and Y, and where Smith votes (or could have voted, had he chosen to bother) for the first-named choice (here X). So V_{xy} is the value to Smith of the voter's "differential" (Down's term) for the shift from Y's election to X's. If for some reason Smith is considering a vote for X but actually prefers Y, V_{xy} would be negative.

We will label benefits (like V_{xy}) that would accrue only if Smith's vote actually changes the outcome "contingent benefits." Naturally, contingent benefits must be discounted by the probability that such an event does occur, which we will write as P_{xy}. (P_{xy}, loosely, is the probability that, if Smith fails to vote, there would be a tie between X and Y.[2])

In addition to benefits contingent on Smith's vote changing the outcome, Smith may be motivated by benefits that, although perhaps contingent in some way on the gross character of the election outcome, do not depend on the effect of Smith's own vote. I will call these Smith's noncontingent benefits (meaning not contingent on Smith's own vote) and label such terms V_x^*, V_y^*, and so on.

Using this notation, Smith will vote for X (in a two-candidate election between X and Y) if

$$wtp(x) \equiv P_{xy}V_{xy} + V_x^* > P_{xy}V_{yx} + V_y^* \equiv wtp(y) \qquad\qquad 7.2$$

and if $wtp(x) \geq C$.

To resolve the puzzle of rational voting we must show how we might plausibly estimate $wtp(x) \geq C$.

Consider first the contingent benefits. Adapting an argument presented by Gordon Tullock, we can judge the significance of this term (the extent to which the conventional model could account for $wtp \geq C$ by invoking contingent benefits) in the following way.[3]

We are dealing with a problem of choice under uncertainty. The voter does not know in advance whether the contingency will arise. What is sometimes called the "sure thing" principle may be invoked to help us (help you, treating this argument as a thought experiment you should try on yourself) decide on the magnitude of $P_{xy} V_{xy}$.

Suppose you are given a lottery ticket, and you can choose whether you will win prize X (in the event the ticket is drawn) or prize Y. The sure thing principle says that if you definitely prefer X to Y, you must prefer the lottery ticket with prize X to the same lottery ticket with prize Y. If the ticket is not drawn, you are no worse off; and if it is you are better off.[4]

Now suppose the lottery ticket costs \$1, and you in fact prefer prize X to prize Y. Suppose further that you would buy the ticket (spend the \$1 for this contingent benefit) if the prize were Y – your less-preferred alternative. Then following the sure thing principle, you would surely spend the \$1 if the prize were X, which you like better than Y. On the other hand, if the ticket with X as a prize is not worth \$1 to you, then the same ticket with only Y as a prize cannot be worth \$1 to you.

Contingent benefits from voting provide a kind of lottery. Here the ticket is free, in the sense that you do not pay \$1 or some other amount for it. But it does have a cost, which will be equivalent to a dollar cost, in the sense that to vote you must take the trouble to go to the polls, wait in line, and vote.

Let us next define a prize that is *better* than V_{xy}, where Smith prefers X to Y. We do this by asking Smith which he prefers: [X is elected] *or* [Y is elected, but Smith receives a tax-free gift of \$Q]. When Q is big enough to get Smith to prefer the second alternative, we have found a value bigger than V_{xy}. For V_{xy} by definition is the value to Smith of X's election instead of Y's. But adding a gift of \$Q would more than offset that value. Casual inquiry indicates that, even for a presidential election, a large fraction of actual voters believe that they would find Q less than \$100,000: often a great deal less. And, for anything but a presidential election, \$1000 seems to be a high value for Q.

We are now ready for the thought experiment. Take whatever you think is a reasonable estimate of Q for yourself, and consider your sense of the probability that your single vote changes the outcome of a presidential election. Now ask yourself how likely it is that you would bother to pick up a free lottery ticket to win a \$Q prize if the probability of winning the prize was the probability that your vote would change the outcome of a presidential election.

You have undoubtedly faced many such choices. It is a common commercial promotional device to offer free lottery tickets (for what is usually described as a contest) to anyone who will bother to come into a place of business to pick one up, or mail in a coupon. Entering the lottery is almost always less trouble (no waiting in line for example) than bothering to vote. Unless you are very zealous for lotteries, you pass up many such opportunities every year, although the prizes are often substantial and the probability of winning large compared to the probability of your vote changing the outcome of a national election.

If you review this argument, I think you will find that it is hard to explain any substantial measure of your motivation to vote by rational calculation with the contingent benefit term of Equation 7.2. And inquiries among colleagues who spend much of their time working on empirical studies of voting confirm the casual impression that, for a very large fracton of actual voters, the paradox of rational voting cannot be more than trivially eased in terms of the conventional notion of rational calculation with the contingent benefit. [5]

Notice that we have not assumed Smith (or you) to be motivated only by narrow self-interest. You are free to be as public-spirited as you wish. But if you are behaving rationally (i.e., in an internally consistent manner) *and* if your motivation can be described in terms of the conventional model of rational choice, then the thought experiment just given will help you decide whether it is rational to bother to vote because of the chance that your vote will actually change the election outcome.

If not, and essentially all the conventional analyses of this issue agree that indeed it is not, then, in terms of rational choice, voting must be accounted for by the noncontingent (V^*) benefits. We can divide these V^* benefits into three categories: (1) demonstration benefits, which turn on the effect of the vote but not on the special contingency in which the outcome is changed by one vote; (2) consumption benefits, such as finding it fun to vote, and certain other benefits that may flow from the act of voting, independent of any utility from the effect of the vote; and (3) psychic benefits (or, more explicitly, moral benefits), which turn on such things as the satisfaction of doing one's duty, following the Kantian categorical imperative, or some other formulation of the view that a person votes because he wants to fulfill what he feels is a responsibility to vote. (As you know from Chapter 5, under FS, moral income is not a component of the utility calculus. But we are dealing here with the conventional model.)

If you are at all familiar with the literature on voter studies, or if you consider your own motivation (if you are a voter), then you will fasten on the third category as the most promising. However, as with the contingent benefits, it is worth taking the trouble to go through a bit of explicit analysis.

Consider the last presidential election and estimate how large Q would have to be for you to prefer $[X + \$Q]$ to $[X + 1000 \text{ votes}]$, where X here is the number of votes received by the candidate you favored. In other words, the choice is between [the actual outcome, but you receive $\$Q$] versus [you receive nothing but your preferred candidate receives an extra 1000 votes in the final total].

You must imagine yourself making this choice after you (but not anyone else) have been told the outcome, which we will assume would *not* have been reversed by adding 1000 votes. For we want to consider here only noncontingent demonstration benefits. Presumably you would in fact prefer that your favorite candidate received another 1000 votes, strengthening his mandate if he won or providing support for his viewpoint if he lost. So presumably Q is not strictly $0. But, whatever Q is, divide it by 1000 to get an estimate of the demonstration value of your own single vote. Unless you believe that politicians are not influenced by the vote-getting effects of their behavior, campaign pledges, and so on, then you will not regard the demonstration value of a vote as strictly zero. Nevertheless, it is unlikely that you will find that your motivation to vote could be significantly accounted for by the prospect of a gain you value at $Q/1000$.

Then let us try the consumption benefits. Imagine you have been given a ballot, stamped and ready to mail, and you are confident that you are not going to change your mind about who you would vote for. Suppose also that there is plenty of time prior to the election, so that you can be sure that if you mail the ballot it will arrive in time to be counted. If you are motivated significantly by consumption benefits from the act of voting, you will not be tempted to use the mail ballot because you will lose all the pleasures of going to the polls, waiting in line, pulling the levers, and so on. Nor will others see that you are voting. But modest inquiries have turned up no one who would not bypass these advantages.

In general, whatever your personal response to these experiments, you are not likely to doubt that large numbers of people who are regular voters would reply to the kinds of questions asked in ways that leave it most unclear how either the contingent or demonstration or consumption benefits from voting, or all three together, can really account for their behavior. We are left, consequently, with the psychic benefits. Further, when surveys are taken of why people vote, or as introspection is likely to tell you, the answer very predominantly is something in terms of citizen's duty or responsibility or of doing one's share.

It is not clear, though, that this answer to the question of why people bother to vote in fact clarifies anything. After all, nothing will make a human being more uncomfortable than to be acting in some way and unable to give an explanation for doing so. So an explanation of voting that amounts to saying "because I ought to," may be just another way of saying, "I don't know why. I just want to do it even if it doesn't make sense in terms of rational choice."

An interesting experiment – not a thought experiment, but a real one often done – involves hypnotizing an individual, leaving him with a post-hypnotic suggestion that on cue (such as the hypnotist coughing) he will perform some odd act: for example, suddenly jump up and open, then close, the door. The subject is awakened (having been instructed to forget the details of his trance), is given the cue, and performs the act. He is then asked for an explanation of his behavior. Typically, the subject will not say that he hasn't any idea, he just got a crazy urge. Rather, he will concoct an explanation, which only he will believe; the others know why he performed the act.

Thus the fact that an individual who votes, such as myself and most probably you as well, feels that he (or she) has a duty to vote does not explain anything unless we can discern a consistent pattern that lets us say something coherent about the conditions under which the individual does or does not behave in a way that can be understood as fulfilling a duty. But if we have a theory that accounts for responding to the personal sense of duty, or social responsibility, or some other variant of psychic income, then the notion of psychic income would no longer be essential to an account of social behavior. (It might or might not be a useful concept, but the theory could in principle be reformulated in terms of the factors that account for psychic income.[6]) The very fact that the conventional theory is driven to rely on psychic income raises the question of whether it has anything very interesting to say about psychic income, or whether it merely treats psychic income as a residual category of motivation to be invoked when the theory otherwise gets into trouble.

Suppose there are three candidates (X, Y, and Z) and that Smith happens to prefer strongly X to Y and, equally strongly, Y to Z. Who will Smith vote for? The conventional model does not yield a definite answer in this commonplace sort of situation. If Smith's psychic income comes solely from the act of voting (not depending in any way on who he votes for), then if the race is close between Y and Z, with X a distant third, the conventional calculus implies that Smith would vote for Y. However, once the conventional analysis leads us to the result that voting must ordinarily depend heavily on psychic income, then it becomes arbitrary to assume that this psychic income comes only from the act of voting and not at all from how Smith votes. But a slight advantage in psychic income from voting for the candidate Smith most prefers would overcome the small (compared to the cost of voting) contingent benefit advantage of voting for his second choice.

One way to avoid this embarrassment is to suppose that a voter maximizes psychic income by voting in whatever way maximizes the expected effect from his vote. (Smith votes because the psychic income offsets the cost even though the expected effect of his vote is too small to move him to do so; but those psychic benefits are maximized if he votes "as if" the expected effect is what motivates him.) However, this may seem arbitrary. In fact, it is very arbitrary. Further, this rule allows the possibility that *whether* Smith votes is unrelated to the expected effect of his vote, although *how* he votes is determined by that effect.

Such difficulties illustrate in a concrete context the point made in more abstract terms at the conclusion of Chapter 2 (and graphically in Appendix A): combining goods altruism, participation, and self-interest is what is needed to obtain a viable model of social choice; and, although that does not at first sight seem difficult, it turns out to be quite unmanageable as long as one is unwilling or unable to make a definite break with the traditional usage in economics.

In any case, the conventional "public choice" literature never advanced to the point of being able to account for voting, in particular to do so in a way that is internally consistent and also consistent with the fact that those who do vote tend to be reluctant to "waste" their vote on third-party candidates.

FS analysis of voting

In terms of the FS utility calculus, S-Smith would neglect any call to duty, for his preference is always to be a free-rider if possible. G-Smith is concerned solely with what he judges to be the welfare of society, and any merely personal psychic satisfaction to Smith would be inconsequential. So, in terms of FS, notions such as duty and social responsibility are not a part of the utility calculus. (Recall the discussion of Chapter 5.) In terms of FS, we must show that we can neglect any notion of psychic benefits and still find voting rational.[7] This would explain the fact that Smith both votes, *and* is conscious of and takes satisfaction in the feeling that he is behaving in a socially useful way. As before, it is worth going through an explicit argument to illustrate this point.

Consider how we might expect a typical Smith to respond (how you would respond, if you think of this, once again, as an experiment to try on yourself) if we explicitly ask for what we may call "S-answers" and "G-answers" to the questions asked earlier about the contingent and demonstration values of voting.

S-answers will certainly be microscopic, confirming that a strictly selfish voter could not be motivated by the effect of his vote on the outcome. For example, with respect to contingent benefits, an ordinary voter could hardly estimate his selfish stake in a presidential election as exceeding a few thousand dollars, or the likelihood that his vote decides the election as better than one in a million. But even judgments like these drive the S-value of Smith's vote down to something on the order of a tenth of a penny.

On the other hand, the *social* value of a presidential election outcome is easily estimated in the billions. (A billion dollars, after all is only a few tenths of 1 percent of one year's federal spending, and the choice of president has some effect on how that money is used, not to mention other matters, such as war and peace, over which a president has some influence.) Discount $1 billion by 1 chance in 100 million that Smith's vote determines the outcome (not 1 in a million as before), and the expected G-value of the single vote still comes to $10.

To make a comparable estimate for demonstration benefits, interpolate from an estimate of the effect of a large enough number of votes to envision the social effect. For a voter who thinks the effect of an additional million votes for his candidate on public policy would have a social value on the order of $10 million (a few thousandths of 1 percent of a single year's federal spending), the demonstration value of a vote comes to $10. So it takes only a judgment that a million votes would have a whisper of a social effect to make the social value per vote comparable to the kind of G-*wtp* that would make voting a reasonable use of G-resources.

At this point a set of psychological issues presents itself, turning on the fact that we get different answers to the question of how much a vote is worth depending on just how the question is framed. A sketch of this topic is given in Appendix G. Here we will move on to consider the FS equations analogous to the conventional calculus Equation 7.2. Generalized to the case of three candidates, we get:

$$wtp(x) = P_{xy}G_{xy} + P_{xz}G_{xz} + G_x^* + S^* \qquad\qquad 7.3$$

$$wtp(y) = -P_{xy}G_{xy} + P_{yz}G_{yz} + G_y^* + S^* \qquad\qquad 7.4$$

where the meaning of the symbols is analogous to the usage in the conventional voting calculus of Equations 7.1 and 7.2. $Wtp(x)$, etc., is Smith's wtp for a vote for candidate X; P_{xy}, etc., is the probability of a tie between X and Y; G_{xy}, etc., is the contingent benefit to G-Smith of X's election instead of Y; G_x^*, etc. is the demonstration value to G-Smith of a vote for X; and S^* is the consumption value of voting to S-Smith.

Equations 7.3 and 7.4 show no terms involving a three-way tie among X, Y, and Z because they would involve probabilities orders of magnitude smaller than those of the two-way ties included. The same equations will also serve for the two-candidate case by setting the probability of ties involving a third candidate, Z, to zero.

Note that, to simplify the equations, I have left out terms that the earlier argument shows will ordinarily be negligibly small, such as $S_{xy}P_{xy}$ and S_x^* – contingent and demonstration benefits to S-Smith, or G^* (consumption benefit to G-Smith). For a secret ballot, consumption benefits (S^*, and G^* in certain situations where it is not negligible) will by definition be independent of *how* Smith votes, so no subscript is needed. Further, in principle we could add a third equation to allow for the peculiar but not impossible circumstance where Smith does best by voting for the candidate that in fact he likes least (here Z).

Finally, notice that in these equations I have taken Smith's *wtp* to be just the expected (in the probability sense) social value of his vote, plus whatever S-value there might be. This is harmless in this context, but of course it is easy to imagine situations in which this simplifying assumption would be untenable. (For example, if we were dealing with a choice where the cost of acting was high rather than very low, then Smith's budget constraint would limit his *wtp*, obviously, to something that he is in a position to spend.)

Consider your own response to the G-components of Equations 7.3 and 7.4. I think that nearly all readers will judge that the demonstration (G_x^*) values are likely to be less important than contingent values except when (1) the outcome is judged to be a foregone conclusion; or (2) the party differential (G_{xy}) is negligible – as when the voter sees no difference between the candidates. In any of these cases, we can see an opportunity for a minor party candidate to garner votes ("send them a message," as George Wallace used to say). Otherwise, we can expect contingent benefits to dominate, with voters strongly motivated to vote (in a plurality system) for whichever of the two strongest candidates is closest to their preference.

Message-bearing minor parties would have the most appeal for a voter for whom (2) holds, who must be motivated (if he is to vote) by demonstration benefits even if the election is competitive, that is, even if (1) does not hold. A familiar illustration of one of the effects is the sharp falloff in voting between the primaries and general elections in the old one-party South, where condition (1) presumably held very widely. As would be expected, this effect has gradually disappeared with the rise of competitive Republican parties in the South.[8]

But an elaborate effort by Smith to refine his benefit estimates would hardly be an efficient way to use G-resources. (Obviously, the cost of voting must be understood to include the cost of making a decision as well as the direct cost.) So the sensible thing for Smith to do – the thing that he can understand in theoretical terms if he is knowledgeable enough about utility theory to know why satisficing is rational in such situations – is to choose in terms of simple rules of thumb sufficient to give some confidence that the resources spent on voting are spent reasonably well, even if not optimally. For example:

1.   Vote unless some exceptional situation arises.
2.   Consider a minor party if both (1) and (2) hold; otherwise vote for the major party closer to your views.

Although such simple decision rules amount to the kind of notion that Tullock characterizes as "duty or habit," their theoretical status under FS is very different than it is in the conventional analysis. They do not reflect a departure from utility-maximizing behavior or an extra component of utility thrown in after the fact to account for an apparent discrepancy between observed behavior and what the basic theory implies. Rather, they reflect the way that, consistent with the basic theory, a rational utility-maximizer should behave in a context where costs and benefits cannot be evaluated very precisely and the total amount of resources involved is small. The rules of thumb are more than artifacts because they affect observed behavior, less so because of the resource savings involved than because behavior will be more persistent than if individual calculations were made at each election. Hence, if Smith uses simple rules of thumb, the best predictor of whether he will vote in this election will be how often he has voted in the past. We expect to see a noticeable difference in turnout only for voters who attach an exceptional value to G_{xy} – either very small or very large compared to their judgments in past elections – and similarly for the effect of closeness.

But something approaching half of those eligible to vote in U.S. elections do not vote even in presidential years. If it is easy to reach a judgment that voting is a reasonable use of G-resources, why do so many fail to reach that judgment? With no pretense of offering a full analysis here, a number of factors come readily to mind.

First, as shown in Chapter 4, allocations to G-spending tend to increase proportionately faster than income if FS holds. Consequently, the better off Smith is, the larger G-Smith's "income," and the easier it is to reach an affirmative judgment about using a bit of G-resources to vote. Poverty, on the other hand, would tend to depress voting.

Second, better-educated citizens (who will also, in general, have higher incomes) face smaller "auxiliary" costs in voting, and the auxiliary costs (knowing enough to have some sense of how you want to vote, knowing how to register, etc.) probably exceed the direct costs. (This will be particularly true to the extent that simple rules of thumb about *how* to vote – party loyalty, most obviously – lose credibility. A consequence of this, one might expect, is that the fall-off in voter participation would be least among the best-educated, other things equal.)

Third, the value of a vote will depend on one's confidence that he is making a sensible judgment. (To the extent you are in doubt about your ability to make a judgment, you will be uncertain whether your vote yields positive or negative G-utility.) As noted under the previous point, this will be particularly important in societies, like the United States, in which simple ideological rules of thumb about how to vote have been losing credibility.

Fourth, for some individuals, G' (voting) is just not salient compared to alternative uses of G-resources. One example would be the individual who leads a narrow life, focused on his immediate neighborhood. His sense of group-interest is focused on that highly localized group, and questions of national policy are remote from his concerns. A very different example would be the scientist or artist who believes that anything that distracts him from his work yields negative social returns. There will also be individuals alienated from the political system, individuals who are narrowly self-interested to a deviant degree, individuals whose group-interested resources are tied up in some nonpolitical activity, and so on – perhaps even individuals who do not vote because they believe that voting has been proved irrational. [9]

Finally, at any given election, there will be people who do not vote even if the rules of thumb given earlier describe their behavior: people who happen to be sick on election day, face some last-minute personal difficulty, are unexpectedly away from home, and so on. Hence the fraction of eligible citizens who vote in any given election will necessarily be smaller than the fraction that votes often enough to be classified as "voters" in the context of the discussion here.

However, although it would be inconsistent with FS for voting in a stable society to decline to such low levels that serious questions are raised about the viability of the political system (for then the demonstration value of voting would increase sharply), FS cannot predict, a priori, the fraction of eligible voters who will vote, any more than conventional economic theory can predict, a priori, the fraction of people who will live in apartments rather than houses. However, FS does provide an explicit framework, consistent with that used in analyzing other respects of social behavior (as illustrated in the balance of the study), which yields predictions about how voting behavior should vary with other contextual and individual variables.

FS and self-interest in voting

The FS voting calculus (Equations 7.3 and 7.4) implies that S-Smith will not much care who Smith votes for: S-Smith would ordinarily be willing to pay neither noticeably more than S^* for a vote favorable to his preference nor noticeably less than S^* if the vote is to be cast contrary to his preferences. Hence, in terms of FS, voting must be understood as an essentially social act, and in particular, given that a person votes, how he votes must ordinarily[10] reflect his social rather than merely private preferences (G-preferences rather than S-preferences). But we need not expect that the social preferences of a voter (as voter[11]) will ordinarily conflict very sharply with his private preferences. Recalling the discussion of group-interest in Chapter 5, we would expect that a farmer, for example, would be especially sensitive to the problems of farmers. His sense of group-interest may include a special concern for farmers; and, even if not, he will be especially aware of the problems of that class of citizens and feel especially knowledgeable about judging the soundness of a political candidate when he listens to what he says about farmers. What to city dweller Jones looks like farmer Johnson's self-interested vote in favor of candidates favoring high price supports may look (must ordinarily look, if FS is sound on this point) to farmer Johnson like a vote in favor of a candidate who understands the problem of farmers.

Is it possible to differentiate between farmer Johnson's favoring high price supports as looking out for his self-interest versus his supporting the group-interest of farmers?

Suppose he retires, sells his farm, and moves to Florida. Now his self-interest would best be served by low price supports; he no longer grows, but he continues to eat. Will Johnson now favor low price supports? Similarly, should we expect a retired scientist no longer to favor generous federal funding of research, or a retired general no longer to favor generous funding of national defense?

Indeed, if FS holds, we should ordinarily find that the farmer, the scientist, and the soldier each feels that the programs he favors are those that serve not merely his "local" group-interest but the national interest. It is those who oppose these programs who will be seen as putting narrower interests above the general public interest in fairness and long-run efficiency, and these views will not change (easily, if at all) with a change in a voter's purely personal situation. In general, in the formalism used earlier, $S_{xy} > 0$ is not in principle inconsistent with $G_{xy} > 0$, and in fact ordinarily will not be judged so by a voter.

But situations certainly arise (for example, in connection with bond issues, or the response of government employees to the Reagan candidacy) in which information on voter attitudes makes it reasonable to impute to certain classes of voters a clear conflict between their sense of what would serve their self-interest and what would serve their sense of group interest: G_{xy} is positive, but S_{xy} is negative. FS would predict such voters would ordinarily vote for X (contrary to self-interest); the conventional theory would predict the reverse. A special challenge in such research would be to devise ways to distinguish between (1) the kind of S-bias to G-preferences in voting that the discussions of Chapter 5 would lead us to expect, and (2) the kind of G-rationalization for S preferences in voting (allowing the voter to enjoy a good conscience while behaving in his narrow self-interest) that the conventional analysis would suggest.

Now in fact, voters are obviously often concerned with issues remote from any plausible self-interest, such as abortion, the Panama Canal, and many others. Even what are often taken as local issues, closer to self-interest, also may have this character. For example, no New York politician could afford to be in favor of Concorde SST landings at Kennedy Airport. Yet, except for a tiny minority living close enough to the airport to be affected by takeoff noise, no New Yorker could be harmed (and a variety could gain) by establishment of the SST route. So the intensity of feeling on this issue is as mystifying in terms of self-interest as the strong feeling voters often exhibit on such matters as abortion, human rights in foreign countries, and many other national and international issues.

However, because representative government legitimizes the efforts of a representative to represent the interests of his constituents, we would expect voters to respond more to local interests in voting for candidates for Congress than in voting for candidates for president. Similarly, we would expect voters to be much more ready to forgive a president who closed a local military base than a congressman who failed to fight hard against the closing.

Consider next the character of political appeals if FS holds. Because we expect voting to be dominated by G-preferences and spending on consumer goods to be dominated by S-preferences, we must expect that a content analysis of commercial versus political advertising would find the formulation of appeals quite different. In commercial advertising, we can expect to see direct appeals to self-interest ("you save," even "other people will be green with envy if you") whereas in political appeals we expect to see appeals to group-interest ("working people, who make America great . . . will save" even, "ask not what your country can do for you").

Would Ronald Reagan's closing gambit in his debate with Jimmy Carter be a counter example? (He asked viewers to think of whether they personally were better or worse off since Carter was elected.) Only, I think, if we believe that voters would be unconcerned about how other people answered. But Reagan hardly expected voters to answer, "Other people may be better off, but I am not, so I will vote for Reagan." Rather, the very asking of the question implied that most people would answer that they were worse off, so that even a voter who had prospered under Carter would not necessarily – in terms of FS we would predict would not in general – be moved toward Carter by this inquiry.

Under what conditions might there be exceptions (consistent with FS) to the basic FS inference. At least three possibilities arise: (1) Smith sees no clear margin in terms of group-interest but is voting anyway, so that a vote in terms of self-interest is just a way of making a choice;[12] (2) Smith is positively wild-eyed on some personal matter and votes contrary to his sense of group-interest in that kind of mood, which he himself will regard as foolish when he calms down; (3) Smith happens, on election day, to be far out of equilibrium, so that it makes him feel better to do something definitely selfish, even if foolishly so. Notice that all of these cases involve peculiar individual situations: they say that it would not be embarrassing to FS to find individual cases in which the basic FS inference is violated, any more than conventional economic theory is embarrassed by individual violations of predicted behavior. But none of these special case explanations could ordinarily be invoked in survey work, for example, where we are looking at what can reasonably be regarded as typical voting behavior.

Another kind of question relates to the role of ideology, given the FS inference on the motivation governing how Smith votes. Ideology plays a role in political choice that has no real parallel in ordinary private choice on how to spend on consumer goods. With respect to private spending, S-Smith must believe only that his spending is good for himself. His choices are those which he is likely to feel uniquely qualified to make. But G-Smith faces a far more complicated problem. He is not only concerned with group- rather than self-interest, but group-interest itself will be complicated given the overlapping and layering of interests that characterize life in a modern society.

Downs deals with part of this by interpreting ideology as something produced by political parties to simplify the task of voters, making it easier for self-interested but inattentive citizens to identify the party that best serves their interest. But mere slogans and symbols would seem better suited to the function Downs describes. Ideology is far more complicated than that, sufficiently so that few truly casual voters could have much familiarity with a party's ideology *beyond* the level of slogans. Yet, even at (or only modestly beyond) the level of slogans, ideology is much more intricate than commercial slogans. In terms of FS, the political function of ideology is to reconcile and integrate the complex layering and intertwining of subnational, national, and (in some cases at least) transnational group loyalties of those committed to a political position.[13]

Nevertheless, when we speak of kinds of voting with which we are familiar, it is difficult to produce FS inferences that are flatly opposed to those obtained by writers using a conventional model. For unless the analyst lacks any sense of empirical politics, he will draw back from inferences that are obviously untenable. Only if we consider a novel kind of decision process, might it be easy for even a politically sophisticated analyst to be led to unsound inferences: he would not have the aid of practical intuition to warn him as to when he should hedge or adjust his model. So it is reasonable, I think, to conclude this discussion with a reminder that until the FS analysis of Chapter 6 became available, no one (even among critics of DR) seems to have noticed how radically misleading the conventional model turns out to be in this context of DR voting.

CHAPTER 8

Leaders and followers

Throughout this chapter, which deals mainly with the work of Anthony Downs and Mancur Olson, what is at issue is how the FS analysis compares with the conventional "economic man" analysis.[1] What is not at issue is the significance of the work by Downs, Olson, Buchanan and Tullock, and others who have followed them in applying economic analysis to political choice. It should be obvious that the present work could not have been undertaken without the basis provided by earlier works, just as (should the FS approach win adherents), the analysis I have been able to produce will eventually be supplanted by something superior.

The FS analysis of Chapter 7 led to the view that it would be reasonable for a citizen to judge voting an efficient use of G-resources. But it would be difficult, and very obviously not an efficient use of G-resources, for citizens to attempt to make any sort of precise evaluation of the components of utility that are included in Equations 7.3 and 7.4. Rational behavior would involve the use of simple rules of thumb and choice based on limited information. We do not expect to see citizens expend substantial G-resources to improve the "quality" of their vote.

This "satisficing" FS argument with respect to gathering information for voting differs very little from that carefully presented by Downs nearly twenty-five years ago.[2] In terms of FS, we would expect citizens to be willing to invest *some* effort into gathering information to make a judgment. But this qualifies, rather than refutes, Downs's point on the "rational ignorance" of voters.[3]

Further, Downs's argument for why a citizen might bother to vote at all is also not very different for the FS view. For Downs's argument relies heavily on the proposition that citizens vote out of a sense of social responsibility, which is not very different from the FS inference that voting must ordinarily be a social act, governed by G- rather than S-preferences.[4]

But this "social responsibility" argument would seem to be inconsistent with what Downs calls the "cornerstone" of his analysis: namely, that "whenever we speak [i.e. Downs speaks] of rational behavior, we always mean behavior directed towards primarily selfish ends." It is from this selfishness axiom that Downs draws his "fundamental hypothesis" about the behavior of political leaders: "they act solely in order to obtain the income, prestige, and power which come from being in office. Thus politicians. . . never seek office as a means of carrying out particular policies, their only goal is to reap the rewards of holding office *per se*. They treat policies purely as means to the attainment of their private ends."[5] But if citizens may vote from a sense of social responsibility, why should they not run for office, in part at least, out of this same sense of social responsibility? And, if they might, why should we accept Downs's "fundamental hypothesis"?

Further, if voting must be explained by social responsibility then are not all of Downs's inferences about voters that derive from his axiom of selfishness thrown into doubt, along with many of the inferences about politicians that depend on how voters will respond to politicians' choices?

However, it turns out that neither of these problems are serious for the Downsian analysis, for the perhaps surprising reason that there turns out to be almost nothing in Downs's analysis that actually relies on the axiom of selfishness. The axiom in fact is never again invoked (for politicians' behavior) once it has served as the basis of the "fundamental hypothesis" quoted above. But that very strong hypothesis (or the variant that Downs often uses, which says that politicians choose policies solely to maximize votes) is in Downs's own judgment empirically untenable.[6] On the other hand, a milder formulation – for example, that politicians are intensely concerned about winning votes – has no need of the selfishness axiom. Whether a politician is motivated by self-interest or group-interest or any compromise between, he must win votes to carry out his purpose. Further, we have already seen that Downs's central proposition about voters – namely, that voters will exhibit "rational ignorance" – also does not require the selfishness axiom. But with these two basic propositions in hand (one dealing with politicians, the other with ordinary voters) almost everything else in Downs's analysis follows.

In fact, Downs effectively abandons the axiom of selfishness soon after he introduces it. His actors, it turns out, may choose altruistically "because self-denying charity is often a great source of [psychological] benefit to oneself."[7] There is no restraint on what form this behavior takes – whatever gives the Downsian chooser psychic benefits will do. This is in contrast to FS, where altruism is tied to Smith's view of group interest, not to Smith's psychic self-interest. Hence, under FS, Smith's group-interested spending must make sense in the light of what Smith can plausibly be supposed to believe about the external effects of his choices. Further, in FS, but not in Downs, there is an allocation rule (defined by Equations 4.1 and 4.2), that determines when we might find behavior reflecting altruistic motivation. Because Downs provides no such rule, we do not have any basis for deciding when we should expect to observe behavior reflecting the self-denying variety of self-interest, as opposed to ordinary self-interest.

Hence, the difference between FS and Downs (as with respect to other analyses in the economic man tradition) is not that FS allows for altruism and other work does not. Advocates of the economic man approach almost unfailingly allow some room for what I will label egoistic altruism (as distinct from the FS notion of separate group-interested preferences). In the terms of Sen's argument mentioned in the Preface, the conventional analysis allows for "sympathy" as distinct from "commitment." But this kind of allowance for altruism would be ruinous for the analytical power of the model unless there were a tacit commitment that effectively says (T1 of Chapter 6) that ordinarily we should always assume behavior is narrowly selfish. The allowance for unselfish behavior is effectively only an escape clause (like "merit goods" in a conventional public goods analysis), not really an integral part of the theory. Indeed, until a model is devised that allows for altruism in a way that is analytically tractable, all of this is only unfortunate and not at all surprising or even unwise.

If we turn from Downs to Olson, the situation is similar in the imagination and shrewdness displayed by the analysis, but the actual role played by self-interest (strictly construed) is much more substantial. Although Olson also allows for altruistic motivation when needed, his book is essentially about the influence of the "free-rider" problem on social outcomes, and the main line of his analysis stays with the strong free-rider inferences of self-interested motivation.

With respect to government programs, the practical solution to the free-rider problem is the imposition of taxes (coerced spending). But there may be a large divergence between ideal choices with respect to government programs (optimal choices, in the sense of Chapter 6) and the actual outcome of a social choice process. What motivated the great interest in DR discussed in Chapter 6 was the possibility that through DR it might be possible to more nearly approximate a Lindahl–Samuelson efficient choice than through the political processes we now use. For, if political choices depend substantially on the effort that citizens make to influence social policy, then the actual outcomes must be understood not in terms of the Lindahl–Samuelson idealization but in terms of a competition for influence over social outcomes. This competition may or may not lead to a result that Samuelson's demon (see Chapter 6) might regard as reasonably efficient, or that you or I might regard as reasonably just.

These individual efforts, in turn, are substantially or wholly voluntary. If a citizen does not choose to contribute to a lobbying effort that is very much in his own interest, no one can require him to do so ordinarily. So, although the government's programs are not directly susceptible to free-rider problems (only to inefficiencies due to "free-rider" disincentives to truthful revelations of preference), they are indirectly susceptible to great distortion due, among other things, to the differential effects of free-rider incentives on the extent to which some views, rather than others, are vigorously pressed in the political process. That is the subject of Olson's book.

Very briefly, Olson's argument is that rational, self-interested individuals will not make voluntary contributions to an organization seeking to advance their economic interest, except to the extent that the organization can offer "selective incentives" so that the individual obtains perceptible gains (or avoids penalties) by making a contribution. If the only gains the organization offers are those which cannot be selectively awarded (for example, higher price supports for farmers, or unemployment insurance for workers), then the individual will rationally choose to be a free-rider. Hence, the main result of the theory: concentrated economic interests (typically, producers) will have a political advantage over diffused interests (typically, consumers). This is partly because it is in small groups that the individual's own contribution can most plausibly have a perceptible effect of the social outcome and that individual pressures to conform to the group interest can most plausibly be applied.

But, ordinarily even more important (since even "small" politically potent groups are ordinarily large enough to face free-rider problems), when economic groups do succeed in organizing themselves politically, we can expect to find that the group has been able to develop selective incentives sufficient to draw members. In the most blatant form, these involve explicit compulsion to join, as in many labor unions, bar associations, and so forth. In subtler cases we will find information services, insurance plans, charter flights, social affairs, and so on. Thus, even though the activities of the organization that are in fact most important to the members may be the provision of nonselective benefits (e.g., favorable legislation), the ability to carry out the socially significant activities must be financed as a byproduct of the selective incentives. The sharply varying ability of some groups to organize to advance their common interests thus turns not on the relative importance of organization to advance that interest but rather, quite incidentally, on the feasibility of providing selective incentives. Professional groups, for example, doctors and lawyers, who provide a market for specialized services (journals, conventions, malpractice counselling, etc.) are well organized to advance their economic interests; whereas the aged, migrant farm workers, and so on are poorly organized.

Empirically, Olson's theory works rather well, provided we are careful to limit its application to economic interests, as Olson is generally careful to specify.

Olson can explain why the theory works (much) better for organizations whose public activity is to advance the economic interests of its members than for other kinds of organizations (philanthropic, environmental, cultural, etc.). To the extent that the benefits sought are narrowly economic gains to a particular subset of society, it becomes hard to invoke whatever propensities potential members have for altruistic behavior. Behavior will thus more closely approximate that of self-interested economic man, and Olson's "logic of collective action" will more closely approximate the empirical result. In terms of the FS model, to the extent that the collective goods gains from organizational activity satisfy S- rather than G-preferences, then individuals will tend to be free-riders even if they highly value the collective benefits the organization seeks. For obtaining these goods is not significantly contingent on their personal contribution. Hence, such organizations must depend heavily on private incentives to attract support. If *only* S-benefits were provided, then only selective benefits (benefits with the character of private goods, attractive to S-Smith) would significantly draw members.[8]

In terms of FS, we would add some further results and also some qualifications. For example, even in organizations that to an outsider look like associations to advance narrowly self-interested concerns there will be a substantial effort (paralleling a point made in Chapter 7) to develop an ideology explaining how the goals the group seeks are actually in the interest of society at large, or consistent with and even required by some higher ethical principle (e.g., meaningful individual liberty is possible only under a free market economy; meaningful human dignity is possible only by the abolition of private capital; etc.), or demonstrating why the class of individuals who are to benefit are especially deserving of whatever consideration is being asked. Obviously these appeals are not mutually exclusive: the ideology will attempt to integrate them all.[9]

It will be very important that the organization take this effort seriously. Otherwise it will face the threat of (1) an organization that can provide the selective benefits more cheaply by neglecting the collective goods; or (generally more serious) (2) a competing organization (perhaps arising out of a schism with the first) that draws off members by appealing more successfully to potential members' G-preferences.

Further, we can expect to find that the organizers themselves will be among those who take ideology seriously; that is, they are not likely to regard it as merely a manipulative tactic. For, other things equal, candidates for leadership who themselves obtain G-benefits from the collective interest activities of the organization, as well as the S-benefits that come with leadership, will work harder and sacrifice more for the organization than will individuals who are merely cynical manipulators.

Finally, we would expect to find significant differences between the ideological notions of the leadership of an organization and those of the mass membership. The "mass market" version of the ideology will be cruder and even to some degree inconsistent with the elite version. We do not expect the Pope's Catholicism to be quite that of the humblest parishioner; or William Buckley's private views on the merits of capitalism to be quite that of the local Rotarian. The function of ideology is to shore up G' (this activity). It cannot be persuasive if it cannot be grasped, or cannot be believed. Hence, the version of the ideology suitable for the casual or naive supporter can hardly be the same as that suitable for the sophisticated and active supporter. What the former can grasp the latter is unlikely to believe and vice versa.

Even in those organizations most clearly motivated by some sense of acting in the public interest (say, the Audubon Society or Common Cause) we can expect to find attempts to provide selective benefits. That is, even when it is clear that the activity depends crucially on G- and not S-incentives, organizers will try to find a way to offer some S-benefits.

After all, the organization has a list of individuals with special characteristics (the far from random characteristics that motivated them to be members of this organization). The organization does not need to be managed by Harvard MBAs to realize that this list is valuable – all the more so since the membership is motivated to give somewhat more attention to communications from this organization than to comparable communications (for example, third-class mail) from other sources. There is almost certainly *something* in the nature of a private good that can be sold to this group, and the organization not only has the list but a certain amount of monopoly leverage in selling to it. Sometimes this private good will be built into the dues (say, the organization's magazine), but there are quite likely to be other things as well (such as charter flights). Often, but not necessarily, the S-benefit is tied directly to the G-benefit (e.g., the umbrella your public television station will give you if you contribute $40 or more).

There are particular advantages in all this to the organization (and yet no penalty to the contributor). S-benefits from Smith's spending on the organization will be charged to S-Smith, as governed by the allocation rules worked out in Chapter 5. Ordinarily we expect to find the bulk of the individual's resources allocated to S-Smith, not G-Smith, so it is highly advantageous to tap the donor's S- as well as G-resources.

None of this depends on the balance between narrow self-interest and the desire to serve the public interest that motivates managers of the organization or the way that the money is used. Whatever the situation, it is rational for the managers of the organization to prefer more resources to less.

Of course, individual tastes vary greatly. There will always be some donors for whom, for example, the organization's magazine is just another damned thing asking to be read and who would be happier if it did not exist. Thus the above remarks, as is almost always true of economic arguments, should not be construed to apply to each and every donor. However, unless the organization seriously misjudges its constituents' tastes the argument will hold for the general case.

A fortiori, all this will hold for an organization substantially devoted to the economic interests of its members. For then there is likely to be a much more important (to the members) set of special incentives that the organization can offer: professional information and counseling, conventions, and so forth. The special offerings will then seem an important element in the membership dues, and, in at least some cases, for some members, the "selective incentives" that Olson argues typically account wholly for participation in a large organization may in fact be sufficient to account for membership. At least, it may not be *obvious* that this view is wrong. But it will not be generally true that selective benefits alone account for membership in such organizations. To leap from the observation that selective benefits are important to members to the conclusion that they alone account for membership would be, from the FS view, reckless and ordinarily empirically wrong.

Olson argues (and one frequently sees analogous arguments by other writers, usually economists) that were it true that individuals are motivated to make nontrivial voluntary contributions to some public good (selective benefits aside), then we would see these individuals undertaking other forms of what would seem to be intimately related cooperative behavior, which clearly is not ordinarily forthcoming. Thus, if a farmer were willing, selective benefits aside, to contribute to an organization that was lobbying for acreage controls (within limits, farmers make more money when the harvest declines), then why would he not try to affect prices directly by voluntarily limiting his acreage, which he doesn't do?[10] As another illustration, Olson notes that if people were willing to make significant voluntary contributions to the supply of public goods, then why has no government ever been able to finance its activities of taxes from voluntary contribution? But coercion seems everywhere essential.[11]

Yet these questions are answered by the first theorem of conventional economic theory: rational actors allocate resources to the use that provides the highest marginal utility so that (at the margin) if the individual allocates to several uses, utility from an incremental allocation is the same for all. This must be true of an efficient (economically rational) allocation; were it not, the actor could gain utility without spending more resources, simply by shifting his existing allocation.

Thus (to simplify a bit), the farmer would not rationally give up $10 worth of income by restricting production a minute fraction if he could have more effect on the likely price of wheat by contributing $10 to an organization lobbying for acreage controls. The same holds for an individual who favors more public spending who gives $10 to the ADA rather than sending $10 to the U.S. Treasury. There is no contradiction between doing one thing and not doing another, even when both have exactly the same goal: a rational actor does what he thinks is efficient, and only an irrational actor would spread his resources indiscriminately among all claimants.

Because this error is both elementary and very widespread, we have a puzzle about why it persists. The explanation, apparently, is that from the viewpoint of the conventional model either expenditure (direct action or contributing to the lobby) is irrational because it provides no perceptible benefit to the actor. So, from the viewpoint of the conventional model, it will seem irrational for the actor to spend even the briefest moment's thought deciding which way is the more efficient way to waste his money: in fact, if he is rational, he will not spend it either way.

However, if we allow that a person might allocate some portion of his spending to social purposes (in FS terms, to G-spending), then this puzzle disappears. From a social point of view both Smith's spending and its effects are microscopic, whether the spending is socially motivated (G-spending) or self-interested (S-spending). But the marginal utilities (G' and S'), which govern the efficient allocation of resources, can be large (that is, the ratio between socially microscopic costs and socially microscopic benefits can easily be large[12]), and the value ratio (G'/S') can also be large. In particular, Smith would make a donation only if he judged the social value of the (say) $10 if given to a charity to be sufficiently greater than spending the $10 on himself that the allocation rule elicits such a donation (i.e., such that $W < G'/S'$ for the donation).[13]

In the case of a large charity raising many millions, Smith personally will not be able to see any difference his donation makes. But his motivation in making that donation, as I have stressed many times now, does not turn on any such perceptible return to Smith personally but on a judgment of social values. G-motivation is not the "egoistic altruism" discussed at the beginning of this chapter in connection with Downs.

Of course, it would ordinarily serve neither his S- nor his G-preferences for Smith to spend any substantial effort deciding how *best* to spend his $10. But if the better outlet for this bit of G-resources is easy to see (or if he has been persuaded of what is efficient by supporters of the lobbying organization), then he will spend the $10 (if he decides to allocate something from G-resources to this good) where it will do the more good, as efficient (economic) allocation of resources insists he should.

Hence, if there is a real problem about the rationality of spending with imperceptible effects, it must turn on a question about the rationality of a person wishing to allocate some fraction of his or her resources to social purposes when he (or she) is only one member of a large society, that is, when the person's social spending (or for that matter the person's existence) has only microscopic social consequences.

It is crucial here to notice that a change in the meaning of the term *rationality* is implicit in the question just presented. As mentioned in the discussion of terminology at the end of Chapter 1, I have been using the term in the narrowly technical sense formally used within economic theory, where "rationality" means "internally consistent." In this technical sense, that an individual might allocate his resources between self-interested and social spending according to some allocation rule (for example, 85 percent self, 15 percent social; or, as we have postulated, such that $W = G'/S'$) is not something that is of itself subject to any test of technical rationality, any more than a preference for vacations in the mountains rather than at the ocean. A problem does arise if we add a requirement that Smith's utility function must depend only on bundles of goods (T2 of Chapter 6).[14] But that would involve either a value judgment (people ought to so behave) which would be irrelevant in our positive context even if it were ethically appealing, or an empirical judgment (people in fact do so behave) that is obviously empirically false. Hence, the belief that contributions with effects imperceptible to the contributor must be irrational depends on a tacit assumption about individual preferences (in the sense of Chapter 6) that is almost necessarily only a tacit assumption because it cannot be defended as empirically reasonable.[15]

In terms of FS, on the other hand, no difficulty arises here, provided we are careful about specifying the point of view that "perceptible" refers to. For S-resources, the referent is Smith himself; but for G-resources, the referent is society. From a social point of view, the effect of Smith's $10 donation to the Red Cross is not less perceptible than, say, a nice lunch Smith might have spent the money on. G-judgments do not turn on Smith's merely personal perceptions.

As a producer or consumer of private goods (as just stressed), Smith's individual choices will ordinarily have no discernable effect on society at large. If Smith is an ordinary citizen, the same will also be true for his choices regarding public goods (broadly construed as including whom he supports for public office and what policies he favors.[16] But the value ratio, G'/S', will be very different for the two cases. It costs me very little in terms of private goods forgone to vote, but it can cost a great deal to compromise my purchases of private goods (pay more than I need to pay; buy what I think is socially desirable rather than what I want) in order to contribute to my perception of group-interest.

If I am a producer facing reasonably competitive markets (even the experience of Ford in trying to promote safety features in automobiles in the mid-1950s is instructive here), then I will scarcely be in a position to do anything very different than produce what the market seems to want. Even if my choices affect only me and my customers, I will not have any customers to benefit unless I offer them things they want at a price they are willing to pay. If there are external effects (environmental side-effects), the dilemma is even worse. [17]

However, if I am in a senior position in my government, my decisions on public matters often affect society in a large way. This being so, there will be no necessary inconsistency between my behaving as a narrow profit-maximizer (to a good approximation) as a private businessman; as a rather casual decision maker, as a voter; and as a very serious decision maker, working very hard and feeling great personal responsibility for the social effects of my decisions as a high public official. For the relation between W on one side and the value ratio G'/S', on the other, will be very different in these very different situations.

I will provide some related detail in Chapter 9. [18] I only wish to say enough here to indicate why Buchanan's and Tullock's "paradox of bifurcated man" seems, from the FS view, to reflect a mistaken assumption that an internally consistent model could not account for a disposition for the same individual to behave in a very public-spirited way in some circumstances and as a profit-maximizing economic man in other contexts. In terms of FS, the supposition that such behavior must be "schizophrenic" is no more realistic than a supposition that different physical laws must govern the way a feather falls in a vacuum versus the way a feather falls in the open air. In terms of a properly specified model, the very different behaviors in different contexts is just what theory leads us to expect.

On the other hand, in terms of FS, many attacks on the application of rational choice models to social choice are equally off the mark. I will use the example of James Q. Wilson's analysis in his *Political Organization,* [19] arguing that Wilson is tactically right (the usual notion of a rational model fails in just the manner he describes) but strategically wrong (it does not follow that a rational model *must* fail). In fact, we will see that precisely the sorts of incentives that Wilson supposes cannot be handled with an "economic" analysis are very much the sort of thing which an FS analysis would lead us to expect to be significant.

Wilson follows Olson in saying that if an outcome is not perceptibly affected – as far as the actor can see, his contribution has made no difference – then the actor will have spent resources irrationally in an act that yields him no perceptible utility. Wilson does allow (as Olson does) that, if we make room for what I described in Chapter 2 as participation altruism, then we can account for acts that have imperceptible external effects. But he argues (as does Olson) that allowing for such psychic motivation in a rational choice model yields a model that is pliable enough to explain anything and hence explains nothing. In terms of the FS argument, this amounts to relaxing T2 of Chapter 6, while continuing to hold onto other tacit commitments; and indeed that leads to just the sort of difficulties that cause Olson and Wilson to reject the use of psychic income.

Hence, accepting Olson's argument about what can be handled in terms of rational choice, Wilson fairly says (on that basis) that Olson's argument gains some important insight into the circumstances under which voluntary organizations are likely to arise and thrive but not enough, it being empirically obvious, and a very important aspect of social and political behavior, that there are circumstances in which people make voluntary contributions that are irrational in terms of that argument. In particular, Olson provides a powerful insight into why concentrated interests are so often more effective politically than diffused interests. But (Wilson argues) Olson's theory does not get too far beyond this insight without running into serious empirical problems.

However, in terms of FS, just the sort of inferences that Wilson argues are empirically indisputable, but beyond the reach of a rational choice model, are easily reached. For example, an immediate corollary of the FS view is that individuals will participate in voluntary organizations under circumstances when self-interest cannot plausibly account for their behavior. Also, individuals are motivated to spend some fraction (governed by the FS equilibrium condition) of their resource on (their perception of) the public good, but because they cannot be expected to have more than a crude sense of the marginal utility of alternative ways of "spending" on the public good (e.g., who can tell if $5 donated to the Cystic Fibrosis Foundation is better than $5 donated to the March of Dimes?), they will have to choose their allocations under a great deal of uncertainty. As has been mentioned before, they will be "satisficers," not optimizers. One consequence of this behavior is that small private incentives will often appear to have surprisingly large effects: nontrivial resources of time and money are devoted to a cause after recruitment appears to have been due to not wanting to say "no" to a friend, or to enjoying the organization's cocktail party, or to being offered a minor office. The discussion in Chapter 5 and Appendix E shows the formal properties of such joint incentives. [20]

The empirical importance of such incentives is the sort of thing that leads Wilson to doubt that social behavior can be studied effectively in terms of rational choice. Yet, the importance of such second-order incentives follows easily from the FS model, requiring only that we follow Downs and Simon in taking account of uncertainty and of the cost of information to reduce uncertainty. The leverage of seemingly minor private incentives is a puzzle only if we suppose (and, of course, FS does not) that these minor incentives alone call forth, rather than only channel, the voluntary contribution.

Consider next the management of public interest organizations, which is another topic that leads Wilson to argue that the behavior we observe cannot be accounted for in terms of rational choice. Some of the comments earlier in this chapter bear on this, but much can be added.

For example, we can see that effective recruitment will be especially important for organizations, which must compete for individual G-resources in a manner that is more nearly analogous than commonly realized to the competition for S-resources by producers of consumer goods. One reason this point tends to be blurred is the radical difference in the nature of G- as opposed to S- appeals, as has already been mentioned in the context of voting (Chapter 7).

We can then notice various factors that would make it easier to keep members, or enlarge their contribution, than to recruit new members: in particular, it will ordinarily be inefficient and even confusing for an individual to try to gather information on the merits of various outlets for G-spending. (The argument is exactly analogous to the role of information in deciding how to vote.) However, once a commitment has been made, it becomes easy to absorb information *consistent* with that commitment: the information fits naturally into a system of beliefs; free information is directed to the engaged individual as a sympathetic recipient; because he (or she) is involved, curiosity about the issue is aroused. On net, therefore, it will ordinarily be "cheaper" (thinking now of the discretionary resources of the managers of an organization) to keep a supporter than to attract a new supporter.

An immediate corollary is that managers will devote more resources per person to maintenance of their existing constituency than to recruitment of new constituents, but with the following important proviso: the largest payoff to the organization will come when it can identify individuals lying between the general mass of prospects (those at least latently sympathetic, but uncommitted) and those already in the constituency. The "economics" of the situation are those we could also expect to find in many private businesses: insurance, stock brokerage, real estate, and so forth. But the nature of the appeals will be reversed: for the voluntary organization whose nominal purpose is to serve some public interest, the prospect must be "sold" by appealing to his sentiments about the public interest (in terms of the model, by appealing to his G-preferences) with private incentives treated as a bonus; for the business venture, the opposite will hold.

Another corollary is that organizers will be opportunists in at least the sense that they will be alert to exploit incidental matters that cheaply (from the point of view of the organization's resources) turn latent sympathizers into prospects. These range from dramatic news developments to the acquisition of a television celebrity as a supporter. On the latter, one might suppose that it is inconsistent with a rational model to infer that it helps to have Joe Namath endorse a charity or a political candidate. However, as is also true in commercial marketing, supposing the endorsement of a celebrity helps implies no irrationality: in part because it is perfectly rational for the audience to be more willing to listen to a message from someone they are interested in than to listen to the identical message from a nonentity; and perhaps also more reasonable to believe the celebrity than an anonymous actor who will say anything he is paid to say.

FS further implies that public interest organizations will seek to maintain themselves beyond anything that can be accounted for in terms of the private interests of its managers. This follows from the previous points. In particular, if it is easier to keep an organization going than to get an organization started, then an organization is an asset that it would be irrational to throw away merely because the cause it was originally intended to serve has been satisfied – or because that cause is no longer sufficiently appealing to keep membership from falling off. Even if the managers are purely motivated by a desire to serve the public interest (solely by G-preferences), they will find that the most effective way to use their G-resources (and of course G-Smith, like economic man and all other utility-maximizers, always seeks the most effective way to use resources) will be to reorient an existing organization that they control to some other good cause. The less perceptible (less jarring) the transition, the easier it will be to persuade the constituency that the new purpose is really the same one that they have already made a commitment to, but better, more up to date, and so forth.

Finally, let me summarize even more briefly a few further points on FS inferences in the context of organizations. First, in contrast to Olson's theory, we do not need different theories, one dealing with organizations concerned with their members economic interests and another dealing with philanthropic organizations. Second, we need not be puzzled when we notice an organization concerned with its members economic interests sometimes engaging in "public interest" activities that conflict with strict economic interests, for example, the American Dental Association's long-standing promotion of fluoridation of water, although obviously dental decay can only help the economic interest of dentists. Third, revolutionaries, resistance movements in occupied countries, and so on need not either be treated as beyond analysis in terms of rational choice, or – much less plausibly, I think – forced into a rational choice mold by supposing that such people choose to engage in such dangerous and arduous modes of life because they have calculated that their self-interested expectations are improved thereby. In terms of FS, the key to their behavior is that G' for such activities, which are aimed at and sometimes succeed in producing radical social change, is very high compared to the perceptions of G' for activities aimed at maintaining or mildly ameliorating the existing state of society. Hence G'/S' is high relative to more ordinary activities, and an extraordinary commitment to group interest is sustained for equilibrium behavior ($W = G'/S'$).

CHAPTER 9

Sketch of further applications

In the past three chapters I have tried to illustrate the application of FS to some issues within economic theory, to the perennially debated question of the rationality of voting, and to a range of topics treated in the well-known books by Olson and Downs. However, if the Darwinian basis of the model is sound, then the theory must have a very much wider range of application. It is not a theory about voting, or about voluntary organizations, or about politics in Western democracies, but about the roots of human social motivation. To the extent that it is empirically tenable, it ought to have implications for any situation in which human beings are faced with the problem of allocating resources between the ordinarily competing ways of best serving social versus private values. The material that makes up this concluding chapter sketches some possibilities. Each of these topics would require a chapter of its own if treated even at the modest level of detail of the material in the preceding three chapters. I have only tried to say enough to stimulate the interest (or the antagonism, for that is also helpful) of a reader with a particular knowledge of a topic. For the more general reader I have tried to provide a rapid tour of the range of possible applications.

Social action

What happens in the event of a sudden emergency that abruptly changes Smith's perception of the utility of actions in group-interest? Suppose, for example, that Smith suddenly finds his country at war. In this context, we would expect the initial reaction to favor group-interest strongly, reflecting an abrupt increase in G', leaving the equilibrium condition strongly positive $(G'/S' \gg W)$. Eventually a new equilibrium will be established, but with a larger allocation of income to G-Smith than in peacetime. (The "rush to the colors" phase will pass.) At the end of the war, the situation will have become either better (the war is clearly being won) or worse (the situation looks hopeless). Especially in the former case,[1] G' declines and the equilibrium condition becomes negative given the crisis allocation between S- and G-spending. People become more selfish.

It is easy to cite examples of such behavior. In an emergency (say, an earthquake) an extraordinary display of social cohesion is often observed. Yet there seems to be a social breakpoint beyond which an attitude of "every man for himself" becomes dominant. In FS terms, up to some point, G' is much higher than prior to the emergency, and (for individuals who have been lucky enough to have escaped personal disaster), S' may remain close to pre-emergency levels. The equilibrium condition is strongly positive. However, as the intensity of the disaster increases, more and more people fall in the class of those for whom S' as well as G' has suddenly increased. Some such people, in fact, become more selfish than in ordinary times (i.e., the equilibrium condition can turn negative even though G' has increased, since the ratio, G'/S' may have decreased, as will be increasingly common as the fraction of the population that has suffered personal devastation increases).

However, utility judgments (empirically, and on the theoretical grounds suggested in Appendix B) reflect relative well-being, not simply absolute well-being. Hence, the effect of the disaster on individual judgments of the value ratio may depend substantially on perceptions of how others are being affected. If so, we should expect the social balance to be more complex when many people are nearly ruined but others are almost untouched, than when everyone has suffered similar losses. Those hard hit will, other things equal, tend to be less socially oriented in the former than the latter case; those relatively unhurt, more socially oriented in the former than the latter. The net effect on social resilience would vary with details of the situation and its side conditions. Further, in the former situations, *class* issues may arise, akin to those discussed in the context of ruling elites (later in this chapter).

A social collapse can result if the situation begins to appear hopeless. For a decline in G' reduces the proclivity to group-interested behavior, which makes the situation look still more hopeless, leading to still further declines in typical values of G'. Hence the crucial role that the imposition of marshall law may play in such situations, arresting the decline of G' and abruptly lowering the perceived value of S'. (The latter is commonly understood: the temptation to antisocial behavior, say, looting, obviously declines if the probability you will be shot on the spot abruptly increases. But FS draws attention to the possibility that an increase – or at least a halt in the decline of G' – as well as the more obvious decrease in S', may be as important.) Along the rough lines sketched, it should be possible to develop a "mathematics of social crisis," with formal properties that would, I think, look very plausible in terms of what is known of the sociology of disasters.

A humbler illustration would be the social dynamics of littering. Other things equal, it should be easier to keep a beach or park clear of litter if the population is prosperous. (Carrying trash to a barrel requires a bit of G-resources; the larger your resources overall, the more likely, other things equal, you are to make the effort.)

More important here, the park or beach with a poorer constituency will also tend to be more crowded so that, even if the "propensity to litter" were equal, there would be more littering per unit area. The more litter on the ground, the less value there will seem in bothering to carry yours to the trash can (G' for this use of resources declines). The less litter per acre, the less cost to the public authorities (or a volunteer group) to keep litter from accumulating to the point where the social value of not littering starts to deteriorate visibly. Further, the better off the community, the more tax money it will have, and/or the easier it will be to organize a volunteer cleanup.

Thus, the same mathematical structure that deals with disaster will also deal with the modest matter of littering, although again I have given only a rough sketch of how such a model would be formulated.[2]

Powerful individuals

If an individual accedes to a position of power, G' will increase because such resources as he expends in group-interest will have greater effect. Hence the equilibrium allocation will shift toward greater G-spending. We expect to see an increase in concern for the "public interest." Further, it will *not* ordinarily be true – as is commonly true for an ordinary citizen considering how much to contribute – that $G'' \approx 0$. In particular the allocation of resources between promoting the best public policy (G-resources) and maximizing the probability of staying in power (S-resources, substantially) will involve richer tradeoffs than those ordinarily faced by a private citizen. The individual will not only be compromising with other actors who share power, in the usual sense of political compromise, but will be compromising within himself. His partisans will note particularly the extent to which he makes choices that involve some cost to his private interests and will admire his public-spiritedness. On the same issues, and even if they do not disagree in a policy sense with him on this issue, his opponents will be alert to any opportunity to suppose that the decision has been tailored to the power holder's political advantage at some cost to public interest, confirming their view of him as a self-serving opportunist. The discrepancy in perceptions on this point will be greatly accentuated by the fact that Smith and his supporters will perceive actions that prolong Smith's tenure in office as a contribution to group-interest as well as self-interest, whereas his opponents will see matters very differently.

Note also that, for a person in a leadership position, the nearly complete indifference of G-Smith to Smith's personal well-being will no longer hold. For Smith is now someone whose health, morale, and relief from merely private concerns (such as money) are a matter of public value far beyond that of an ordinary citizen. Further, these matters can ordinarily be most generously attended to at trivial social cost compared with the social cost of the leader's failing to work very hard on matters of public policy. The leader himself will be too busy with public matters to bother with such things, but the model suggests that he will not mind – and may even take a moment to arrange – that a subordinate sees that such things are attended to.

In short, in terms of FS motivation, we expect to see more genuine concern in political leaders for the public interest than will ordinarily be found in a private citizen; at the same time, we would not be surprised to find the advantages of office used for private enrichment. But the former does not reflect a general superiority of character of politicians to the citizenry at large; nor does the latter reflect a comparable inferiority. Rather, both reflect the responses expected under FS when the social power of an individual increases greatly beyond the ordinary.

The tailoring of decision to election prospects will be particularly striking because, as has been noted already, S-Smith and G-Smith both will have a strong interest here. We need not doubt that Smith feels that group-interest as well as self-interest will be served if he, rather than his opponents, holds office. Finally, we see that there is no inherent inconsistency (in terms of FS motivation) between deep public concern and private indulgence, as long as the private indulgences do not require personal resources needed for more substantial matters. (Private wealth would reduce this temptation, as would a social context in which effectiveness in public matters depends on an impeccable reputation with respect to private enrichment; the effectiveness of both would depend on the probability that privately greedy behavior would be exposed.)

To take a concrete case, an FS view of Richard Nixon will not make us admire him more – or less – than before. But FS would warn us not to suppose that, if we judge his behavior despicable on matters that *he* regarded as socially unimportant, we can presume that his handling of matters he perceived as important lacked any reasonable measure of responsibility and political courage. We should find similar propensities in all who achieve political power – or even all who achieve a special measure of social power in any way, or indeed even those who merely delude themselves into believing they enjoy a position of special social power. But the difference between "all politicians are similar" and "all politicians are the same" is extremely important.

Social choice experiments

The ultimate test of a theory is whether it helps us to understand how the world works. But the place where it is easiest to test a theory is in the narrow domain of artificial situations – laboratory situations – in which it is possible to isolate the phenomena we want to examine (or, at least, possible to analyze closely those phenomena we can contrive to isolate). At the other extreme are phenomena that are very extended in time and other dimensions, rendering it difficult to make anything more than plausibility arguments for a particular account.

In this section, I give an example of how the FS analysis can be applied to the closest thing we have in the study of social choice to the natural scientist's laboratory experiments. A considerable literature on such social choice experiments has appeared in recent years. On issues where the two views diverge, the results almost routinely falsify the economic man model of motivation, mainly because the free-rider problem repeatedly turns out to be less severe than the conventional analysis would lead us to expect.[3] The example considered here, however, deals with a subtler effect, which illustrates how differently things are apt to be "seen" (in Kuhn's sense) under the FS view compared to the way they are seen from within the analytical framework provided by economic man.

The experiments I will discuss were part of an extensive series organized by Morris Fiorina and Charles Plott of California Institute of Technology.[4] Here, groups of five strangers (different in each trial, with careful precautions taken to rule out the possibility of collusion) were asked to choose a single point from a large grid of points. Unknown to the players, the payoffs were arranged so that, given a choice between any two points, if every player always voted for the point that gave him the higher payoff, the status quo would always move toward a unique dominant point – point D in Figures 9.1 and 9.2).[5] The process of moving the status quo from one point to another would continue until a majority voted to end the game.

In sum, the experiment was arranged so that, if the players behaved egoistically, the status quo would always move closer to D. Further, since one player's best payoff came just at D (player 1 in Figures 9.1 and 9.2), that player had an incentive to propose D as the outcome, and point D would always command a majority against any other point.

A detail of the situation that is important from the FS view is that, except for the player at D, payoffs declined only slowly for some distance from a player's assigned best point. Then they began to decline much more steeply. For example, player 3 lost $0.14 per unit distance from his best point up to eight units, but the ninth unit cost him almost $3. I will call this the player's "payoff break." The distance at which the payoff break occurred varied from player to player. As a result, although the location of

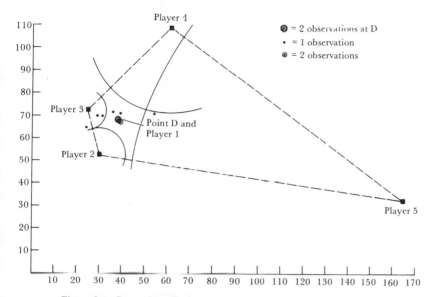

Figure 9.1. Best points (D, 2, 3, 4, 5) for the five players, payoff breaks, and outcomes for the ten Fiorina and Plott experiments with high payoffs and a dominant outcome, but no communication.

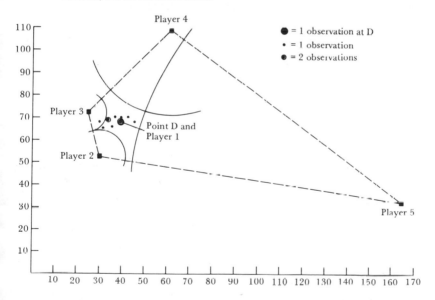

Figure 9.2. Best points, payoff breaks, and outcomes for the ten Fiorina and Plott experiments with high payoffs and a dominant point, but *with* communication. The location of the best points and payoff breaks are the same as in Figure 9.1.

D inside the quadrilateral formed by the best points of the other four players was well away from the middle of the figure, if we draw in the location of the payoff breaks we find that D is located roughly in the middle of the zone where payoffs become very sensitive to the outcome choice. These payoff breaks are shown by the curved lines in Figures 9.1 and 9.2.

The experiment described was run twenty times. In the first ten trials, no overt communication was permitted other than proposing and voting.[6] (Each player knew only his own payoff schedule.) In the second series, players were allowed to say whatever they wanted (reveal their best points, describe the shape of their payoff schedules), but with the restriction that only qualitative – never quantitative – information about payoffs could be discussed.[7] In both sets of experiments, the basic instruction to the players was: "You should decide what decision you want the committee to make and do whatever you wish within the confines of the rules to get things to go your way."[8]

The article, which reported the results of the twenty trials, summarized the results graphically with Figure 9.3. The authors saw no significant difference between the ten trials with communication and the ten trials with no communication, so they pooled the results. The payoff breaks were not shown in their figure, and indeed the existence of the payoff breaks is never mentioned, although a reader who studied the payoff equations in the appendix to the article could discover that they existed.

As with the DR thought experiment of Chapter 6, there are two different but related points to the FS analysis of these results. One concerns the helpfulness of FS in understanding things about the empirical situation beyond what was obtained from a conventional analysis; the other concerns the tendency of analysts working within the conventional framework to fail to "see" aspects of the situation that are likely to be striking not only from an FS viewpoint but even from the viewpoint of common sense unaided by theory.

Here, the authors interpreted the results as showing strong support for an egoistic model. They describe the results from the two series as essentially the same (as is implicit in the way the data are displayed), pointing out that there is no significant difference between either the mean or the variance of the two series. Further, the mean for each series was very close to the dominant point, D. If you look at the whole space of possible outcomes, or even at the space of possible outcomes that are not worse for everyone than some other points (in the figures, the space within the dotted lines), it is obvious that the outcomes are clustered in the vicinity of the dominant point. Hence the authors announce themselves favorably impressed with the power of an egoistic model to account for the experimental results.

Yet this interpretation leaves some startling anomalies. Why should

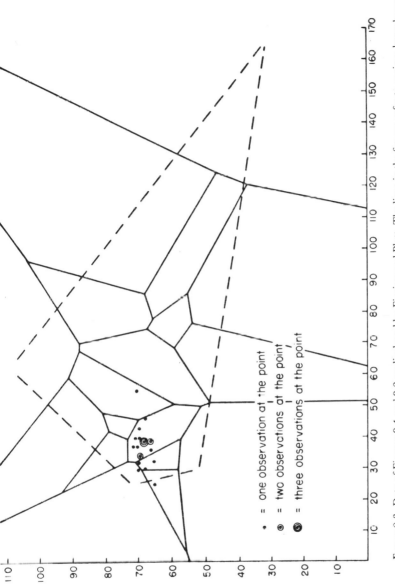

Figure 9.3 Data of Figures 9.1 and 9.2 as displayed by Fiorina and Plott. The lines in the figures refer to various hypotheses considered by the authors in analyzing the data. Reproduced by permission from *APSR* (June 1978).

egoistic players fail to arrive *at* the dominant point? In particular, why should the players fail to do so when, as in these experiments, D is located in a region where the payoff to each player was very sensitive to just how far the outcome was from the player's preferred point, so that egoistic players would be sharply motivated always to vote for the point closer to their respective preferred points. (The consequence, as mentioned earlier, would be that the outcome at each stage in the game would always be moving closer to D; once D was reached, it could be beaten by no other point.) But as can be seen in the figures, the process failed to hit this easy target with eight of the ten sets of players when there was no communication; and it missed nine times out of ten when there was (qualitative) communication.

Furthermore, in the trials with communication (where some information on the payoff breaks could be exchanged) we would expect an outcome chosen solely for social reasons to lie within the payoff breaks.[9] The plausible range of outcomes, therefore, was not the entire field of possibilities, or even the pareto-optimal field given by the dashed boundary in the figures, but the much smaller zone indicated by the payoff breaks in Figures 9.1 and 9.2

The clustering of outcomes does not look tight, therefore, whether we consider the region within which egoistic motivation was strong for all players or consider the (same) region, within which we could expect the outcomes to fall even if egoism were excluded completely.

Finally, when we read the description of the experiments, we find that no sophisticated argument about coalitions and daredevil bargaining can explain what happened. The authors tell us there was little effort at coalition formation, and the discussion was generally in terms of picking a fair or reasonable outcome. In fact, we are told, on several occasions the tentative outcome actually was the dominant point, and the group then voted to move away from it!

In view of all this, only workers within the conventional rational choice community would interpret these results as showing clear *support* for an egoistic model of choice. From a common-sense point of view, I should think it is obvious that something other than pure self-interest must be involved.

Of course, that is a congenial insight from the FS point of view. We expect the results of social choice to reflect self-interest but not only self-interest. Further, from the fundamental equilibrium condition of the model, we expect the payoff breaks to have special significance, for, from the point of view of any player, there would be an abrupt shift in the value ratio (G'/S') on crossing a payoff break. In fact, the payoff breaks provided the only salient clue to the area within which a socially reasonable outcome could be assumed to lie. Further, from the superior good result (illustrated by Figure 4.2), we expect that, if what we may term the "culture" of this simulation of social choice evoked social motivation at all, the most generous among the players in each group would ordinarily be the one who was likely to deem himself holding the favored position: This would be the player at D and indeed the authors report that it was the player at D who would most often vote contrary to his self-interest. Finally, given the calibration of this game provided by the observations of the no-communication series (Figure 9.1), FS implies something about what to expect in the communication series.

First, any outcome beyond the payoff breaks (where G'/S', as judged by any player, would fall sharply) is anomalous, provided of course that the players were aware of the breaks. For the no-communications series (Figure 9.1), groups missed the zone inside the payoff breaks four times in the ten trials. FS implies that to the extent the communication permitted in the later series allowed players in these groups to learn of the existence and precise location of the breaks, outlier outcomes should be less in the communication series. In fact, in the communications series (Figure 9.2) players did exchange information on their payoff breaks, and there is but one outlier among the ten trials in that series. There is no reason to expect this shift under the conventional analysis because an egoistic player knows all he needs to know: namely, what is best for himself, whether or not there is any communication.

Second, absent communication, a player, even if not motivated solely by self-interest, would have no clear way to judge outcomes in terms of group-interest. Indirect clues were possible, for example, it is possible that one player looked just miserable at the way things were going, or in chatting before the experiment began one player might have mentioned how much he needed the money he hoped to earn. Whatever the possibilities for such communications of need or pain in the nominally no-communication series, though, they would be much enhanced for the ten new groups who would be involved in the series with communication during the choice process. Hence, one would expect that not only would outlier outcomes be reduced, but outcomes inside the payoff breaks would be spread wider, reflecting firmer (although still only subjective) judgments made, mainly by the player at D, about the direction in which a desire to be generous might best be exercised. If you compare Figures 9.1 and 9.2, you will see that this also occurred. The outcomes *inside* the breaks in Figure 9.2 are decidedly more spread out than those in Figure 9.1.

Obviously, caution is required in treating the significance of these after-the-fact inferences applied to a small set of data. But, if you compare the conventional analysis illustrated by Figure 9.3 with the FS analysis illustrated by Figures 9.1 and 9.2, I think a reasonable claim can be made that one approach proves to have considerably more analytical power than the other. The FS analysis leads easily to noticing effects that the conventional analysis apparently misses easily. Conventional analysis attributed no special significance to the payoff breaks (presumably because in terms of egoistic choice they have no special significance), just as in the DR context of Chapter 6 the question of what a voter could buy if he were willing to spend a penny had no special significance in terms of egoistic choice.

In terms of FS we are led to look closely at just these matters; and in each case asking questions that are obvious in terms of FS leads to striking results. The FS viewpoint makes us expect to see some difference between the results of the two series and makes us expect that this difference will be linked to the payoff breaks. We are therefore led to plot the results as shown in Figures 9.1 and 9.2, rather than as shown in Figure 9.3 from the conventional analysis. Having done so, we can see that, even though the mean and variance of outcomes was about the same for the two series, two shifts had actually occurred, both as would be expected under FS. However, because neither shift involves a shift in the expected mean and the effect on the variance would be in opposite directions, the effects easily uncovered under an FS analysis were missed by the conventional analysis.

FS correspondence within the conventional model

What happens in a context where, to a reasonable approximation, we need consider only private goods? If we are only concerned with standard topics – existence of competitive equilibria in a private-goods-only economy, exposition of income and substitution effects, and so on – then the "correspondence" relation mentioned in Chapter 1 holds. The FS analysis can then be replaced by a standard analysis. Essentially, if we are dealing with a situation in which Smith's U-map (as developed in Appendix C) will not change during the analysis, then Smith can be treated as if his preference structure was such that it could be described by a fairly conventional indifference map, and analysis of an economy under these conditions could not diverge very far from the conventional analysis which allowed for altruism in the way discussed in Chapter 1.

This does not mean that FS has no observable implications in a private-goods-only context. We can see *within* the theoretical framework (i.e., without invoking some special notion, such as "merit goods") why Smith may prefer to give bread to the poor (adding to his own total demand for bread) rather than give money (loosening the income constraint on the benefited poor). For Smith reveals that he sees more G-utility from the poor eating better than from the poor having more general spending power to be possibly expended on drink. This is hardly very surprising as an expression of Smith's perception of group-interest. And it is fundamental to the FS model that it is Smith's own G-function, not the preferences of his poorer neighbors, that he is seeking to maximize.

Similarly, we can see why Smith as a businessman seeks to maximize profits and yet may give away some of those profits he has sought to maximize. To sell something at less than the market price is a "virtual" expenditure of G-resources. Situations may arise in which Smith the businessman sees this as a sensible (efficient or, more accurately, satisficing) way to use this bit of G-resources. Thus, we are not surprised to see him occasionally extend credit, for example, to an individual in desperate straits who is unlikely ever to be able to pay. Ordinarily, though, Smith's customers are not, by coincidence, the people he sees as the most favorable outlet for funds spent in group-interest. So ordinarily it is rational to maximize profits and then use the portion of the profits that is allocated to G-Smith in another way. Indeed, Wicksteed saw that a long time ago. [10]

If we now allow for public goods, we find that FS ameliorates the basic free-rider inferences of the conventional analysis. Under strictly self-interested motivation, as Coleman remarks in the quotation on page 1, human societies as we know them could hardly exist. Voluntary social action would be found only in the special situations that strictly meet the conditions described by Olson (and summarized in Chapter 8). Essentially anonymous social activity (such as most voting, many charitable donations, and help to total strangers) would not occur. Everyone would cheat whenever it was safe to do so; hence everyone would also have to be continually concerned with being cheated. With various qualifications, some would argue that all this is true in existing societies. Yet the qualifications are important, and their influence on the way we behave and the way we anticipate others will behave are of enormous importance.

One can avoid the severe implications of the standard analysis by interpreting self-interest as meaning only what the individual prefers to do. This has already been discussed in Chapter 1, and in Chapter 6 we saw (by way of the DR thought experiment) the technical difficulties that arise when an attempt is made to incorporate this kind of notion into the formal structure of a theory of choice. In the light of those results, we can understand why the loose sense of self-interest has been used only in an ad hoc way – invoked when convenient, neglected when not so – essentially serving as an extratheoretical source of motivation invoked to "save appearances" when the standard analysis runs into difficulty. In a private-goods-only context, this takes place subtly and is likely to seem harmless even if noticed. Once public goods enter the analysis, this is no longer so. There is neither opportunity for such waffling under FS (under FS self-interest means strictly self-interested, and group-interest means strictly group-interested) nor a need for it (untenable inferences of the conventional free-rider analysis do not arise).

However, absent coerced spending (government spending financed by taxes), there would be a suboptimal supply of public goods, as under the conventional analysis, although less severely so. Absent government programs, G' for voluntary spending would be higher than with such programs (see the more detailed discussion in the section to follow); hence, allocations within individuals to G-spending will be larger. But now even activities that we could expect to be financed essentially from S-resources under government programs (fire and police services, for example) must now be financed mainly by G-resources, S-spending for such public goods being limited to what is elicited by "other people are watching you" motivation. At equilibrium, individuals will be spending more voluntarily. But the total supply of public goods must be less than at an efficient level with government programs.

More formally, suppose (recalling the discussion of Chapter 6) that the mixed S-Lindahl, G-Nash equilibrium is pareto-optimal and that the society is at this optimal (extended Lindahl–Samuelson) situation. However, abandoning coerced spending, the government now announces that all taxes henceforth will be voluntary. Since taxes now become G-spending (rather than a mix of G- and S-spending[11]), W abruptly increases for each citizen who voluntarily pays his full tax. Imagine that initially, all did so. Each would then find his equilibrium condition is negative ($G'/S' < W$). Accordingly, tax receipts fall, hence government spending falls, driving up G' for voluntary contributions. Each individual allocates more to G-spending than under the coerced arrangement. At the new equilibrium, though, the total amount of G-spending will be less than (in a large society, we would expect, much less than) the total of voluntary G-spending plus coerced G-and S-spending of the earlier arrangement. For most individuals in the society (but not necessarily for all) the shift from coerced-plus-voluntary spending to pure voluntary spending will involve a loss of S-utility as well as a loss of G-utility. (Each S-individual would prefer to be a free-rider; but he is better off – ordinarily – at the coerced outcome than in a situation in which all S-individuals free-ride.)

Evolution of social spending

Starting from the particularly simple context in which there are only private goods and only private (individual-to-individual) charity, consider how FS would account for the evolution of public voluntary charities and tax-supported charities.

If we suppose Smith to be reasonably well off, we expect to see him wish to spend some fraction of his resources (increasing with wealth) for social purposes. But if Smith is a member of a large society, then the business of discovering and seeking to allocate his G-resources among those most deserving and in need would be a drain on his G-resources. Note well that deservingness as well as need will be important to G-Smith; as already stressed, he acts to optimize his use of G-resources in his perception of group-interest, not in the interest of particular beneficiaries, except insofar as helping them happens to coincide with G-Smith's preferences.

So here – in our imagined context where there is no organized philanthropy – we have a situation in which there are obvious welfare gains through introduction of some division of labor. There is a function for a service that will search out efficient ways to use G-resources – not Smith's alone, of course, but for all those who have G-preferences sufficiently similar that it serves their G-preferences well to allow the service to distribute the resources, relieving individual contributors of the problem of gathering and evaluating information on need and merit.

Indeed, if no such service exists, it will be an excellent use of G-Smith's resources to organize one, so excellent that (G' being high) Smith may find himself "spending much more time on this than I really intended." Not only is the service useful to G-citizens (G-Smith and others), but it raises more money than would be provided by individual action because it effectively improves the benefit–cost ratio and hence increases G-wtp for contributions to group-interest for those who believe that the "tastes" in group-interest of the service are congruent with their own.

This model can be elaborated in a straightforward way, accounting for the rise of different public charities (to some extent competing, to some extent complimentary); the amalgamation of charities (e.g., Community Chest) to increase the efficiency of fund raising; incorporation of S-Smith's resources, to some extent, into such voluntary activity (most obviously by exploiting the possibility that certain kinds of visible charitable activity may be "good for business").

The same line of argument would also account for the eventual rise of government (tax-supported) charitable programs. It is more efficient to raise money if the money must be paid under penalty of law than if donors must be approached and individually persuaded of the value of the activity. Equally important, money can be obtained from individuals who otherwise would contribute very little, or not at all, either because the activity does not look attractive in terms of *their* G-function or because they are unusually selfish people who simply allocate less to group-interest than do most other people with comparable incomes.

Even if we were to limit the discussion to G-resources, there would be a temptation for like-minded individuals to form a coalition if there is a prospect of thereby gaining effective control (through the power of government) over others' resources. Note that this holds even though by definition here the purpose is entirely divorced from self-interest (is concerned solely with a particular view of social interests). However, on many issues, a government program could draw on S- as well as G-resources, even where the government program is concerned with activities that otherwise would be provided only through charities.

Social stability (ordinarily) serves S-Smith's interest; at least some social programs will have (or may be believed to have) a favorable influence on social stability or perhaps some other effect favorable in a personal way to Smith. S-Smith would not contribute voluntarily, preferring to be a free-rider. But a government program may be in his interest, on the usual public goods argument. Undoubtedly, some programs that as voluntary action could be financed only by G-resources would be paid for entirely out of S-resources as a government program. [12]

Thus you can see that there are a number of reasons to expect that G-preferences would tend to be favorable to the growth of government social programs. This takes on special importance when you recall that in political contexts (voting, volunteer organizations, and so on), it is G-preferences mainly that we expect to see elicited.

Once social programs are enacted, given diminishing marginal returns, G' (charitable activities) declines as government programs grow. Further, to the extent that G-spending is coerced (taxes are charged to G-Smith, according to the process in Chapter 5), there is less discretionary G-spending to be done. Hence, other things equal, private charitable giving should fall.

However, there are partially offsetting effects so that we would not expect private G-spending to decline on a dollar-for-dollar basis as government programs take over (and ordinarily extend) what were previously voluntary programs. The very fact of government activity creates new opportunities for G-spending – for example, partially shifting the activity of the charitable organization from doing directly what it deems socially valuable work to influencing the way government-coerced spending is used. Further, as with private goods in the market context, wants are expandable. Needs satisfied (or satisfied to a level that earlier might have seemed meeting all reasonable requirements) will lead to new wants. If income is growing, the new needs effect may be important. Further, private charities will now find niches, where a significant constituency of G-people sees the government efforts as inadequate; that is, where G' for this particular endeavor is higher than G' from marginal government spending. To elicit any resources from Smith, G' for this "neglected" activity must be high (high enough to create an incentive for funds to be reallocated from

S- to G-Smith, even though the equilibrium conditions may be negative ($G'/S' < W$) at the level of G-spending enforced on Smith by the tax program). Undoubtedly some and possibly many such specialized niches could be found; to the extent that they are, donations will be forthcoming even in a context in which government charity, in dollar volume, far exceeds the total private charity that would exist in the absence of government programs.

Empirically, it appears that another factor intervenes powerfully that is compatible with FS but not predictable. Citizens may perceive an element of group-interest in the very existence of voluntary charity. If indeed G-Smith perceives that it is good for the morale and sense of justice in the society that voluntary charity exists, then G' from a dollar spent by a private charity will be higher than G' from a dollar spent by the government for exactly the same purpose. The lower the resources available to private charity the greater this discrepancy will become. If this motivation exists, as appears to be the case, a measure of private charity would continue to exist even if there were no specialized niches available.

But the equilibrium condition works in both directions. At some level, government spending would be so high that many people would begin to be out of equilibrium in ways beyond their control (because they cannot as individuals control their spending on government programs). This presumably could stimulate some of the nonrational behavior discussed (in the context of voting) on page 95, and (in a more general context) in Chapter 5. Further, if this malaise should become general enough (and it would be combined with other significantly social – not merely self-interested – concerns, of the kind familiar from recent political debates in this country) then a social basis for opposing (more, or as much) government spending would arise, and G-preferences for increasing numbers of citizens with respect to government spending would come into accord with S-preferences. Because these effects turn on how individuals perceive the situation, they would presumably vary a good deal with the traditions of various societies, the extent to which government controls access to information, and so on. Here I only wish to make the point that the argument (like the first argument of this chapter on reactions to crisis) is one that must allow for the specifics of the situation. The basic FS inference is that individuals will act to move themselves closer to equilibrium, which can lead to radically different responses as the social situation evolves.

Evolution of ruling elites

Through almost all of recorded history, societies have been marked by exceedingly sharp class cleavages. Put overly boldly, a small part of the population was very rich, and almost everyone else lived on the border of subsistence. Why did the many submit, by and large, with remarkable docility? Why has this pattern been substantially overturned in recent centuries, with the downfall, or at least severe weakening of the power of hereditary aristocracies in every part of the globe. (The Saudis now are the leading exception. And who believes the probability is high that they will long outlast the century?)

The following brief FS account of how ruling elites evolve is certainly no more than a caricature of what has actually happened. [13] But I hope that, like a good caricature, it yields or stimulates some real insight. For it provides a framework around which more serious efforts to construct theories of the evolution of societies and of ruling classes might be made. There is a certain resemblance of this account to the work of Mosca and Pareto; but my familiarity with those writers is casual, and I must leave it to others to say to what extent the argument here qualifies or supports this older work.

The whole argument grows out of the basic FS result (p. 41) that, other things equal, the better off an individual is, the larger the share of his (her) resources tend to be allocated to (his or her perception of) the interest of the group. As mentioned in Chapter 4, we can easily imagine particular situations in which we would expect to see this inference violated. But looking at long-run tendencies and the grand sweep of history, we expect it to hold. Now combine this inference with a view of societies as structures that emerge at the deepest level by a biological evolutionary process (making man by nature a social and political animal), but which take particular forms by cultural evolution, and even, as in the founding of the American republic, by conscious construction. [14] We are led to the following sort of account. I give the argument first in its boldest and simplest form; and then add some qualifying remarks.

Under FS, we expect to see a close link between private wealth and political power. The more wealth you have, other things equal, the more generous you will be in donating time and resources to the provision of public goods, in the strong sense that not only does the amount of G-spending increase, but even the fraction of all spending allocated to G-spending. At the earliest stages we may expect that (on the positive side of human activity) water management – flood control and irrigation and (on the negative side) organizing to exploit one's neighbors, and as a consequence organizing to defend against one's neighbors – would have been especially important, providing the potential of very large returns to a favorably situated society that was able to organize itself beyond the level of small kin groups and loose tribal affiliations. [15]

Those who took the lead in organizing such activities would be those for whom talents and circumstances, and possibly greater wealth, combined to yield a value ratio favorable to this work. But, at the earliest stage, the last could easily have been quite unimportant, as it would be if we are dealing with what were essentially undifferentiated primitive communities. Such activities serve visibly valuable (and, in fact, once the society has become accustomed to them, vital) social functions, and those who perform them are visibly of special value to the society. Further, as has been mentioned, FS qualifies but does not overturn the basic free-rider inference of the conventional theory. A reasonably adequate supply of public goods, once a society has grown much beyond the tribal stage, requires coercion (taxes, work gangs). On the other hand, given the rise of coercive institutions, much more ambitious ventures in organized social activity become feasible. But it is those who take the lead in organizing the supply of public goods into whose hands the coercive powers will most naturally fall.

Given power, the opportunity will arise and be exploited to enrich oneself. In part this reflects the FS inference that self-interest is a normal good: increase a man's control over resources, and he will devote some fraction, even if a declining fraction, of the increment to himself. A modest fraction of social resources devoted to a private individual will make him a much richer man than his fellows not enjoying this advantage. In addition, the special role of these public individuals will justify some degree of enrichment as serving group-interest, and might rationalize a good deal more. [16] Finally, private wealth can be provided out of the surplus that accrues with a higher level of organization, so that a larger share to the elite need not imply less absolutely to the masses.

Thus a powerful source of positive feedback exists, with social leadership leading to political power leading to enhanced wealth, which in turn enhances the propensity to social leadership and the wherewithal for acquiring political power. As generations pass, the resulting division between those who manage and defend the state (often enough at real personal cost and risk) and those who labor comes to seem to accord with the natural order. What gives that presumption special potency is that there is some substance – something more than a self serving myth – in the presumption that the noble and commoner are motivated in different ways. In terms of FS, that presumption is false at its roots but nevertheless consistent with observed behavior. Our modern colloquial usage of words like "noble" and "peasant" is an anachronism but not necessarily a libel. [17] Particularly as long as the society is not visibly deteriorating, it easily seems obvious that power and responsibility are the natural domain of the nobility; mundane labor and concern with day-to-day private concerns mark the natural function and natural propensity of those who failed to be born to power, duty, responsibility – and wealth.

However, the modern age greatly weakens this, and for many reasons, almost all of them rooted in technology – the means of production, broadly understood. Only a noble knight, trained for many years and richly out-fitted, could fight in a suit of armor on horseback or, in much older times, in a war chariot, but put a musket in the hands of a peasant who has never handled one before, and the knight must back away. The state grows more complicated as commercial life becomes more complicated; bureaucracies arise, and the need for aristocrats to manage and defend the state becomes less obvious the more obvious it becomes that it is mostly managed by paid functionaries and defended by conscripted citizen-soldiers. The rise of science – itself very much tied to the revival of commerce that marked the closing of the Middle Ages – challenges tradition as the primary font of wisdom. Beyond this there is a vast increase in wealth that comes as the industrial revolution takes hold: wealth from novel sources, that is, not from land tenure, on which the aristocratic class has no traditional claim. At first the business class, whose claim to wealth does not depend on any claim to nobility or duty, and later a much wider segment of society rises above mere subsistence. But with wealth comes a propensity to increasing concern with public as against private matters (with group-interest as against self-interest).

None of this says that allocations to group-interest come to compare ordinarily with allocations to self-interest. But the many are many and the aristocrats few. The widening propensity to expend *some* effort on public affairs is rising while the unique socially important functions of the aristoc-racy are waning.

Finally, the same feedback process postulated to account for the original rise of artistocracies applies again. Those commoners who are better off or more talented, and especially the combination, are the first to take on some public responsibilities. Responsibility increases G' (with power, such resources as are spent on public affairs has more effect), which increases the fraction of resources allocated to G-spending (from the FS condition). But it also brings opportunities for private enrichment.

The process cannot go as far as before, however. The function of the person motivated to volunteer time and resources to public affairs is far less crucial than in times when there was little alternative to getting the public business done. Competitors can arise far more easily. Hereditary aristoc-racies disappear, and, although elites continue, they are far more transi-tory, and the extent to which they can enrich themselves privately is very severely limited in comparison with the old days.

Many complications can be imagined to both weaken and enrich this basic account. In particular, as noted in Chapter 5, the theory of rational choice does not tell us what governs tastes and hence what governs an individual's sense of group-interest (his G-utility function). The Darwinian viewpoint suggests – and there is a good deal of sociological research that finds a similar result empirically – that group-loyalty is triggered by perceived similarities. We feel attached to people who seem like ourselves. We are also stimulated by symbols that identify our group. Hence group-loyalty is encouraged toward others who look like us, have similar tastes, follow similar customs, speak the same language, and so on. As stressed in Chapter 5, this leads in the modern world to very complex patterns of overlapping loyalties.

One aspect of this, which we could expect would be more marked in older times when travel and communication were vastly more difficult than today and when differences in wealth were much greater, is that class loyalty (with a partial exception for crowded urban proletariats) would be very much more important for the wealthy (and politically powerful) than for ordinary citizens, who would rarely see anything of the world beyond their village. The possibility arises from this that members of the ruling class would come to identify social welfare with the welfare of the ruling class itself, regarding whatever is worthwhile in their society as the product of the ruling class.

Further, since the ruling class is very small compared with the rest and also lives an inherently more public life, a certain amount of public commitment would be elicited by the motivation that "others will see what I'm doing." But this could even more easily turn into class loyalty rather than loyalty to the society at large. Finally, the value ratio (G'/S') for working to help the common people in periods when there is no economic growth or during the whole long period when the very idea of progress was scarcely imagined might seem very unfavorable: if there really is nothing to be done, there is no reason to make sacrifices to try. It is easy in those circumstances to believe that God intended the poor and miserable to be poor and miserable.

Hence, especially in older times, it is easy to imagine situations in which, by modern standards, the ruling class seems narrow and self-serving, with the claims to higher service seeming a sham to us. We need not admire the result to allow that, subjectively, the individuals involved may have taken their proclaimed ideals more seriously than seems easy to believe today.

On the other hand, to the extent (and it is not trivial) that many of these conditions have been reversed in modern times, we should not be surprised to observe commitments with some bite (that affect allocation of resources) that are broader than anything that could have any real hold in premodern times. As is characteristic of the human dilemma, the consequences may not always be to our taste, or what the actors intended.

A miscellany

Even more briefly let me note a scattering of other areas of inquiry.

Anarchism

Consistent with much comment on this point by anarchists and nonanar-
chists, anarchism would seem most feasible for small groups. [18] The focus
of group-loyalty can be most intense in small, self-sufficient communities,
and it is in a small community that S-spending is likely to be most nearly
congruent with G-spending, for reasons akin to those mentioned in the
context of class loyalty in the previous section. In a small society behavior
is more likely to be observed, and individual actions will more often have
visible social consequences. Hence the value ratio will easily seem larger
than in a mass society. [19] However, even though FS also implies (as discussed earlier in this chapter) that elimination of coercion would increase
voluntary social action, overall the FS analysis does not add anything substantially favorable to arguments for the feasibility of anarchy in societies
larger than (say) a small village. Serious questions would arise about the
costs associated with such social organization. These include not only
economic costs turning on the loss of economies of scale and on the problem
of supplying goods whose "publicness" crosses community lines (scientific
research, for example) but also on the social effects of focusing loyalties on
small communities. One might argue (I *would* argue) that for most purposes, such as the general peace, quite the opposite kind of social evolution
is desirable, diffusing loyalties far beyond the currently dominant boundaries
of national states. Of course, advocates of small, autonomous social organizations are (in the current revival of such views) generally very much in
favor of small organizations *and* global loyalties, but on the arguments
given earlier with respect to the triggering of group-loyalties, that would
seem unlikely.

The underworld

A reader interested in evidence that would undermine the FS hypothesis
might look to the sociology of subgroups within a society whose very mode
of life appears to be antisocial. Can such individuals be construed fruitfully
as being in equilibrium with respect to allocation of resources between self-
and group-interest? On the other hand, if FS holds, then study of such
groups should produce striking insights; their members must (ordinarily)
be in equilibrium, but in a way that is not easily appreciated by those of us
who live under a more conventional morality. One would expect to find,

for example, that a more elaborate subculture exists than would be supposed in terms of interpreting the underworld as antisocial, or at least amoral, selfishness run wild, so that an exceptional commitment to subgroup loyalty is developed. Hence, perhaps, some insight into the notion of "honor among thieves," the patriotism of criminals, subculture practices that enhance subgroup loyalty, and others that make the risk of being observed to be disloyal high. One need do no research to be aware of the role of penalties.

Conspicuous consumption

The FS argument was developed in response to the apparent need for a theory of motivation that could account for more social behavior than could be understood within the conventional framework. But the notion of FS equilibrium has implications in the opposite direction as well. In order to be in equilibrium, individuals who are very well off but nevertheless acquire yet more wealth to dispose of must spend some (even though a decreasing fraction) of that wealth on themselves. Beyond a certain point, that raises problems: where to spend the money once all reasonable objective needs are satisfied. Lacking real outlets, yet with the psychological urge to spend on oneself, more and more artificial ways of spending on self-interest develop. Hence, one might suppose, some insight into the roots of the behavior zestfully studied by Veblen and its modern extensions and reformulation in the hands of writers like Lindner and Scitovsky.

Neuroses

In terms of FS, one is led to look for various psychological disorders that seem implicit in the theory, given that we may suppose that, as with other physiological mechanisms, malfunctions sometimes occur. Some obvious examples would be: (1) Incompatibilities between G- and S-functions (i.e., so that the normal internal compatibility discussed at the end of Chapter 4 does not hold); (2) disequilibrium favoring G-spending, or favoring S-spending, even though objectively the individual could move toward equilibrium (i.e., the individual feels out of equilibrium, but some internal problem blocks his ability to adjust his allocation); (3) disequilibrium under coercion (the individual is out of equilibrium and would adjust but something external prevents him from doing so); (4) extreme regret (the individual is in equilibrium but he feels he has grossly misused his resources; for example, having learned that the charity to which he has devoted much time was a fraud or that the glorious car he bought to raise his status is regarded by everyone as evidence that he is an ostentatious fool, and so on). In general, the listing moves from deeper-seated, presumably harder to treat, difficulties to ones that seem likely to be transient in nature.

Academic work

The rewards here are notoriously modest compared with more practical activity. Yet able people are attracted to it. But the pursuit of knowledge for its own sake almost by definition is an activity in group-interest. If G' is judged (wisely or not) by the individual to be high compared with other ways of earning a living, then he will feel good – feel in equilibrium – about work that involves a virtual contribution (in the form of income forgone) to group interest. As in all these applications, and as developed in detail in Chapter 5, we do not, of couse, assume that those attracted to such activities are immune to more mundane concerns.

A. Diagrammatic treatment of goods versus participation altruism

We can sum up the situation discussed in Chapter 2 in terms of Figures A.1 to A.3, which assume convex indifference maps for Smith as (depending on how we interpret the budget lines) a pure goods or a pure participation altruist. Figure A.1 is for the case in which Charity is some individual; Figure A.2 will be used to discuss what happens if we apply the goods or participation model to the case where Charity is a large public charity, like the Red Cross. We will consider the pure goods case first.

(Readers who know the Hochman and Rogers and the Becker models should note that both are pure goods models, so the figures here can be interpreted in terms of those models. Figure A.1 is the Hochman and Rogers diagram with axes shifted,[1] and it is the Hirshleifer diagram for the Becker model with the production frontier (which is irrelevant here) deleted.[2] As Hochman and Rogers pointed out in their original article, their model is a special case of the Becker model.[3])

Figure A.1 shows two budget lines, I and $I+$, and Smith's indifference curves tangent to each. The budget lines show the sum of Smith's + Charity's income (Becker's "social income") for the two cases; and the line labeled IS is Smith's preferred Income-Spending path, showing the locus of all such preferred points (preferred, of course, by Smith the goods altruist, not necessarily by Charity).

If the initial endowment were at Y in Figure A.1, Smith would prefer that Charity transfer resources to him, moving the ex post redistribution to his optimal allocation at P where IS intersects the budget line, II. If the ex ante allocation were at X, then Smith would voluntarily donate resources to Charity, moving the ex post situation to his optimal outcome.

But this pure goods model is not plausible. Suppose, for example, that Smith ex ante had $7000 and Charity had $4000, whereas Smith's preferred outcome (for $I = $11,000) happened to be: Smith, $6000; and Charity, $5000. Then Smith would give $1000 to Charity. If (still with $I = $11,000) Smith's ex ante income were $10,000, with Charity's $1000, then Smith would give charity $4000, thus again reaching his preferred ex post outcome.

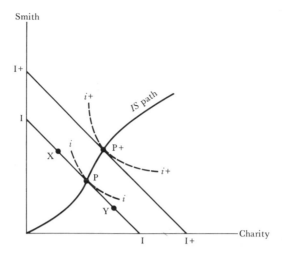

Figure A.1. Smith's income-spending (*IS*) path, showing his preferred allocation of income between spending on Smith and spending on Charity.

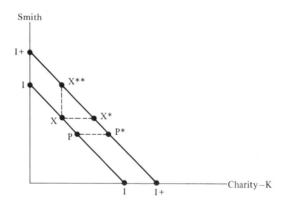

Figure A.2. Smith's preferences under goods altruism, when Smith is a typical individual and Charity is a large public charity.

In other words, if indeed Smith were a pure goods altruist, as assumed by Becker and by Hochman and Rogers – as by most formal models involving altruism found in the economic literature – then a shift in the initial endowment in Smith's favor (social income remaining constant) would have no effect on the ex post outcome: Smith would give all of his increase back to Charity. This is plausible in certain special cases, for example, in the case of altruistic behavior between parent and child. But it is certainly untenable as a general model of altruistic behavior.

Still more serious problems arise if we try to extend this model to large public charities. Now, to get a diagram in which all the action is not crowded into a microscopic sliver along the horizontal axis of Figure A.1, we shift the axes over, obtaining Figure A.2, where K will be some amount vast compared with Smith's individual contribution, or even compared with Smith's entire income.

Where in Figure A.1 we imagine the shift from I to $I+$ as being substantial relative to either Smith's income or to Charity's, in Figure A.2 we are considering the (entirely realistic, of course) situation in which a shift in Charity's income – the total amount raised by the Red Cross, for example – which is fractionally microscopic to the charity is substantial relative to Smith's own income.

For this case, if we imagine that Smith's IS path looks at all like that of Figure A.1 (where a shift in Charity's income that sets Smith + Charity from I to $I+$ leads to a gross shift in Smith's own contribution[4]), then we have the absurd result that Smith's charitable behavior would shift wildly with fractionally trivial shifts in the total amount raised by the charity.

A model that implies this can hardly be tenable, so let us suppose, on the other hand, that Smith's contribution does *not* change significantly when there is a (fractionally) very small shift in Charity's income. Then (Figure A.2) let Smith's preferred point be P, when social income (Smith + Charity) is I, and put Smith's endowment at X. Now let Charity's income increase, moving the social income to $I+$, which will move Smith's ex ante position to X^*. Because we are now assuming (realistically) that Smith's contribution will not be affected by this slight shift in Charity's income, Smith's preferred point must now be at P^*.

But suppose social income grew to $I+$ not because Charity's income increased by a fractionally trivial amount but because Smith's income increased by a fractionally substantial amount. We would still be on the budget line $I+$, but now Smith's ex ante position would be at X^{**}. However, his preferred ex post position, under the goods model, must still be P^*. Smith will therefore, if the goods model holds, give his entire increase in income to Charity. Combining this result with the previous one, we see no matter what we assume about how Smith reacts to a fractionally slight shift in Charity's income (that is, whether Smith's contribution is sensitive or insensitive to the shift in Charity's income), the goods model leads us to a bizarre conclusion. All of this is a generalization of the "voluntary contribution" paradox discussed in Chapter 2.

Further, you can see intuitively why these odd results occur. As long as we are working with a pure goods model, Smith will not distinguish between an increase Becker's "social income" (Smith + Charity), which comes from a change in his own endowment, and an equal increase from a change in Charity's endowment. His set of preferred points will remain unchanged, with the unacceptable implications discussed.

Obviously, these problems would not occur in a pure participation model. However, other untenable results then occur. We can interpret Figure A.1 as a pure participation model by interpreting the budget lines as referring to Smith's own income. (In other words, his ex ante position is at the upper left-hand extremity of the budget line; and the horizontal axis measures the amount Smith donates to Charity, not Charity's income.) But now Smith's donation is completely independent of Charity's income: even a very large shift in Charity's income would have no effect on the amount Smith gives.

Further, no *simple* combination of the goods and participation notions will resolve the difficulty. Figure A.3 illustrates what happens if we suppose (as in fact has often been supposed) that utility from participation can be added to utility from goods altruism.[5]

In Figure A.3, the equilibrium income-spending path is defined by sliding a horizontal line in the figure, where the curve on the left shows the marginal utility (MU) of self-interested spending, the lower line on the right shows the essentially constant MU from goods altruism, and the slanting line on the right is the MU from participation. The horizontal axis (in both directions from the origin) measures spending. So at income I, Smith is spending $x on self-interest; and $y altruistically. At income $I +$ he is spending $x +$ on self-interest, $y +$ altruistically. If you think about the geometry of the figure, you will see that, for every income level, a unique equilibrium spending choice is defined.

The gross failure of the pure goods or pure participation models are now eliminated. Smith no longer necessarily exhibits a bizarre income-spending path under the conditions considered earlier; nor is his altruistic spending · independent of how much good he sees in that spending. However, if the goods component of the total altruistic marginal utility is comparable in magnitude to the participation component (as it is in the figure as drawn), then perfectly feasible changes in the goods component – for example we offer to match Smith's donation – imply an enormous shift in the way he spends his income. Indeed, there is a strict upper limit on the amount to be spent on himself, which is x^* in the figure as drawn but would shrink to almost nothing if goods altruistic MU doubled.

However, supposing that individuals find the goods utility component of their altruistic motivation very small does not solve the problem of defining an empirically viable model. For if the goods motive is small compared to

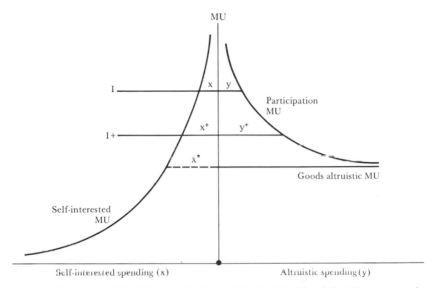

Figure A.3. "Tree" diagram for determining Smith's *IS* path if self-interest, goods altruism, and participation all represent additive components of utility. Note that income is increasing as the horizontal line slides down the vertical axis: $I = x + y > I^+ = x^+ + y^+$.

the participation motive, then we can be led to the equally untenable inference that the goods component could shrink to nothing, or even turn negative (implying that Smith perceives his participation as socially harmful), without having a large effect on Smith's spending.

These problems can be ameliorated in part if we suppose that participation utility depends on the fraction of resources – rather than only on the absolute amount – spent altruistically. Further, by making sufficiently complicated assumptions about the interactions between self-interested and altruistic sources of utility (to start, by dropping the separability assumption implicit in the figure as drawn), we can define a model that works any way we please. Nevertheless, what we really want is much more than merely a model that does not lead immediately to empirically implausible results. To be clearly useful, the model must be able to handle not only all the difficulties discussed in this appendix, but also all the empirically important complications sketched at the conclusion of Chapter 2.

B. Detailed introduction of the FS model

This appendix supplements the discussion of Chapter 4, defining terms more precisely and providing some detailed discussion of points treated very briefly, or not at all, in the main text. Topics that have already been treated in detail in the main text (for example, intuitive interpretation the FS equilibrium condition) are not repeated here. The notation, except where defined at first use, is that of the main text.

Formal specification of the FS model

The basic model

To restate the basic equations developed through a Darwinian argument in Chapter 3 and later reframed in terms of the introspective argument of Chapter 4, Smith is in equilibrium if and only if,

$$W = G'/S' \qquad \text{(FS equilibrium)} \qquad \text{B.1}$$

where

$$W = W(g, s); \quad \partial W/\partial g > 0; \quad \partial W/\partial s < 0 \text{ (Weak FS)} \qquad \text{B.2}$$

or

$$W = W(g/s); \quad W' > 0 \qquad \text{(Strong FS)} \qquad \text{B.3}$$

The W-function

Equation B.2 (the same as Equation 3.1) gives only a minimal characterization of how a W-function must behave to be consistent with the Darwinian argument of Chapter 3, and it is not strong enough to give us the "superior good" result presented in connection with Figure 4.2. On the other hand, Strong FS (here Equation B.3; also Equation 3.3) is stronger than we require for that result, but I have thought of no simple characterization of necessary conditions. The analysis to follow in Appendix C may be helpful for the reader interested in getting some sense of just how strong Weak FS must be to yield the superior good result.

138

As mentioned in Chapter 3, I postulate the Strong FS form as the simplest characterization consistent with Weak FS and also because it is the simplest form consistent with stability under the "good times/bad times" stresses mentioned in the text. We expect that individuals will be concerned with relative (not only absolute) well-being, as is certainly observed empirically. For in addition to the point of the text, under stable conditions (constant population size) genetic fitness will depend very much on relative situation of individuals within the group, for the usual Darwinian reason that the number of members born into the population ordinarily exceeds (in nature, generally greatly exceeds) the number who can be present in the next generation of adults. The mathematical conclusion of Appendix C suggests how Strong FS could contribute to the ESS effectiveness of the W-function in this regard also.

Two further issues that arise with respect to the W-function take us well beyond the level of detail that is needed for the discussion of this study. However, a few comments may be useful.

First, the Darwinian argument leaves open the specific functional form for W (even assuming Strong FS) and also the value for $W^o \equiv W(g = 0)$. On the functional form, see the discussion in Appendix C. On W^o, it is plausible and simplest to postulate $W^o = 1$, and I do that, though the Darwinian argument only requires that $W > 1$ if $g > 0$ (so $W^o \neq 1$ is possible, and it is not necessarily the case that W^o is constant across individuals.)

Second, as mentioned in Chapter 3, spending is sometimes simultaneously optimal for both G- and S-Smith: that is, special situations arise for which $G' = S'$. Nonsubversiveness (Chapter 5) suggests that such spending is charged neither as S- nor as G-spending. If we assume that, then Smith's income constraint would be:

$$I = g + s + \overline{gs} \qquad\qquad \text{B.4}$$

where s and g are as defined on page xii and $\overline{gs}$ is spending that is jointly optimal for both S- and G-Smith. This $\overline{gs}$ spending would mainly consist of minimum subsistence for Smith, plus a component of S-wtp and G-wtp in the context of voluntary spending for public goods (Appendix E). Only the former is likely to be significant in an FS analysis, for the reason discussed in Appendix E.

Further, as long as we suppose that we are dealing with income levels beyond subsistence, we can leave $\overline{gs}$ implicit because it will play no active role in the analysis. Except where gs is specifically mentioned, I do assume as much in the balance of the discussion.

The G- and S-functions

Let

$$G = G(M,N) \qquad \qquad \text{B.5}$$

where G is Smith's utility from the point of view of perfectly group-interested G-Smith; $M = [M_{ij}]$ gives spending on private goods, indexed by i, as distributed across all members of the society, indexed by j; and $N = [N_k]$ is spending on public goods in the society, indexed by k. As you know, in this G-function no *special* weight is given to the vector of private goods for which $j =$ Smith himself, nor to public goods that happen to be of special value to Smith himself.

Parallel to the G-function, we have:

$$S = S(m,n) \qquad \qquad \text{B.6}$$

Here S is Smith's utility from the point of view of perfectly self-interested S-Smith; $m = [(M_i)_j, \, j =$ Smith$]$, the vector of spending on private goods for Smith; and $n =$ spending on the subset of N that happens to be personally significant in terms of Smith's self-interest. (So if Smith is not blind, the provision of Braille books in the public library is a public good that enters N but not n, as illustrated by Figure 5.1.)

Defining S in terms of m and n instead of M and N is merely to emphasize that there are aspects of the situation of interest to G-Smith that may be of negligible interest to S-Smith: by definition, S-Smith's marginal utility with respect to goods in the sets $[M\text{-}m]$ and $[N\text{-}n]$ is negligibly small.

The Darwinian argument of Chapter 3 requires, and I have accordingly defined, the S- and G-functions to be pure goods functions, in the sense specified by Equation 2.2. (Hence, as stressed in Chapter 5, neither G- nor S-utility involves "psychic income.")

We can rewrite Equations B.5 and B.6 as:

$$G = G(g : s, \cancel{M}, \cancel{N} ; K) \qquad \qquad \text{B.7}$$

$$S = S(s : g, \cancel{m}, \cancel{n} ; K) \qquad \qquad \text{B.8}$$

where all the arguments to the right of the colon are parameters for the chooser. (S-Smith has no control over g, nor G-Smith over s.) $\cancel{M}$, $\cancel{N}$, $\cancel{m}$, $\cancel{n}$ include relevent portions of $\overline{gs}$ (as discussed above), but otherwise they are respectively M, N, m, n of Equations B.5 and B.6 *except* that goods provided by spending by Smith himself are excluded. Thus, if Smith's own consumption of private goods, m, is provided entirely out of Smith's own spending, then (aside from $\overline{gs}$) $\cancel{m}$ will be empty.

In Equations B.7 and B.8, K refers to any constraints on Smith's spending, most obviously to mandatory contributions to government-supplied goods (taxes). How taxes are allocated between charges to G spending and charges to S-spending is discussed in Chapter 5 and will be developed further in Appendix E.

In sum, Equation B.7 says: G-utility is a function of Smith's G-spending (g), *given* the resources available to S-Smith (s), the distribution of goods in Smith's society aside from Smith's G- and S-spending, taking account of any constraints (most obviously taxes) on how Smith spends his income. Equation B.8 is the analogous function for S-utility.

Dual significance of s and g

In Equations B.7 and B.8, s and g implicitly represent the way that S-Smith and G-Smith, respectively, will use S- and G-resources. If you know my preference structure, along with my spending opportunities and any constraints on the way I use my income, then you do not need to be told just how I spend my income to evaluate my utility function. You already know everything you need to know to deduce my spending on particular goods.

However, in the W-function (Equations B.2 and B.3) s and g are simply accounting categories (not, even implicitly, the goods that Smith will obtain with that spending). The W-function has nothing to do with the particular goods Smith may spend his resources on or, better, that G-Smith and S-Smith, respectively, spend resources on (s for S-Smith, g for G-Smith). Where S and G would be insufficiently defined unless we supposed that the entity evaluating the functions knew Smith's situation (M, etc.), the value of W is defined by simply knowing the aggregate quantities of resources (g and s) allocated to G- and S-spending.

It may be helpful to think of the W-function as an overlay on what I will call Smith's "value map." (Smith's V-map, see Figure B.1.) The V-map is defined by Smith's value ratio as a function of Smith's bundle of goods. A shift in M and N that is just compensated for by a shift in Smith's income would amount to a shift in the origin of Smith's own spending (hence the origin from which g and s would be measured), as indicated by the shift from 0 to 0' in Figure B.1. Following this shift, the value ratio at any fixed point (such as P in Figure B.1) remains the same as before. For the G- and S-functions are defined solely by Smith's goods situation, which has not changed. The W-function, however, would be moved with the shift in endowed point. It would have the same value at 0' that it had at the original origin because the W-function does not depend at all on Smith's goods situation but only on the way he has used his own resources. Thus, at any fixed point (such as P), W will ordinarily change with a shift in the origin of Smith's spending, whereas G'/S' will always remain the same.

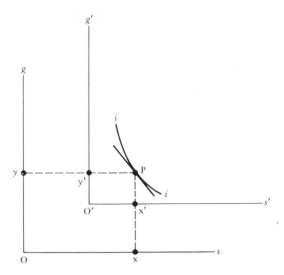

Figure B.1. A shift in Smith's endowed point from O to O' does not affect his V-map: S'/G' at $(x,y) = S'/G'$ at (x',y'). But his W-map moves with the shift in endowed point, so that in general $W(x,y) \neq W(x',y')$.

As will be described in Appendix C, taking the inverse of the value ratio (i.e., S'/G') yields contours that look like indifference curves, such as is illustrated in Figure B.1. As drawn, O' lies almost on a line joining O and P (hence $g'/s' \approx g/s$). So under Strong FS the values of W would change only a little in the particular case illustrated.

Comparability of G' and S' "inside Smith"

The value ratio, G'/S', will be well defined only if we have some condition that rules out transformations of the utility functions that would change the ratio. In the Darwinian context of Chapter 3, that issue would not arise because utility in that context meant genetic fitness in its technical sense of expected number of reproducing offspring. Further, for the reason discussed at the conclusion of Chapter 4, we expect Smith's G- and S-functions to be based on a common value function, differing only in that S-Smith cares only about Smith and hence ignores all effects except those which pertain directly to Smith. So Smith's value function is also G-Smith's utility function. But whereas G-Smith maximizes that function, S-Smith cares only about a subset of the values and allocates S-resources to maximize only that subset. However, for the special case in which external effects due to S-spending is negligible, we will have:

$$S' \equiv S_s = G_s \qquad\qquad\qquad \text{B.9}$$

The existence of this single value function as the basis of both G- and S-utility is highly plausible in terms of the Darwinian viewpoint. However, even with the single value function, to assure that the value ratio (G'/S') is stable, it is necessary to restrict permissible transformations of the G- and S-functions to linear transformations: in other words, we require interval scale cardinality. However, since the Darwinian argument makes even ratio scale cardinality plausible for the G- and S-functions, that is not a strong additional assumption for the model. (For the case of a typical individual in a large society, it is possible to derive cardinality of the internal G- and S-functions as a property of the model, as shown in P5, Appendix C. But that is in addition to the direct argument given here.)

Mathematically, the linkage between the G- and S-functions through Equation B.9 assures that a transformation of one function must simultaneously transform the other. Consider the transformation, $G^* = f(G)$; $S^* = f(S)$. The derivatives G^* and $S^{*'}$ are then $G_G^* G'$ and $S_S^* S'$. But in contrast to the situation in a conventional model, where the ratio of marginal utilities will be invariant under any positive transformation, here $G_G^* \neq S_S^*$, so that the value ratio would in general shift. However, if the transformation was limited to linear functions, we would have: $G^* = a + bG$; $S^* = a + bS$. The transformed marginal utilities would be $G^{*'} \equiv G_g^* = bG'$, and $S^{*'} \equiv S_s^* = bS'$, which would leave the value ratio, G'/S' unchanged.

The FS standard case

What I will label the "standard case" invokes the usual convexity assumption (C) of the conventional model (loosely, positive but diminishing marginal utility); plus two assumptions unique to the FS model, which I will label "conditional separability" (CS) and "G-separability" (GS).

CS holds if G' can be treated as independent of Smith's own S-spending and S' is similarly independent of Smith's own G-spending.

GS holds if G' can be treated as constant with respect to Smith's own G-spending: in other words, even though (if C holds) $G'' < 0$ (declining marginal utility), the spending of a single individual has only a negligible effect ($\Delta G' = G'' \Delta g \approx 0$). If you give to the Red Cross or public television as an ordinary citizen, you can see no difference in marginal utility from your first to your tenth (or even thousandth) dollar. ($G_{gg} \approx 0$, which defines GS.) In symbols, the standard case holds if: $G', S' > 0$; $G'', S'' < 0$; $G_{gs}, S_{sg} \approx 0$; $G_{gg} \approx 0$.

I emphasize that none of these conditions can be treated as universally applicable (as conventional models cannot ignore the possibility of empirically significant situations in which C fails – nonconvexities occur). But parallel to the assumptions of the standard competitive model of microeconomics, the specially simple cases in which C, CS, and GS characterize the situation mark out a particularly important context.

Methodologically, the analysis of this standard case is the counterpart to the analysis of an atomistic society in conventional microeconomics, important partly because it sufficiently describes an important class of situations and partly because it provides a point of departure for analyzing nonstandard situations.

There are three major classes of situations in which one or more of the standard assumptions (C, CS, GS) would not apply.

First are exceptional individuals. Departures from the standard case will be commonplace for major figures in a society: leaders of political factions, labor federations, large corporations, and so on, as well as "opinion leaders," even those with no formal power base (see Chapters 8 and 9).

Second are exceptional situations for ordinary individuals. These are harder to define; by their nature any particular example will appear rather bizarre. But in a large society there will be a substantial number of ordinary individuals at any moment who have opportunities to do things in extreme self-interest (criminal acts) or extreme group-interest (acts of heroism) such that one or more of the standard conditions do not hold. Although from an individual point of view these situations may be rare enough to be of little interest, from a social point of view they are consequential because how ordinary individuals in the society respond in such situations in the aggregate has social significance.

Third are increasing returns. With respect to social goods, increasing returns to scale are common. (If I am the only person carrying my trash to the barrel, the effect is not as large from my act as if almost everyone is doing it.)

In the first two classes, CS or GS or both are easily violated; in the third, convexity is violated. The essential point, though, is only to make it clear that, although the standard case plays an important role in the analysis, the FS model is not built on the assumption that these conditions necessarily hold. Empirically, as we have just seen, many situations arise in which those assumptions become empirically implausible, and nothing in the arguments leading to Equations B.1–3 requires that they hold.

In addition to cases in which we can see that the standard assumptions would be unrealistic, there are cases in which the standard assumptions appear to be violated empirically even though on the logic of the model they should hold.

Suppose that Smith, who had not previously owned a television, now buys one, becoming an enthusiastic watcher of public television. We will not be terribly surprised if he now becomes a contributor to public television, whereas we would be surprised to find he was a contributor before he had become a viewer. This certainly appears to be a case in which spending on a private good for Smith (the television) changed his marginal utility for an item of G-spending. For although S' (contributing) would certainly be increased by the purchase of a television, that value would remain far too low to motivate any nontrivial S-wtp. On the other hand, G-Smith has no special concern for Smith, and the improvement in the value of public television for some single individual – here Smith – would not significantly affect G' (contributing to public television).

There are a variety of possible explanations, however. For example, human beings exposed to new environments, opportunities, and so on do have the capability to become somewhat different persons: tastes change, sometimes (as stressed by James Buchanan in an interesting paper on this topic)[1] by deliberate choice, but sometimes by happenstance. In any event, we should not wholly neglect the possibility of changes in taste with change in experience.

A second kind of issue, more plausible in the context here, concerns how Smith chooses to use G-resources when in fact it will rarely be possible for him to make other than very crude judgments about G'(alternative social goods). See the discussion of rules of thumb in Chapter 5, in particular, the comments on salience and Kantian rules.

A third possibility arises from the role of mixed spending (G- and S-resources jointly spent), because it is valuable to S-Smith to be observed to contribute, or because goods of interest to S-Smith are part of the incentive to contribute, or because S-motivation gains Smith's attention, giving this outlet for G-spending salience, although it is only G-Smith who would be motivated to spend anything. See the discussions of Chapter 5 and Appendix E. Again, some concrete illustrations are given in Chapters 8 and 9.

Spending as arguments of the G- and S-functions

The G- and S-utility functions (Equations B.5 and B.6) were defined in terms of spending on various goods rather than (as is usual) in terms of quantities of goods. But nothing of substance is at issue here; it is simply a matter of convenience. The functions could be reformulated in the more usual manner, provided only that we add to the specification that the entity evaluating these functions also knows the price structure faced by Smith. Because this entity, to repeat that point, is strictly "inside Smith," this would amount to no more than saying that Smith knows the price structure facing Smith.

Of course, for cases in which changes in prices are not at issue, it is the same if we define utilities in terms of spending *or* in terms of quantities of goods but choose units such that each good costs \$1 per unit.

Contrary to usage in economics, however, I will use spending as arguments even in contexts where it is possible that prices may change. (If so, then Smith's whole V-map changes, in contrast to usual usage, where the contours of Smith's indifference map would be undisturbed, with all the effects of the price change captured by a change in the slope of his budget constraint. In our usage here, the slope of the budget line is -1, always: a dollar of G-spending obviously costs exactly the same amount as a dollar's worth of S-spending; namely, a dollar: a change in prices implies a change in the value ratio.

The first reason for this convention is that, for most of the choices we are concerned with in a political context, the chooser's own focus is on spending, not on units of goods. Smith will most often be concerned (whether as an ordinary voter among millions, or as a political leader) with how much he thinks ought to be spent on defense, or scientific research, or whatever. He will have to make decisions about how much to contribute to a political candidate or a charity. In few of these cases would it be helpful if the utility per dollar that determines Smith's choices was based on separate consideration of utility per unit and price per unit. Often such a formulation would be meaningless, for often the only well-defined measure of "goods" at issue in a political context is in terms of resource use (spending).

Even more important, in a political context it would be wholly implausible to make the customary "tastes as given" assumption of an economic analysis. In economics, we can ordinarily take the individual's preferences as given, focusing the analysis on what happens when prices or income changes. These are important in a political analysis but not particularly more important than what happens when individual preferences change, either due to the efforts of other actors, or due to a change in circumstances (war is declared, social fashion changes, and so on). With these effects so important to the analysis, it is more convenient – even though in a conventional economic analysis it would generally be less convenient – to think about what happens when G- or S-utility per dollar changes for expenditure in various directions, with changes in prices being just one possible cause of such changes.

In sum, then, my definition of the S- and G-functions in terms of units of spending rather than units of goods reflects what is convenient, given our primary interest in social (rather than private, market-oriented) choice.

C. Some properties of the FS model

Discussion of the V- and U-maps

Smith's V-map (defined in Appendix B) is analogous to a conventional indifference map. If illustrated by a figure drawn with g on the vertical axis as in Figure 4.2 or B.1, we can obtain contours with the usual properties of indifference curves by assigning a slope equal to $-S'/G'$ at each point. (The reason for the orientation of the axes in Figure 4.2 is that noneconomists find it easier to "see" the meaning of the superior good result if the IS path bends upward, rather than to the right, as it would if we put s on the vertical axis.) By analogy with a conventional indifference map, we will call the absolute slope of contours in the V-map the V-MRS. So if FS equilibrium holds ($W = G'/S'$), then $W \times V\text{-}MRS = 1$.

Contours in the V-map will have the usual properties of indifference contours. I hope I have made it clear, though, that there is no entity, not even a metaphorical entity, that is indifferent among points along a given V-contour.

Smith's U-map is derived from the V-map by setting (at each point in the map) $U\text{-}MRS = W \times V\text{-}MRS$. Because we have defined the G- and S-functions in terms of spending, the slope of Smith's budget constraint will always be -1, and Smith's IS path in the U-map will be just the set of points such that U-MRS is tangent to Smith's budget line, since at these points $W \times V\text{-}MRS = 1$.

Details of the FS model worked out in the next section could be developed using geometrical arguments like those employed in connection with Figures 4.1 and 4.2, and with a little extra trouble this can be done using the U-map. (The arguments are more direct in terms of the V-map.) Nevertheless, readers accustomed to indifference map analysis are almost always tempted to try to think about FS in terms of a U-map (or some variant of a U-map). For the U-map presents the FS model in a way that looks closer to a conventional model. As I have stressed repeatedly, that does not seem to me a helpful way to proceed.

In any case, note well that the U-map incorporates g and s in *both* the senses discussed in Appendix B (in the G- and S-functions and, simultaneously, in the W-function). Hence a given U-map (or U-function, as will be developed in a moment) applies only with respect to a given situation (given perceived spending opportunities and a given endowed point for Smith). It does not have the stable properties that make a utility function convenient in a conventional analysis. The G- and S-functions can be defined (conceptually) without our knowing anything about the situation in the world because they are defined by Smith's preferences, not his situation. We could then (conceptually, again) "plug in" the situation in the world (fill in the values of the arguments in Equations B.5 and B.6) and evaluate the functions.

That could not be done with the U-function, however. The slope of the indifference contours at each point depend on the location of the origin. If Smith's endowed point shifts, then the value of W at each point, hence the value of $W \times V\text{-}MRS$, hence the entire U-map will be altered.

The U-function

Various economists have provided me with suggestions of how the FS model could be presented within a more conventional framework. Nearly all of these suggestions have turned out to be some variant of the U-map. An anonymous reviewer provided the suggestion from which the following discussion was developed, using a "separable utilities" function of the kind studied by Archibald and Donaldson.[1]

Let Smith's "total utility" function be:

$$U = U(G,S) \qquad\qquad\qquad \text{C.1}$$

where we will stipulate that the assumptions of the standard case (C, CS, and GS) hold, and in addition that in U, both G- and S-utility yield diminishing marginal total utility. Specifically, suppose U_G and $U_S > 0$; but U_{GG} and $U_{SS} < 0$.

The derivatives of Equation C.1 with respect to s and g will then be:

$$U_g = U_G\, dG/dg \equiv U_G G' \qquad\qquad \text{C.2}$$

$$U_s = U_S\, dS/ds \equiv U_S S' \qquad\qquad \text{C.3}$$

An equilibrium allocation will be such that (setting $U_s = U_g$ and rearranging terms):

$$U_S/U_G = G'/S' \qquad\qquad\qquad \text{C.4}$$

Taking spending by anyone but Smith as a parameter, we can define $W_g^* = U_G$, $W_s^* = U_S$; and the equilibrium condition can be written:

$$W_s^*/W_g^* = G'/S' \qquad\qquad\qquad \text{C.5}$$

Now let $W = W_s^*/W_g^*$. The equilibrium condition then is:

$$W = G'/S' \qquad\qquad \text{C.6}$$

where $\partial W/\partial g > 0$; $\partial W/\partial s < 0$, which is exactly the FS model of Equations B.1 and B.2.

The U-function will describe how Smith chooses, given his situation. It is the algebraic equivalent of the U-map, and it is subject to the comments. Because of its lack of stability, it would be misleading to speak of this choice function as equivalent (although for some purposes it is analogous) to the utility function of a conventional analysis.

The U-function does exhibit the sense in which the FS model can be interpreted as an extension of the notion of diminishing marginal utility to the issue of social versus self-interested spending. But if you think it plays a significant role in the analysis, you will find yourself immersed in such problems as how to define Smith's *real* utility function (from which this choice function can be derived). How, next, do you generalize the results to allow for situations in which the standard assumptions are violated? How would you reformulate the results to deal with the public goods context discussed in Appendixes D and E? And so on.

All this work is completely unnecessary, and in fact obfuscatory, in terms of the Darwinian viewpoint; yet it is the Darwinian viewpoint that must be called on to resolve many of the issues that arise in thinking through details of the FS view. So the very viewpoint that helps us repeatedly in working with the model tells us that it is pointless, and in fact misleading, to focus on problems related to total utility.

Thus, although I hope that mathematically inclined readers will be entertained by the formal elegance of this U-function, they will be taking the least promising road to understanding this theory if they take that function seriously.[2]

Further properties of the FS model

The analysis that follows reviews and somewhat extends results given in Chapter 4. The extension of results and the alternative technique used to reach them may be of interest; and they provide the basis on which the results of the next section will be built.

We have earlier defined the IS path as an income-spending path such that at each point we have:

$$W = G'/S' \qquad \text{(FS equilibrium)} \qquad\qquad \text{C.7}$$

This condition holds everywhere on the IS path, so it must be true that between any two points:

$$\Delta(WS') = \Delta(G') \qquad\qquad\qquad\text{C.8}$$

and if the allocation is efficient we will also have:

$$\Delta g + \Delta s = \Delta I \qquad\qquad\qquad\text{C.9}$$

In other words, the allocation of an increment to income, ΔI, must be divided between increments to G- and S-spending (Δg and Δs) such that the change in WS' just equals the change in G'.

Given CS, we will have (in the limit, taking derivatives):

$$W_I S' + WS'' ds/dI = G'' dg/dI \qquad\qquad\text{C.10}$$

where $ds/dI + dg/dI = 1$ \qquad\qquad\qquad\qquad C.11

and $W_g dg/dI + W_s ds/dI = W_I$ \qquad\qquad\qquad C.12

Like Equation C.7, Equation C.10 is an equilibrium condition, not an identity: Smith must choose ds/dI (hence $dg/dI = 1 - ds/dI$) such that equilibrium holds (just as in Equation C.7, he must choose s and g such that $W = G'/S'$).

Inspection of Equations C.10–12 yields the following properties for an equilibrium allocation, given CS and Weak FS, plus the normal convexity conditions (C).

P1.   Neither G- nor S-spending is an inferior good.

Suppose Smith, given an increment to income, allocates all to g ($ds/dI = 0$), or even also gives to g some resources previously allocated to s ($ds/dI < 0$). From Equation B.2, W_I will be > 0; hence (given C and CS) the first term on the left in Equation C.10 will be greater than 0; and the second term on the left will be ≥ 0. The term on the right will be ≤ 0. So $ds/dI \leq 0$ cannot be an equilibrium allocation.

Similarly, for $dg/dI \leq 0$ (G-spending is inferior), both terms on the left are negative, but the term on the right must be ≥ 0. Therefore the equilibrium allocation can only be one such that $ds/dI > 0$ and $dg/dI > 0$.

P2.   There exists a unique equilibrium allocation.

Let ds/dI vary monotonically from 0 to 1. Inspection of Equation C.10 shows that the sum on the left will be > 0 if $ds/dI = 0$, and would decrease monotonically, becoming negative by the time we reach $ds/dI = 1$. But the term of the right, which is negative when $ds/dI = 0$, increases monotonically, reaching 0 when $ds/dI = 1$ (hence $dg/dI = 0$). Since the functions are all continuous we must have a unique equilibrium (as in Figure 4.1).

P3. If $W > G'/S'$, a shift of resources from g to s moves closer to equilibrium; and the converse.

The monotonicity argument in P2 yields P3 as a corollary.

To this point, the assumptions used have been weaker than those used in Chapter 4, and they do not yet give us the superior good result of Figure 4.2. However

P4. Under Strong FS, C, CS, and GS, S-spending is a normal good and G-spending is a superior good. As income increases, the fraction of resources allocated to G-spending increases, although the absolute amount allocated to S-spending also increases.

Given GS (hence $G'' \approx 0$), Equation C.10 can be reduced to:

$$W_I S' = -WS'' \, ds/dI \qquad \text{C.13}$$

But at equilibrium the right side of Equation C.13 will be positive, since $-S''$, W, and ds/dI (from P1) must be all positive. Therefore at equilibrium the right side must also be positive, which from the definition of Strong FS, will only occur if $dg/dI > g/I$.

P5. Given CS, the G- and S-functions are cardinal, up to a linear transformation.

That separability implies cardinality is well known. Let $G^* = f(G)$ be some permissible transformation of G. Differentiating with respect to g yields:

$$G_g^* = G_G^* G_g \qquad \text{C.14}$$

and differentiating again with respect to s yields:

$$G_{gs}^* = G_G^* G_{gs} + G_{GG}^* G_g G_s \qquad \text{C.15}$$

But given CS, $G_{gs}^* = G_{gs} = 0$. Since G_g and G_s are ordinarily positive, Equation C.14 implies that $G_{GG}^* = 0$. Hence $f(G)$ can only take the linear form,

$$G^* = a + bG. \qquad \text{C.16}$$

Strictly, CS requires only that $G_{gs} \approx 0$, not $G_{gs} \equiv 0$, so that sufficiently small departures from linearity are not ruled out. But they will be negligibly small.

P6. However, the U-function is ordinal.

Any monotonic positive transformations can be used, indifferently, to number the contours in the U-map: one numbering system can give no less or no different information than any other. Specifically, in the U-function (Equation C.1), let $U^* = f[U(G,S)]$, where f is again (as in P5) any permissible transformation. Differentiating yields $U_g^* = U_U^* U_G G'$ and $U_s^* = U_U^* U_S S'$. The rest of the argument leading to Equation C.6 then follows, given any function f whatsoever. However, since we want to maximize, not minimize, the U-function we require also $f' > 0$.

See the discussion in Appendix B dealing with these points (permissible transformation of the utility functions).

Cardinal FS analysis

The material that follows extends the analysis of the previous section in a frankly speculative manner. We examine what happens to the expressions for equilibrium marginal allocations (Equations C.10–12) when we consider what seem to me salient assumptions about functional forms for G- and S-utilities and for the W-functions.

I consider only the simplest situation: Smith is an ordinary citizen in a large society; Strong FS, C and CS hold; there are no spending constraints; and we need analyze only generalized S- and G-spending, as if there were but two goods, a pure private good, which is the preferred spending opportunity for S-Smith, and a pure public good, which is the preferred spending opportunity for G-Smith. The argument is taken from the early paper referred to in the preface.

If we follow Bernoulli and a long line of subsequent writers in assuming logarithmic utility functions (i.e., of the form $u = K + k \log x$), marginal utility for our G- and S-functions will take the form,

$$S' = k^S/s \qquad\qquad \text{C.17}$$

$$G' = k^G/g^* \qquad\qquad \text{C.18}$$

where k^S and k^G are constants of the S- and G-functions, respectively; s is as already defined; and g^* is the sum of spending on the public good, which includes Smith's contribution, g.

From Equations C.17 and C.18, we get:

$$S'' = -k^S/s^2 = -S'/s \qquad\qquad \text{C.19}$$

$$G'' = -k^G/g^{*2} = -G'/g^* \qquad\qquad \text{C.20}$$

But, at any point along Smith's IS path, $WS' = G'$; hence (substituting into Equation C.20) we must have:

$$G'' = -WS'/g^*$$
C.21

From Equation C.19, we can write:

$$WS'' = -WS'/s$$
C.22

Then dividing Equation C.21 by C.22 gives:

$$G''/WS'' = s/g^*$$
C.23

Because this will certainly be microscopic for our case of Smith as an ordinary citizen in a large society, we can henceforth assume $G'' \ll WS''$. It will also be convenient to simplify the notation, as follows: let $f = ds/dI$, the fraction of a marginal increment to income allocated to S-Smith (hence, $1 - f = dg/dI$); let $F = s/I$, the fraction of Smith's total income allocated to S-Smith (hence, $1 - F = g/I$); and let $R =$ Smith's ratio of G- to S-spending $= g/s$.

Using the result of Equation C.23, $S'' = -S'/s$ (from Equation C.19), and this new notation, we can approximate Equation C.10 as:

$$f = W_I s/W$$
C.24

where, using Equation B.3 and writing out the derivative,

$$W_I = W' dR/dI = W'(F - f)/F^2 I$$
C.25

Now substituting Equation C.25 into C.24 and rearranging terms, we get:

$$F/f = 1 + FW/W'$$
C.26

where (since F, W, and W' are all positive), P4 follows by inspection: at equilibrium obviously $0 < f < F$. Note that in this argument, we did not need to assume $G'' = 0$ from the outset because it followed from Equation C.23.

Equation C.26 has the virtue of transparency, but it does not really lead to any inferences beyond those yielded by the earlier analysis. To go further, we must postulate something about the form of the weighting function, $W = W(R)$. Further, unlike the hypothesis on the utility functions, there is no long history indicating a "usual" assumption that has recommended itself to the leading writers. (The long history of the logarithmic hypothesis at least makes it clear that the hypothesis was not arbitrarily chosen for the immediate purpose at hand.)

My own intuition is that the simplest assumption about the W function that is empirically promising would be an exponential decay function. Casual observation suggests that practically everyone makes some voluntary contributions, but the weight we give our own interests apparently increases rapidly as R (the ratio of altruistic to private spending) increases. Few people of ordinary income spend a large portion of their income altruistically. On the other hand, apparently $1/W$ (the weight attached to altruistic spending), although near unity but rapidly declining near $R = 0$, never quite reaches zero as R increases. However large the fraction of income an individual has already spend altruistically, a sufficiently persuasive or touching appeal is likely to bring some further contribution.

A specification that captures all this sets:

$$W = W_{max}(1 - e^{-R/a})$$ C.27

where $W_{max} = W(R = \infty)$, and a is a second parameter of the function. (If attempts were made to fit the function to empirical data, one of these parameters might be interpreted as reflecting individual variability within a culture and the other as reflecting variability across cultures.) The specification differs from that of Appendix B by using W_{max} as a parameter in place of W°. As the simplest guess about W° would set $W^\circ = 1$, the simplest guess about W_{max} would set $W_{max} = N$, the number of individuals in Smith's society. However, none of this involves issues that can be resolved in the present study. The model can be specified in detail in a variety of ways consistent with the points of Appendix B, and only empirical work could tell us which is most effective or convenient.

Proceeding here by differentiating Equation C.27, we next obtain:

$$W' = e^{-R/a} W_{max}/a$$ C.28

Substituting Equations C.27 and C.28 into Equation C.26, we then get:

$$F/f = aF(e^{R/a} - 1) + 1$$ C.29

which does not depend on W_{max}.

For small values of the exponent, $e^x - 1 \approx x$; and $R = (1 - F)/F$. So for $a \approx 1$, R less than, say, 0.1, Eq. C.28 yields:

$$f \approx F/(2 - F)$$ C.30

leaving a decision rule that is trivially simple.

Further, there is a simple way Smith might estimate when he has reached the minimum level of well-being that first elicits $f < 1$. Call it income I^*, all spent on subsistence for Smith and charged to $\overline{gs}$ as defined in Appendix B. Suppose that Smith first senses $W < G'/S'$ when a dollar's spending on the good under cooperative conditions (everyone contributes a dollar) would lead him to wish to spend the dollar on the public good out of pure self-interest. This can be criticized in various ways (it supposes that the value of Smith's dollar to everyone can be approximated by the value to Smith alone of everyone's dollar). But it is a reasonable satisficing rule of thumb. Certainly the availability of this simple rule means that there is no first-order problem of how Smith could make a judgment about I^*. Beyond I^*, we have the rule of Equation C.29, or even the simpler yet rule of Equation C.30.

This discussion is best interpreted in terms of the programmed versus calculated responses discussed in Appendix F, with a rule like that of Equation C.30 representing a cognitive response that may or may not be overridden in particular situations. Both the rule for locating I^*, and the rule of Equation C.30 fit well with the "good times/bad times" argument for Strong FS discussed at the beginning of Appendix B.

D. Extended Lindahl–Samuelson equilibria

Chapter 6 summarized the FS analysis of how the Lindahl–Samuelson equilibrium for public goods might be extended to allow for social as well as strictly self-interested preferences. This section deals with some technical details.

Suppose that G-Smith, given his perception of group-interest, would be willing to pay \$0.70 to add \$1 to the supply of some good when the supply is \$$Q$; and G-Jones, given his (possibly very different) perception of group-interest, would be willing to pay \$0.30. If S-Smith and S-Jones were in the same situation, it would be consistent with their interests to jointly spend the incremental dollar, S-Smith paying \$0.70 and S-Jones paying \$0.30. But for G-Smith and G-Jones that kind of arrangement yields no necessary or even probable advantage. In this case, G-Smith and G-Jones would be jointly paying \$1 of funds dedicated to group-interest to buy an increment that neither thinks is worth a dollar to the group. Like the family purchase example discussed in Chapter 6, their individual *wtp*s are not summable to reach group *wtp*. For each G-individual *wtp* already represents a judgment about the group.

Now imagine a society that contains only G-Smith, G-Jones, and so on. As an analogy, we might think of the board of trustees of some public interest institution, where the peculiar arrangement holds that each trustee controls a certain fraction of the institution's budget, as G-Smith, G-Jones, and so on control whatever portion of Smith's, Jones's, and so on, resources are allocated to group-interest.

For each possible budget (so much for Project A, so much for B, etc.), each individual trustee would have some preferred way to use his own resources. If, to trustee Smith, it seemed that A was seriously underfunded, he might wish to allocate all of his own budget to A; or, if uncertain about what was best, he might prefer to spread his resources over a number of projects. In any case, if we make the usual assumption of the basic market analysis of economics, supposing that there are large numbers of trustees each controlling only some tiny portion of the total budget, we can imagine

156

an equilibrium budget, analogous to the market equilibrium for private goods in the conventional analysis, such that no actor wishes to change his allocation, given the allocation of all others (Nash equilibrium). Analogous to our trustees, for G-Smith, G-Jones, and so on, the appropriate counterpart of S-Smith's demand function for a public good is the amount that G-Smith would supply. For S-people, we must sum demand functions; for G-people, we must sum what might be labeled G-supply functions.

In the general equilibrium context, difficult technical issues arise with respect to proof of existence, stability, uniqueness, and so on of the equilibrium. For the conventional model, these issues were not resolved for many years after the original presentation of the notions, and I make no pretence of having dealt with them here for the FS model. However, in the partial equilibrium context the situation is straightforward. We will have G-supply schedules, $q = D(Q)$, where, for the good at issue, q is the amount Smith would allocate (donate) to the supply of that good when Q is already available. Summing these schedules across all members of our G-society, we will have a (Nash) equilibrium outcome where $\Sigma q_i = Q$.

It is convenient to convert these G-supply schedules into summable wtp schedules. We will label these as G-wtp^* schedules to remind ourselves that we are defining a synthetic notion of willingness to pay that is designed to have the desired property of summability across actors. As mentioned in the main text, the S-wtp ordinarily used in the Lindahl–Samuelson analysis also has a synthetic character, and we will here relabel that notion S-wtp^*. (See the more detailed discussion in Appendix E.)

We set G-wtp^* at each budget level, Q, equal to q/Q. Summing these schedules across all voters would then locate the (Nash) equilibrium where ΣG-$wtp^* = \$1$. Assigning each G-person a tax price equal to his or her G-wtp^* at that outcome, each would be charged just the amount he would wish to donate, given the supply of all others. Of course, as we have already seen, we could reach the same result by directly summing the q's across voters. It is exactly the same thing to say that equilibrium occurs where $\Sigma q_i = Q$, or where ΣG-$wtp^*_i = 1$. However, because we will want to broaden the context to account for the S-preferences as well as the G-preferences of all citizens, using G-wtp^* is helpful. We can now conveniently define Q^* as the point such that ΣG-$wtp^*_i + \Sigma S$-$wtp^*_i \equiv \Sigma FS$-$wtp^*_i = 1$. Assign each individual his appropriate tax price, S-$wtp^* + G$-wtp^*. The total taxes will then just equal the budget for each good; and (from the argument of Chapter 6 on nonsubversive allocations) all entities (S-Smith, G-Smith; S-Jones, G-Jones, et al.) will simultaneously be in what I will call a *mixed* equilibrium. If you review the argument, you will see that the equilibrium with respect to S-people is the coerced but pareto-efficient (Lindahl–Samuelson) result; but with respect to G-people, the equilibrium is a Nash equilibrium, the analog here of the conventional model's competitive equilibrium.

This may leave us short of a fully efficient outcome. Consider, for example, the good mentioned at the beginning (call it good A) for which G-Smith would be willing to pay \$0.70, and G-Jones \$0.30. Now suppose that under Nash behavior G-Smith would spend his last dollar on good B, which G-Jones regards as having zero social value; whereas G-Jones would spend his last dollar on good C, which G-Smith regards as a socially perverse "good" (perhaps free beer at the town meetings), with a social value of $-\$1$. Then unexhausted gains from trade exist (the outcome is not pareto-efficient). If the \$2 were spent on good A the value to G-Smith would be \$1.40 (instead of \$1 + \$0), and the value to G-Jones would be \$0.60 (instead of \$1 − \$1). Both Smith and Jones are better satisfied than if Smith spent his dollar on B and Jones on C.

In contrast to the situation under the conventional analysis or with respect to S-people under the FS analysis, it is not obvious that G-Nash outcomes will ordinarily depart grossly from pareto-efficiency. It is possible that, for the large numbers case, the Nash outcome would be a reasonable approximation of an efficient outcome, given only mild assumptions. My conjecture is that that will not turn out to be the situation. In any case, the single illustration given is sufficient to show that, as for C-Smith and S-Smith, a kind of free-rider analog, including a revelation of preferences problem, can exist for G-people. Although the problem is certainly not as gross as for C-Smith and S-Smith, it is not trivial. Especially given increasing returns to scale, as will commonly be encountered in the context of public goods, serious inefficiencies may exist under Nash behavior. Further, we could not expect G-individuals (*even* if they could act independently) to reveal their demand honestly. If gains from trade are possible, it becomes strategically advantageous to understate one's demand for some goods and overstate it for others to enhance one's bargaining position. (Do not confuse group-interested behavior with ethical behavior; although from the point of view of group-interest ethical behavior may be presumed to have a positive value as such, it is not infinite.) In the same way, absent coercion, we could not count on universal compliance with an announced efficient outcome, even if it were possible to invoke the help of Samuelson's omniscient demon to design the outcome.

Notice also that I have tacitly treated the issue in the static context (as defined in Chapter 5), taking the allocation inside Smith, Jones, and so on as fixed. This seems generally plausible, although important counter-examples can be defined (revolutionary situations, for example), some of which would also be cases in which significant gains from trade remain in the mixed equilibrium. Finally, it is not obvious that even with the assistance of Samuelson's demon a stable pareto-optimal solution would always, or even generally, exist. A new kind of Arrow paradox could arise.

E. Coerced and voluntary spending

Appendix D dealt with a conceptual problem (extension of the Lindahl–Samuelson formalism) that concerns the special case of coerced spending obtained when (waiving all revelation of preferences questions) we seek to define an outcome meeting the Lindahl criteria. As mentioned in the text, this conceptual problem is not of any direct practical significance, although we may expect that it will prove helpful in analyzing various practical questions, particularly in the normative context of what government ought to do (such as, given what we know of the properties of an ideally efficient outcome, would political process A be more or less likely than political process B to approximate such a solution.)

However, in positive analysis we need to deal with a quite different sort of question: namely, (1) how does Smith behave when he faces a voluntary choice, including choice involving spending that affects both S- and G-utility (we will call this the "voluntary context"); and (2) how are his taxes allocated between charges to S- versus G-spending in the context where spending is chosen by the government and Smith is assigned a tax share (the coerced context). The issue of Appendix D is then the special case of (2), where the FS analog of the Lindahl-Samuelson marginal conditions hold. More precisely, our problem was to see what form the Lindahl-Samuelson conditions took when extended to allow for G-preferences. A choice was to be made by society, not by particular individuals (Smith, Jones, and so on).

The formal process *inside* Smith that is equivalent to the conventional public goods analysis is the first context: Smith is making a choice governed only by preferences of the entities (G-Smith and S-Smith) "inside," as in the Samuelson pseudomarket, the choice is determined solely by preferences of the entities (Smith, Jones, et al.) in the society of which Smith is a part.

If choices in the real world were actually made under the Samuelson mechanism, then the issues of this appendix with respect to the second problem (how to allocate coerced spending) would not arise. For each individual within the society, as for the society as a whole, the extended Lindahl–Samuelson marginal conditions would hold so that, for each individual, tax price would just equal $S\text{-}wtp^* + C\text{-}wtp^*$, as discussed in Appendix D. Nonsubversiveness would then assure that tax shares inside Smith be just $S\text{-}wtp^*$ and $G\text{-}wtp^*$ to S-Smith and G-Smith, respectively.

But since choices about public spending in the real world are made by a political process, the neatly balanced marginal conditions of the conceptual solution will almost never hold. We face the issue of whether the logic of the FS model together with the logic of the Samuelson analysis can guide us to an appropriate rule for dividing this coerced spending between charges to G-Smith and charges to S-Smith.

To start, notice that in the voluntary context (1), Smith (G-Smith or S-Smith or both[1]) may stand to gain by being observed to behave in a way that Smith's fellow citizens regard as socially useful (or to lose, as for example if Smith holds revolutionary social views, and observed activity serving this conception of group-interest would be dangerous). However, if the behavior is anonymous, there will be no such side effect. I will write $S\text{-}wtp$ to mean S-Smith's wtp for a marginal unit, given the amount available, and assuming no side effects. I will write $S\text{-}wtp+$ for the case in which there may be side effects.

Ordinarily, with respect to a public good, $S\text{-}wtp$ will be only some trivial fraction of the actual cost of providing an incremental dollar's worth of the good. But $S\text{-}wtp+$ need not be negligibly small, although for an *anonymous* donation, by definition, $S\text{-}wtp+ = S\text{-}wtp$. Finally, there is the $S\text{-}wtp^*$ of Appendix D (the summable wtp that we are most familiar with from its role in the Lindahl–Samuelson analysis), which will equal $S\text{-}wtp$ if income effects are negligible, although conceptually they are entirely distinct (one dealing with units up to Q, the other with units beyond Q.)[2]

Now consider what form the equivalent notions for G-Smith will take. $G\text{-}wtp$ (analogous to $S\text{-}wtp$) is what G-Smith would pay for a marginal increment to the supply of the good, given the amount that will be available anyway, and supposing the spending to have no side effects, that is, assuming the anonymous spending situation just discussed in connection with $S\text{-}wtp$. The relation between this $G\text{-}wtp$ and $G\text{-}wtp+$ (analogous to $S\text{-}wtp+$) is just that already explained in the S-context. The relation between $G\text{-}wtp$ and $G\text{-}wtp^*$ of Appendix D is given by Figure E.1.

The solid slanting line is a segment of G-Smith's $G\text{-}wtp$ schedule, showing marginal wtp for units beyond Q°, the amount that would be provided aside from anything C-Smith provides. The actual cost of \$1 added to the budget is of course just \$1, shown by the horizontal line in the figure marked \$1/\$. The amount that G-Smith would supply (donate) is then \$$q$, where his marginal demand curve intersects the cost curve. This supply, q, can then be converted into what I have called G-Smith's supply $G\text{-}wtp^*$ (the

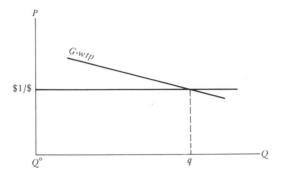

Figure E.1. G-Smith's preferred voluntary donation, q, to the supply of a public good, given his marginal valuation of the good (G-wtp), and the supply that would be provided aside from Smith's donation ($Q°$). G-Smith's G-wtp^* schedule will be determined by the set of such points for all possible values of $Q°$, with G-$wtp^* = q/Q°$.

summable willingness-to-pay equivalent we want for constructing a public goods equilibrium) by dividing q by $Q°$: G-wtp^* at $Q = Q° \equiv q/Q°$, as described in Appendix D.

In the Samuelson "pseudomarket" context of Appendix D, it was unnecessary and in fact would have been meaningless to sum S-wtp^* and G-wtp^* for particular individuals (Smith, Jones, etc.) in choosing the efficient outcome, Q^*. In the aggregation to reach a social outcome, nothing depends on linking wtps for S-Jones and G-Jones; S-Smith and G-Smith; and so on. A single choice is being determined for all of society, and the logic of the process lets us treat S-Smith, S-Jones, G-Smith, G-Jones, and so on "as if" they were all separate individuals. In particular, notice that there is a qualitative difference between wtp for S- and G-Smith in this aggregation process. For S-Smith the relevant wtp concerns units *up to* Q; the process is intended to locate an optimum for S-people who would otherwise individually choose inefficiently. But for G-Smith relevant wtp concerns units *beyond* Q. Thus G-wtp^* in Appendix D was separable from S-wtp^* in the sense required by the logic of the Lindahl–Samuelson analysis. That is, we cannot encounter any double-counting problem (for example, the family wtp example of Chapter 6) if we sum these wtps because they do not apply to the same units.

But in the voluntary context (1), where the choice will be determined solely by Smith's S- and G-preferences, and where, for S-Smith as well as G-Smith, the issue concerns wtp for units beyond Q, the question does arise as to whether independence between S- and G-preferences holds in the sense required to make S-wtp and G-wtp summable.

However, Chapter 6 showed that the separability required by the Lindahl–Samuelson logic will hold if either T1 or T3 holds. But T1 holds by definition for S-Smith; and whereas T1 and T3 are both in general violated by G-Smith, for the special case in which we are concerned with G-Smith's judgment about S-Smith, T3 will hold, for the reason discussed at the conclusion of Chapter 4. Essentially, G-Smith may apply his own tastes to what is good for other people, but his own tastes about what is good for S-Smith will not differ from those of S-Smith, so the problem of paternalistic choice does not arise. Hence, the Samuelson pseudomarket analytics can be applied directly to Smith's choices in the voluntary context, giving the results described in the discussion of mixed spending in Chapter 5.[3]

Finally, then, we come to the coerced context (2), where how much to spend is a decision imposed on Smith so that our only concern is with the allocation of this coerced spending between S- and G-spending. Any allocation such that $p_s + p_g = p$ will be efficient (pareto-optimal "inside Smith"), as discussed in Chapter 5. The problem, then, is reduced to dealing with the requirement that the allocation be nonsubversive. But the principle of nonsubversiveness is sufficient to lead us to the rule for coerced spending defined in Chapter 5: charge S-Smith according to S-wtp*, and charge any balance to G-Smith.

The simplest way to see this is to imagine that Samuelson's demon were available, telling us both the equilibrium result for S- and G-people (where we will assume that the G-Nash equilibrium happens also to be pareto-optimal) and also the Lindahl equilibrium for S-people alone. If the allocation process inside Smith is nonsubversive (as we require), then it should make no difference whether the G- plus S-equilibrium was implemented or only the S-equilibrium. For it would make no difference whether the social budget was based on charging Smith (and Jones, Green, et al.) a tax price, S-wtp* + G-wtp*, or only S-wtp*. What was lost in taxes would be gained in voluntary contributions.

That necessary (for nonsubversiveness) relation would obviously hold if the allocation rule just noted holds. But suppose that at the S-equilibrium, G-Smith has a positive G-wtp, or even a positive G-wtp*. If this leads to any share of the tax price at that equilibrium being charged to G-Smith, then G-Smith (and G-Jones, G-Green, et al.) will be somewhat poorer (having been charged for a share of the S-only demand), and the result must be that the final supply of the good will be less than if the G- plus S-equilibrium had been implemented. Spending in the society to satisfy S preferences would be greater, spending to satisfy G-preferences less than the FS allocation principle implies. But that is just what nonsubversiveness forbids.

An interpretation in Darwinian terms might go as follows. Coerced spending that Smith would willingly incur in the absence of any propensity to spend in group-interest (spending that could be accounted for in pure selfish gene terms: kin altruism + reciprocal altruism) will be charged to S-Smith; spending that S-Smith would never favor, even on a cooperative basis where others must also pay, must be paid for by G-resources.

F. Interaction of FS and Schelling's "inner struggle"

This material supplements remarks in Chapter 5.

It is a commonplace that rules of thumb apparently built into the structure of the human mind sometimes produce misperceptions that we cannot wholly escape. At least it is commonplace that such things occur with visual stimuli (e.g., two parallel lines of equal length, but with inward versus outward arrows on the ends). We suppose that what has happened is that a good rule of thumb, in general, leads to a bad result in certain unusual situations. In Darwinian terms, a wired-in rule of cognition that in general contributed to fitness nevertheless may be misleading in particular circumstances.

It is not so commonplace, but not really surprising to notice, that similar rules of thumb might operate (and sometimes mis-operate) even in the logical processes of our minds, or closer to logical processes than just visual examples suggest.[1] For example, deal three cards face down and ask someone whether he would rather bet that two or more are the same suit, or bet against that. Most of us will sense some degree of an intuitive urge to bet "no" on this, including people who can easily do the calculation that shows "yes" is better. Now deal again, but ask: would you rather bet that all three cards are different, or bet against that. Again people (this time correctly, objectively) want to bet "no." But the two questions are logical inverses. Betting "no" on the first is exactly the same (logically, although obviously not so cognitively) as betting "yes" on the second. Yet, even when you know the situation, I expect that you will find that your mind "sees" the answers as first indicated, even though you know what the right answers are, just as your mind sees the two parallel lines as different in length even though you know they are not. (This suggests, incidentally, an interpretation of the Allais paradox in decision theory.[2] In the example here, no one is likely to insist on the logically inconsistent preferences, in part because the exact inverse relation between the two propositions leaves no room at all for rationalizing an inconsistent choice and in part because the nature of the question is such that one can readily satisfy himself with a hands-on experiment in card dealing that, if you prefer more money to less, there is only one reasonable way to answer the pair of questions. In the Allais paradox neither condition holds, so it is possible for an individual to rationalize his choices – to deny their inconsistency. However, because the response in fact is based on a cognitive rule the individual cannot "see," it is impossible for two people with opposing responses (say Raiffa and Allais) to compose their differences.)

Apply this viewpoint to Schelling's struggle for inner control. Suppose, as would hardly be very surprising, that people have some built-in behavioral rules of thumb that were advantageous in hunter-gatherer times, such as, "if you have a chance to eat, *eat*"; "if you are tired, and no physical danger is present, ignore what is disturbing your sleep." If we are alert and in good spirits we (may, depending a lot on whether we have developed a strong habit before we rationally decided we wanted to behave differently) have no great difficulty ignoring these primordial promptings, just as we can override the message our eyes send us that the two lines are of different length, or our intuitive judgment telling us to bet against two of the three as the same suit. We can't change the ingrained message, but we can rationally decide that it is wrong and override it. However, that may be more difficult to do when the message prompts us to physical gratifications, when we are trying to change a long-standing habit, and/or when we happen to be tired or under unusual stress.

This interpretation of Schelling's inner struggle leads to the dichtomous-in-two-dimensions structure illustrated by Figure 5.2. I have commented in the text on how these might interact and on research that might be based on these interactions. I will only add here a remark or two on the discussion to this point. For one thing, it would be a mistake to treat the good kid and lazy kid that Schelling uses at one point to illustrate his article, or equivalent formulations, as qualitatively similar entities in the way that both S-Smith and G-Smith in the FS dichotomy are both rational utility-maximizers, sharing common tastes, and differing solely in that one is oriented toward Smith's private interests exclusively and the other to his sense of group-interest. Schelling's dichotomy turns on a completely different kind of division. His pair (perhaps we should think of a pair of pairs, one for G-Smith, one for S-Smith) are – sometimes, for we have no reason to suppose that programmed Smith is usually, much less always in conflict with calculating Smith – in conflict over how best to use resources, even given an allocation between G- and S-Smith. Programmed Smith is dumb, but persistent; calculating Smith is weaker but clever, able to choose a strategy that takes account of what the other will do because programmed Smith (being programmed) has no surprises.

Finally, it is stimulating, I think, to take note of the possible interactions of the structure of analysis sketched here and (see the comments at the end of Chapter 3) Lumsden and Wilson's mathematical analysis of interactions between genes and culture. The line of analysis here would also lead to some obvious extension of the remarks on neuroses near the conclusion of Chapter 9.

In a forthcoming study (*Political Cognition*) I hope to begin to address this set of issues, especially the way that social judgments are shaped by reasoning that is constrained by unconscious cognitive rules and habits. I expect these constraints will turn out to be reasonably loose in terms of what is wired into the human brain, but strong in terms of culturally induced mind sets broadly construed (paradigms in science, ideologies in politics). This line of inquiry can tell us a lot, I think, about social phenomena such as polarization and response to risk.

G. Notes on further psychological issues

The predominant tendency of economic theorists has been to stay clear of psychological issues. In particular, and despite Veblen, the almost universal tendency has been to take "tastes as given." For example, Olson (and many others have taken the same position) essentially defines the domain of economic theory as the study of efficient choice, *given* preferences. The study of preference formation itself he assigns to the other social sciences.[1] In recent years, however, there has been some break with this tradition of no psychology in the work of such prominent figures as Scitovsky, Schelling, and Leibenstein.[2]

As already illustrated in Appendix F, the FS analysis would push further in that direction, although I will do no more now than give several illustrations of psychological issues that arise in the context of working through the implications of the FS utility calculus applied to voting (Chapter 7).

1. Few people seem inclined to doubt that voting is a reasonable use of resources from the point of view of group-interest. Nevertheless people are often surprised by the quantitative confirmation of this point reviewed in Chapter 7. In other words, people are often "surprised" to find that something they already believed is in fact a reasonable belief.

2. The answers we get to questions about the value of voting turn sensitively on just how the question is posed. From the point of view of social psychology, this is not very surprising; much work has been done on the subtle ways in which the precise framing and context of questions (as in opinion polling) influence the elicited judgment.

   From the point of view of rational choice, though, it comes as a surprise to realize that, if we ask what Smith thinks a vote is worth, the answers we get are very different from those we get if we ask specifically for "S-answers" and "G-answers". The logic of the theory says that Smith's value is just the sum of S-wtp and G-wtp. Part of the problem here seems to stem from a triggering effect of focusing Smith on S-preferences if we ask in terms of what Smith is willing to pay, G-Smith not being especially interested in Smith and S-Smith being interested only in Smith. But it also seems to reflect Smith's existing allocation between S- and G-resources. Given that allocation, he is apt to misjudge drastically how he would choose in a situation that presents him with radically unfamiliar spending opportunities.

3. Voting is a little like choosing to redeem the deposit on a bottle. You have something of value in hand; and suppose the value is perishable (as when you are leaving the area in which the bottle can be redeemed, as may happen on a vacation trip). How likely are you to redeem the bottle as a function of how much bother it is to do so? (How likely is Smith to bother to vote, given his judgment of the value of voting?) In terms of S-preferences, the vote is unlikely to be worth more than a small fraction of a penny, and it will hardly seem worth bothering to vote even if Smith happens to be walking past the polling place and there is no waiting line. But in terms of G-preferences, a substantial effort may be made – with perhaps some nontrivial part of the effort reflecting the psychology of the redeemable item. This would add also to the "salience" effect on voting noted in the discussion of social rules of thumb in Chapter 5, and to the discussion of programmed versus calculated judgments in Appendix F.

Inquiry into the kind of issues sketched here falls mainly to social psychology rather than economics or political science. For example, the remarks under point 2 imply that, given an actual opportunity to change the outcome of an election, Smith's behavior would be far more self-sacrificing than he realizes. Dealing with a situation in which Smith has no experience, even secondhand vicarious experience (as he might imagine how he would behave if given the opportunity to save a drowning child, for example), we should not be terribly surprised if Smith's answer to the "how much would you sacrifice" question in the voting context is colored by his existing allocation of resources between group- and self-interested spending. If he is now in equilibrium, it will be hard for him to envision making some enormous sacrifice to benefit his view of group-interest. Given the actual opportunity, though, he would find G'/S' has suddenly assumed an enormous value, and only a correspondingly large shift in his resources to group-interest will bring him back into equilibrium.

This prediction of FS is not directly testable. We can hardly arrange for Smith actually to be able to determine the outcome of the next presidential election. But it would certainly be possible to study situations in which extraordinary opportunities for acts highly advantageous to an individual's sense of social values arise and examine the extent to which individuals act in ways that reflect a stronger commitment to social values than they themselves realized beforehand they were capable of. Similarly, one could examine situations in which G'/S' suddenly diminishes and look for whether selfish behavior follows, to an extent unexpected by the individual beforehand.

Indeed, if FS works empirically, one would expect it to be possible to arrange experiments in which the same individual behaves both more generously and more selfishly than he himself would have predicted, with the behavior in each case predicted beforehand by contrived changes in the value ratio.

This topic has some bearing on the controversy within social psychology over the relative merits of attributional versus situational accounts of behavior.

Notes

Preface

1. John Chamberlin, "Provision of Public Goods as a Function of Group Size," *APSR* (June 1974).
2. Amartya Sen, "Rational Fools," *Philosophy and Public Affairs* (1977). I am not conscious of being directly influenced by this, but I have learned that memory is an unreliable guide on such matters. I first saw the paper sometime in 1978, or perhaps 1979; so it may or may not have had some specific influence. In any case, Sen, starting with an economic theorist's awareness that technical difficulties arise when allowance is made for altruism within the conventional framework, was led to a distinction between what he called "sympathy" and "commitment"; he concluded that to allow for the latter it seems necessary to allow that individuals have more than one set of preferences. Sen's distinction is, I believe, essentially the distinction between what I call egoistic altruism and group-interested motivation. See the discussion of this point at the beginning of Chapter 8.

Introduction

1. The notion that my G- and S-functions might be interpreted as if there were a two-person society "inside Smith" comes from Joshua Cohen's comments on an early draft.

   The preceding material, along with parts of Chapter 4, is reprinted from my "A New Model of Rational Choice," *Ethics* (January 1981), with permission of the University of Chicago Press.

Chapter 1. Overview

1. See, for example, Jacob Marschak, "Decision-Making: Economic Aspects," in *The International Encyclopedia of the Social Sciences* (Free Press, 1968).
2. The technical term *public goods* must be understood as defined by the property that such goods can be available simultaneously to more than one (ordinarily to many or all) members of the society. Such a good is not *necessarily* a good provided by the government, nor is it necessarily a good in the usual economic sense of a commodity or service. An election outcome, or a choice of policy, or a law are all public goods: every member of society "has" this good. This usage is due mainly to Samuelson and (with respect to its natural extension to policies, etc.) to Olson in his *Logic of Collective Action* (Harvard University Press, 1965).

171

The best textbook treatment I have run across is James Buchanan, *The Demand and Supply of Public Goods* (Rand McNally, 1968); but it is essential to read Samuelson's own papers, most conveniently in his *Collected Scientific Papers,* 3 vols. (MIT Press, 1966, 1972). Not all of these are technically difficult, and the later ones are often concerned with clearing up misinterpretations of the notion, including one or two by Buchanan. Finally, note that the term *good* itself is a term of art, carrying no evaluative connotation: national defense is perhaps the most commonly cited example of a public good. But if you are a pacifist, you may see nothing good about it. The same "good" may have positive value for Smith, zero for Jones, and negative for Williams.

3. For a recent survey of this work, with an extensive bibliography, see Dennis Mueller, *Public Choice* (Cambridge, 1979). A short list of the best-known work would have to include at least: Kenneth J. Arrow, *Social Choice and Individual Values,* rev. ed. (Wiley, 1963); Paul Samuelson, "Pure Theory of Public Expenditure and Taxation," in *Collected Scientific Papers;* James Buchanan and Gordon Tullock, *The Calculus of Consent* (University of Michigan Press, 1962); Anthony Downs, *An Economic Theory of Democracy* (Harper & Row, 1957); M. Olson, *The Logic of Collective Action;* Albert Hirschman, *Exit, Voice and Loyalty* (Harvard University Press, 1970); and Thomas Schelling, *Micromotives and Macrobehavior* (Norton, 1978). For a sympathetic, yet critical, appraisal of this kind of work, see Brian Barry, *Sociologists, Economists and Democracy* (1970; reprint, University of Chicago Press, 1978).

4. Because of the ambiguity with which economists use the term *self-interest* (see Chapter 6), it is hard to be quite sure when this view is being taken, in contrast to that of the next point.

5. A particularly eloquent statement can be found in Phillip Wicksteed, *The Common Sense of Political Economy* (1910; reprint, Kelley, 1962). Another important statement of this view is in Lionel Robbins, *On the Nature and Significance of Economic Science* (1935; reprint, St. Martins, 1962), which is read by nearly every reasonably well-trained economist. Certainly this is the prevailing view among contemporary economists.

6. In addition to Barry, *Sociologists, Economists, and Democracy,* see Mancur Olson, "Economics, Sociology, and the Best of All Possible Worlds," *Public Interest* (Summer, 1968).

7. Leon Feistinger, *A Theory of Cognitive Dissonance* (Row, Peterson, 1957).

8. Quoted in William Niskanen, *Bureaucracy and Representative Government* (Aldine-Atherton, 1971), p. 8.

9. See the further comment related to this, Chapter 4.

10. A general survey is given by David Collard, *Altruism and the Economy: A Study in Non-Selfish Economics* (Oxford University Press, 1978). An especially interesting paper in our context, one concerned directly with an economic view of altruism in the context of a Darwinian model, is Jack Hirshleifer, "Natural Economy vs. Political Economy," Department of Economics Working Paper, no. 114, University of California at Los Angeles, 1979. See also, Norman Frohlich and Joe Oppenheimer, "I Get by with a Little Help from my Friends," *World Politics*

(October 1970), for an approach to altruistic motivation in formal modeling by political scientists; and "The Value – and Limits – of Sociobiology" by Roger Masters for a political philosopher's exploration of a Darwinian approach to social analysis, in Eliot White, ed., *Sociobiology and Human Values* (Lexington, 1981).

11. The problem of finding a plausible explanation of voting in terms of rational choice came to prominence in Downs, *An Economic Theory of Democracy.* For a sampling of efforts to deal with these issues after nearly twenty years, see the symposium in the *American Political Science Review,* June 1975. The issue is discussed in detail in Chapter 7.

12. Downs gives a particularly good account of his argument in an article summarizing his book, "An Economic Theory of Political Action in a Democracy." *Journal of Political Economy,* 1957). One of the best post-Downs contributions is in Gordon Tullock, *Toward a Mathematics of Politics,* (University of Michigan Press, 1967), which was the book that first aroused my own interest in this field.

13. Dennis Mueller, *Public Choice* (Cambridge, 1979).

14. An elegant survey, with many original results, is Amartya Sen, *Collective Choice and Social Welfare* (Holden-Day, 1970).

15. In Vilfredo Pareto, "Mathematical Economics," reprinted in J. Gerrity, ed., *Economic Theory: A Historical Anthology* (Random House, 1965).

16. A partial exception to these remarks is the way that Sen sometimes uses the notion of utility in his work on social justice. The exception is only partial in that, although Sen is an economist and uses mathematical techniques familiar mainly to economists, this work is essentially moral philosophy. As it happens, in terms of the theory I will be developing Sen's usage is essentially congenial. The internal S- and G-utilities that I use turn out to be cardinal in character and could be interpreted in Sen's fashion. However, a "total" utility function fitted to the theory could not. See the technical discussion in Appendix C.

Chapter 2. Paradoxes

1. See note 11, Chapter 1.

2. The most elegant and insightful treatment of PD (extended to multiperson contexts) is Thomas Schelling, *Micromotives and Macrobehavior* (Norton, 1978).

3. Robert D. Luce and Howard Raiffa, *Games and Decisions* (Wiley, 1957).

4. See, for example, the results reported in Anatol Rapoport and Abraham Chammah, *Prisoner's Dilemma* (Michigan University Press, 1965).

The following comments on the paradox may be of interest, although they are not essential to anything in the main text:

If the payoffs are in units of utility, then the paradox is just a description of a terrible situation, like dying of thirst on a raft in the middle of the ocean. However, no real world game can have payoffs defined in utiles, which are psychic entities existing only in the mind of the evaluator. The payoff must be things in the external world, such as dollars. The *players*, not the organizer of the game, make the evaluation in terms of utiles. Since that evaluation rationally must include the effect of behavior on the first play on expectations of payoff from the balance, there is no necessary reason why the PD dollar payoffs imply (even for perfectly selfish players) PD utility payoffs. For in this situation, how could Smith be certain (as is essential to the logic of the paradox) that Jones will defect early? If not, why should he?

There is a paradox here, but not (I think) a paradox in utility theory. Rather, it is a linguistic paradox akin to the self-referential paradoxes brought to prominence by Bertrand Russell ("Smith says he is lying. Is he telling the truth?"). "The rational thing for a perfectly selfish man to do in this situation is to behave as if he were not perfectly selfish. He behaves as if he were not perfectly selfish. Should his behavior be described as perfectly selfish?"

5. I give an account in "Public Goods and Group Size," unpublished paper, September 1974. As mentioned in the Preface, it was apparently the paradoxical result of this paper that stimulated my first notion of the equilibrium condition around which the present study is built.

6. John Chamberlin, "Provision of Public Goods as a Function of Group Size," *APSR* (June 1974); Martin McGuire, "Group Size, Group Homogeneity, and the Aggregate Provision of a Pure Public Good Under Cournot Behavior," *Public Choice* (Summer 1974). Chamberlin does not give the result explicitly, although he was aware of it (personal communication); McGuire's Equation 5 does give the result, but without comment.

7. See, for example, Gary Becker, *The Economic Approach to Human Behavior* (University of Chicago Press, 1976); Harold Hochman and James Rogers, "Pareto Optimal Redistribution," *American Economic Review* (September 1969).

8. By a serious effort, I mean one in which some effort at sustained analysis is made so that the work faces the difficulties developed here and in the diagramatic treatment in Appendix A. There are, of course, many papers in which "psychic income" or some variant is inserted into a verbal discussion or (more rarely) into a formal model to "save the appearances."

Chapter 3. A Darwinian argument

1. Edward Wilson, *Sociobiology* (Harvard University Press, 1975).

2. "Economic man" is always understood to include his family.

3. The best popular account, with references to the technical literature, is probably Richard Dawkins, *The Selfish Gene* (Oxford University Press, 1976). The ESS notion and its role in recent discussions of the evolution of altruism is due to John Maynard-Smith, *On Evolution* (Edinburgh University Press, 1973).

4. Up to the point, of course, when further increases in W yield no further advantage in within-group competition. Roughly, we can think of W as being in the range of 1 to N, where N = number of members in the group.

5. We have, I think, strong grounds to postulate something along the lines of Equation 3.3 for the reason given. But the argument given does not necessarily lead to the simple ratio form, although it seems to me entirely reasonable to choose this form for the work described here. For some further discussion of this matter, see Appendix B.

6. George Williams, *Sex and Evolution* (Princeton University Press, 1975). Williams, in turn, credits Maynard-Smith with strongly influencing his argument. It is, I think, worth noting that these two writers are among the most frequently cited critics of group-selection. My impression, frankly, is that the most adamant denials of the plausibility of a significant role for group-selection, especially in the context of human evolution, are not the leading theorists themselves but their interpreters in the social sciences.

7. Stephen J. Gould, "Evolutionary Biology of Constraints," *Daedalus* (Spring 1980); David Layzer, "Altruism and Natural Selection," *Journal of Social and Biological Structures* (1978).

8. The work of writers such as Williams, Trivers, Maynard-Smith, and Hamilton has pretty well driven the earlier versions of group-selection from the field. See Dawkins's review of this work in *The Selfish Gene*. Virtually no one now proposes evolution of characteristics merely as "for the good of the species." But a variety of writers in recent years have been working on mechanisms for group-selection that are not (obviously, or even at all) vulnerable to the earlier criticism, among them, those noted in the text. Others (such as Lumsden and Wilson and Eldredge and Gould, cited here) propose theories that, although not specifically addressing the question of group-selection, are nevertheless compatible with such a view.

9. Roy Eldredge and Stephen J. Gould, "Punctuated Equilibria: An Alternative to Phyletic Gradualism," in Thomas Schopf, ed., *Models in Paleobiology* (Freeman, Cooper, 1972), which has helped stimulate a large literature on "cladistics."

10. Layzer, "Altruism and Natural Selection."

11. See the concluding chapter of Wilson, *Sociobiology*, or of Dawkins, *The Selfish Gene.*

12. Charles Lumsden and E. O. Wilson, *Genes, Mind, and Culture* (Harvard University Press, 1982).

13. The usual claim is that the selfish gene view provides the most rigorous and parsimonious model. But this claim becomes vacuous to the extent that its exponents then allow themselves resort to such notions as "synthetic kin," fossil reciprocal altruism, and ad hoc appeals to cultural influences when the theory gets into trouble, as it frequently does in trying to account for the human behavior we can observe around us (including our own behavior). This is very much the kind of pseudorigor found in the economic analysis when a writer first postulates strictly egoistic choice but then feels free to invoke "psychic income," or what I call "egoistic altruism," when the theory gets into trouble. See the discussion on psychic income in Chapter 5 and on egoistic altruism in Chapter 7.

Chapter 4. A new model

1. For a discussion within the framework of this long philosophical tradition, see, for example, Stephen Salkever, "Who Knows Whether It's Rational to Vote?" *Ethics* (1980). One could compile an anthology of references to this insight: "Two hearts beat within my breast" (Goethe); "If I am not for myself, who am I; if I am not for others, what am I" (Hillel); Dr. Jeckyll and Mr. Hyde; and so on.

2. Kenneth J. Arrow, *Social Choice and Individual Values,* rev. ed. (Wiley, 1963); James Buchanan, "Individual Choice in Voting and the Market," *Journal of Political Economy* (August 1954); John Harsanyi, "Cardinal Welfare, Individualistic Ethics, and Interpersonal Comparisons of Utility," *Journal of Political Economy* (August 1955). A later article by Harsanyi is closer to the spirit of the present study, "Rational Choice Models of Political Behavior vs. Functional and Conformist Theories," *World Politics* (July 1969).
3. Harsanyi, "Cardinal Welfare," p. 315.
4. Ibid.

Chapter 5. Applying the FS model

1. These remarks are to be read in the context of the discussion that concludes Chapter 3. Perhaps it would be useful to add that saying that group-motivation presumably arose out of motivation that was strictly "selfish gene" in character is not a qualification of the earlier Darwinian argument any more than saying that a bird's wing developed from a reptile's claw implies that the wing is really "just" a claw.
2. Notice that this side-steps the most difficult problems that arise when we take note that various components of an individual's sense of group-interest will compete – at least in the sense of providing alternative uses for a given bit of resources, and sometimes in a more direct sense. However, one device that will be mentioned in later chapters is the role of ideology in integrating diverse components of group-interest into something that the individual – if not an outside observer – can find internally compatible.
3. Paul Samuelson, "Pure Theory of Public Expenditure and Taxation," in *Collected Scientific Papers,* vol. 3 (MIT Press, 1972). This is a restatement and elaboration of the seminal 1954 paper mentioned earlier.
4. Sigmund Freud, *The Ego and the Id,* trans. Joan Riviere (Norton, 1963), p. 52. The second half of the quote is Freud's footnote to the first.
5. Thomas Schelling, "The Intimate Contest for Self-Command," *Public Interest* (Summer 1980).
6. William Riker and Peter Ordeshook, "A Theory of the Calculus of Voting," *APSR* (March 1968); for Mueller's use of psychic income, see his *Public Choice* (Cambridge, 1979), p. 121, which also cites Barry.

Chapter 6. Translating across paradigms

1. Amartya Sen, "Rational Fools," *Philosophy and Public Affairs* (1977).
2. Thomas Kuhn, *The Structure of Scientific Revolutions,* 2d ed. (University of Chicago Press, 1970).
3. Dennis Mueller, *Public Choice* (Cambridge, 1979), ch. 4 gives a survey of this work. T. Nicolaus Tideman and Gordon Tullock give a relatively nontechnical account of their version of DR in "A New and Superior Process for Making Social Choices," *Journal of Political Economy* (December 1976). Theodore Groves and John Ledyard give a highly mathematical version of a variant mechanism

in "Optimal Allocation of Public Goods: A Solution to the 'Free Rider' Problem," *Econometrica* (May 1977). The basic idea behind DR was worked out a few years earlier by Groves and (independently) by Edward Clarke. Some of the comments in this chapter appeared in my review (*APSR*, July 1981) of Clarke's *Demand Revelation and the Provision of Public Goods* (Ballinger, 1980). A more detailed account of the thought experiment, with responses from Tullock and others was scheduled to appear in the journal *Public Choice*, 1982.

4. For a detailed introduction, see James Buchanan, *The Demand and Supply of Public Goods* (Rand McNally, 1968). But any reasonably recent microeconomics text will include a treatment of this topic.

5. That is, the outcome will be pareto-optimal, which means "efficient" in the sense that it is not possible to make anyone better off without making someone else worse off. Although that is all you need to know for the argument here, it may be helpful for noneconomists to emphasize that pareto-optimality has nothing to do with fairness or even with plausible judgments of reasonableness. If you and I are given $100 to divide, then any division that wastes nothing (for example, me $100 and you $0; or even me $110, you − $10) is pareto-optimal. Any division that wastes something (for example, me $49.95 and you $49.95, 10 cents thrown in the sewer) is not pareto-optimal. Things could have been improved for you without harming me by giving you the last dime. As this illustration shows, departures from pareto-optimality can be trivial, and it is easy to give examples where almost everyone would judge a given non–pareto-optimal outcome preferable to a given pareto-optimal alternative.

6. For a nonmathematical reader, the Tideman and Tullock paper would probably be the most easily grasped. I have tried to make the argument even simpler in my Public Choice Society paper (March 1981), but the presentation there is very condensed.

7. The somewhat roundabout wording of the two preceding sentences reflects, again, my argument of Chapter 4.

8. Gary Becker, *The Economic Approach to Human Behavior* (University of Chicago Press, 1976); Harold Hochman and James Rogers, "Pareto Optimal Redistribution," *American Economic Review* (September 1969); John Harsanyi, "Cardinal Welfare, Individualistic Ethics, and Interpersonal Comparisons of Utility," *Journal of Political Economy* (August 1955).

9. I have run across two kinds of exceptions. The first involves utility functions that allow for some variant of psychic income, as in William Riker and Peter Ordeshook, *An Introduction to Positive Political Theory* (Prentice-Hall, 1973), ch. 3; the other involves functions, as in Gary Becker, *The Economic Approach to Human Behavior* (University of Chicago Press, 1976), which use as arguments such things as social standing and self-image where (in contrast to the psychic income versions) these satisfactions can themselves be expressed as goods functions. As I mentioned in Chapter 2, I do not know of any case where the pure psychic income approach has been seriously sustained. On the other hand, in the Becker-like situations, the work has sometimes led to interesting results, but the utility functions do not violate T2 in any essential way.

10. As in the great majority of papers on DR, I will ignore all merely practical

questions: for example, the possibility that a person may not know his *wtp* for a public good or may feel that it is not worth the bother of thinking through a precise answer, or that the tax may be too small to collect, and so on. The only thing that is not assumed away here is the possibility that, even if given perfect information, real human beings may not want to respond to DR incentives the way the conventional theory says they ought to want to respond.

11. For if (as we have supposed) the sum of the tax prices per dollar across all citizens just equals the required dollar, and if the DR prices summed to the tax prices gives us the social *wtp* described above, then social *wtp* for a marginal dollar just equals the required dollar when the sum of the DR prices is zero. Notice that a voter's assigned tax price will be the same for any budget, Q (so his regular tax is Q times his tax price per dollar); but his DR price will depend on Q. Ordinarily it is assumed, and we assume here, that the voter's *wtp*, and hence also his DR price, declines as Q increases. In what follows, when I refer to the voter's DR price I mean the DR price at the value of Q that turns out to be the DR social outcome, Q^* (strictly speaking, but a trivial distinction in a large society, at the outcome that would have been chosen had this voter abstained).

12. If I value a good positively and I am interested only in myself (*or* if I obey T3), the sum of my tax price and DR price (which is my *wtp* at Q) must be positive. So the negative DR prices of a voter who thinks the budget is too high cannot be larger (in fact cannot be as large) in absolute magnitude as his tax price; hence, barring some very peculiar distribution of voter preferences, the DR prices near Q^* of typical voters who favor a larger budget also cannot vary much from the average tax price. But anyone who "spends the penny" will have an enormous DR price, as illustrated by the first column in Table 6.1, positive if he prefers a larger budget, negative if the opposite.

13. See, for example, Tideman and Tullock's calculation, which estimates the total DR taxes across all U.S. taxpayers for the total U.S. federal budget as $2000. Scaled to the $1 billion item considered here, the DR tax on a typical voter must be, as shown in Table 6.1, on the order of .00001 cent.

14. The elasticity will equal the percent change in the social *wtp* if Q is increased by 1 percent. It will ordinarily be a number fairly close to 1. Following Tideman and Tullock, I happen to have used 2 in the calculations here.

15. Specifically, the conventional analysis (tacitly) assumes that T3 holds, even if T1 does not.

16. Edward Clarke, *Demand Revelation and the Provision of Public Goods* (Ballinger, 1980); Jerry Greene and J. J. Laffont, *Incentives in Public Decision-Making* (North Holland, 1979).

17. One of the oddities that results from the fact that these assumptions are almost always only tacit is that this important result is *not* one that will ordinarily be found in an economics text. Because the assumptions are tacit, the question of what happens if they are violated just does not arise. The result, however, is well known to theorists. See, for example, G. C. Archibald and Donald Donaldson, "Notes on Economic Equality," *Journal of Public Economics* 12 (1979).

18. I have avoided discussion of normative questions, but not because I judge them either unimportant or not very usefully examined in terms of the FS view. The basic claim of the argument is that the FS model works empirically: it describes (much better, at least, than any alternative I know) how people actually choose. It seemed to me that it would only invite confusion on this vital point if I gave anything more than passing reference in the study to questions of how people *ought* to behave or what government ought or ought not to try to do.

Chapter 7. Voting behavior

1. See, for example, the *APSR* symposium of June 1975, or the discussion in Brian Barry, *Sociologists, Economists and Democracy* (1970; reprint, University of Chicago Press, 1978).
2. This can be elaborated on as circumstances and taste for detail require. The probability that your vote changes the outcome is the probability that your vote breaks a tie (or makes a tie), discounted by the probability that your preferred candidate wins in the event of a tie. I show a simple way to estimate the probability of a tie as a function of uncertainty, size of electorate, and so on, in "Probability of a Tie Vote," *Public Choice* (Winter 1977).
3. Gordon Tullock, *Toward a Mathematics of Politics* (University of Michigan Press, 1967), p. 112.
4. Suppose, however, that as a gesture to a friend you chose the ticket with the prize he or she would prefer, even though if given the direct choice you would not have done so. But that would illustrate exactly the distinction between contingent and noncontingent benefits. There is a value to the gesture (noncontingent benefit), and it is not inconsistent with the sure-thing principle that a situation arises in which the contingent benefit of your preferred prize (the differential in value, discounted by the probability you have a winning ticket) is less than the noncontingent benefit.
5. The qualification "the conventional notion of" in this sentence is needed because, in terms of FS, we will be led (as you will see in a moment) to frame the questions for rational calculation differently, and for reasons discussed in Appendix G this turns out to lead to a different result.
6. We need to distinguish here between the personal sense of duty, yielding Smith personal psychic income, and the objective finding – for example, by polling – that the general view is that a citizen has a duty to vote. The remarks here deal with the former. We could probably develop a viable account of duty if in fact people act out of a sense of duty whenever the behavior is generally regarded by members of their society as a duty. Notice that in this case we could eliminate (personal) duty from the actor's decision calculus: we could say, "Smith votes because he follows a general sentiment in his society that citizens ought to vote," instead of, "Smith *feels a duty to vote because he* follows the general sentiment, and therefore he votes."

   As it happens, this treatment of personal duty in terms of social norms (Smith does his duty when he thinks others think he has a duty) does not work very well to account for voting. For one thing, the response that a citizen has a duty to vote turns out to be highly correlated with whether that individual votes. So we have the ambiguity of cause and effect noted in the hypnosis illustration of the text. Furthermore, we would not be surprised to find that most people report that a citizen has a duty to pay taxes, but we would hardly conclude that taxes would be paid voluntarily or that those who vote would also pay taxes voluntarily.

7. I do not mean, of course, to rule out the rule-of-thumb role (see Chapter 5) of the sense of citizen duty to vote, which is discussed a little later. But there the role of the sense that there is a duty to vote is a satisficing rule, which simplifies Smith's decision making, not an excuse for choices that are otherwise inexplicable as a rational use of G-resources.

8. Tullock has pointed out that turnout was also low even in the primaries. But poll taxes, segregation, and the difficulty of establishing easily understood differentials absent party competition seem sufficient to account for that.

9. This point would apply mainly to someone who attached a high social value to demonstrating his adherence to (his conception of) rational choice. If I could convert Gordon Tullock to FS, I might also persuade him to vote.

10. Exceptions consistent with the basic theory do arise, as discussed below.

11. Except in an opportunity cost sense, this will also ordinarily hold for spending in general: the way Smith uses G-resources is not ordinarily contrary to his S-preferences, and vice-versa, for the reason discussed at the end of Chapter 4. Taking account of opportunity costs, of course, the situation is very different. Ordinarily, as Mosca notes in the remark from which we started, there is a clear conflict between the *best* way to use a bit of resources as between maximizing self-interest versus group-interest. The point here is that for Smith as voter there will often be little conflict even in an opportunity cost sense. The positions of candidates are themselves like public goods, not like private goods, which can be tailored to an individual's tastes. So, even in a world where individuals in fact acted only out of narrow self-interest (were social life, hence politics, possible in such a world) political appeals would have to be wide appeals to the electorate as a whole or to groups within the electorate, with care taken to frame those appeals so as not to alienate other groups avoidably. Only if (to use a term from Olson) selective appeals were possible – as, for example, if vote buying were legal – would it ordinarily be true that Smith's self-interest could easily diverge far from his sense of group-interest in the context of voting. But as noted in the text, it is just where such a divergence arises that we can test the model best.

12. Why would Smith vote in that context? Aside from the peculiar situation noted in (2), he may go to the polls undecided but expecting to be able to decide. However, if he still cannot make up his mind in terms of G-preferences, S-preferences would govern (the cost of voting then being a sunk cost). Or, Smith may go to the polls knowing whom his G-preferences favor for senator, but he has no G-preferences with respect to some local offices, so he votes his S-preferences for those offices.

13. Some further remarks on ideology will be found in Chapter 8.

Chapter 8. Leaders and followers

1. Anthony Downs, *An Economic Theory of Democracy* (Harper & Row, 1957); Mancur Olson, *The Logic of Collective Action* (Harvard University Press, 1965). Of the books cited in note 3, Chapter 1, these are the only two that both deal with empirical issues and explicitly postulate (for purposes of the analysis) self-interested choice. Of the others, Kenneth J. Arrow, *Social Choice and Individual Values,* rev. ed. (Wiley, 1963), and James Buchanan and Gordon Tullock, *The Calculus of Consent* (University of Michigan Press, 1962), are normative; Arrow again, Albert Hirschman, *Exit, Voice and Loyalty* (Harvard University Press, 1970), and Thomas Schelling, *Micromotives and Macrobehavior* (Norton, 1978), do not assume specifically self-interested motivation.

2. The best statement of Downs's argument, I think, is not in his book, but in his summary article, "An Economic Theory of Political Action in a Democracy," *Journal of Political Economy* (1957).

3. Downs, "Economic Theory," p. 259.

4. Downs, "Economic Theory," p. 267. Downs goes on to argue (p. 268) that social responsibility itself can be understood in terms of (indirect, long-term) self-interest. A citizen may vote, Downs says, because he does not want to act in a way that, if everyone acted that way, would be bad for himself. But this argument requires as a premise that the individual be prepared to act in terms of social responsibility; otherwise he would prefer free-riding.

5. Downs, "Economic Theory," pp. 27, 28.

6. "In reality, men are not always selfish, even in politics. They frequently do what appears to be individually irrational because they believe it is socially rational, that is, it benefits others even though it harms them personally. For example, politicians in the real world sometimes act as they think best for society as a whole, even when they know their actions will lose votes." (Downs, "Economic Theory," p. 27.)

7. Downs, "Economic Theory," p. 37.

8. The experience of auto clubs illustrates this point. In an early enough period, many members probably saw themselves as serving not merely their self-interest but a wider social interest (naturally, most readily perceived by car owners) in good roads and the rest of the infrastructure that would support this revolutionary mode of transportation. With time, the plausibility of a social need for an organization to speak for car owners has weakened. Auto clubs have come to depend almost entirely on selective benefits. Yet they are not really a model for the Olson analysis, because in the course of this they have become almost irrelevant to public policy affecting automobiles, especially outside of California. Before the passage in 1970 of the Muskie amendments to the Clean Air Act, environmental organizations and the auto industry were active, but the automobile clubs appear to have played no role, although by far the largest economic stake was that of the automobile owners (see my "Politics of Auto Emissions," *Public Interest* (Fall 1977). Hence, even when strong individual incentives were available, a dispersed (but in the aggregate very large) interest was not mobilized when, in the mood of that time, the interest could not be

easily identified with some plausible notion of the public interest. At the other extreme, organizations such as the Sierra Club appear to partially subsidize some of their more nearly selective benefits (trail huts for hikers, and so on) from funds raised mainly on broad environmental appeals – precisely the opposite of the Olson thesis. See Russell Hardin, *Collective Action* (Johns Hopkins University Press, 1982), ch. 7. That is why it is important to note that Olson allows that the theory may work poorly to the extent that the interests an organization promotes depart from narrow economic interests.

9. Of course, the organization is also motivated to create arguments useful in propaganda to outsiders. However, ideology goes beyond that, as discussed near the end of Chapter 7. And, of course, there would be no point to such an effort unless the targets of the appeal could in fact be moved to some extent by appeals not directed at their own self-interest.

10. Olson, *The Logic of Collective Action,* p. 64. Olson presumably means to exclude highly dramatic (hence publicity-generating) variants of this, such as milk-spilling in the context of farm protests.

11. Ibid., p. 13.

12. A derivative can be infinitely large although it is the ratio between two infinitesimally small quantities.

13. An important qualification, which has already been mentioned in the context of voting in Chapter 7 and in the more abstract discussion of Appendix E, concerns donations that may be observed by others whose good will Smith has reason to value. Strictly, then, the remark of the text applies only to an *anonymous* donation. See the further comments later in this chapter and in Chapter 9.

14. See Paul Samuelson, "Social Indifference Curves," which does (tacitly) assume T2, in his *Collected Scientific Papers,* vol. 3 (MIT Press, 1972).

15. The argument about perceptibility is not quite justified even in terms of the conventional model. Suppose Smith takes a vitamin pill this morning. Surely this has no perceptible effect on his health (as opposed to skipping the pill this morning). In fact, taking the pills every morning is hardly likely to have a perceptible effect. All that the economic man view requires is that Smith believe that taking the pills is good for him. Why then should we require that Smith see the effect of his $10 donation, or the effect of his vote? So the reason such behavior is hard to account for in terms of the conventional model is not simply that the effects are imperceptible. It is because, if we go through the kind of analysis given in Chapter 7 with respect to voting, or through the abstract analysis of "shiboleth" allocation rules in Samuelson, "Social Indifference Curves," tacitly using T2, we are led to the conclusion that Smith's behavior is inconsistent with his behavior on other matters. Hence the conclusion that such contributions are irrational under the conventional model is correct, but the mere appeal to "imperceptibility" elides some of the argument needed to support the conclusion. Under FS, of course, T2 does not hold, and the (apparent) inconsistency does not arise.

16. See the discussion of the term *public good* in note 2, Chapter 1.

17. Because I face both the problem of informing the customer (for example, that my product costs a little more than my competitor's because I am being more

careful about the environment) and the problem of persuading the customer that accepting my higher costs is a good use of *his* G-resources.

18. In particular, we will see why Smith's G-motivation does not ordinarily lead him away from profit-maximizing behavior.
19. James Q. Wilson, *Political Organization* (Basic Books, 1973).
20. Of course, if the friend is a competent recruiter, he will certainly have something to say about how terrible the disease is, or why it is getting less financial support than it deserves; and if sufficiently persuasive, this could elicit resources to this outlet for G-spending which Smith otherwise would have spent on his self-interest. However, when this happens, it is no longer a pure case of Smith's behavior being triggered by a minor private benefit.

Chapter 9. Sketch of further applications

1. For the loser, G' (fighting the war) will decline; but G' (helping with recuperation) may remain high.
2. I have not discussed, in particular, the S-component of such behavior, which will be negligible when the behavior is anonymous (not littering when walking alone on the beach at night), but not ordinarily so otherwise.
3. Vernon Smith, "Experiments with a Decentralized Mechanism for Public Good Decisions," *American Economic Review* (September 1980); and Friedrich Schneider and Werner Pommerehns, "Free-Riding and Collective Action," *Quarterly Journal of Economics* (in press).
4. Morris Fiorina and Charles Plott, "Committee Decision Under Majority Rule: An Experimental Study," *APSR* (June 1978). See also, in the same issue, Richard McKelvey, Peter Ordeshook, and Mark Winer, "The Competitive Solution for N-Person Games Without Transferable Utility, with an Application to Committee Games," *APSR* (June 1978). Superficially, the two sets of games are very similar; but the results are sometimes strikingly different. What this reflects is the great importance, in such a gaming simulation of social choice, of what may be termed the "culture" of the game. Essentially, in the Fiorina and Plott experiments, the decision process was much closer to the kind of decision process used in actual social choice contexts. Within the (important) constraints noted in the text, the game was a kind of parliamentary process in the small. On the other hand, in the McKelvey, Ordeshook, and Winer game, the decision process was arranged in a way that looked like a competitive parlor game, such as musical chairs, and the results reflect that.
5. An easy geometrical argument shows that, given any four points, which form a quadrilateral, there will exist a unique dominant point in the interior, located at the intersection of the diagonals.
6. The players were in the same room, so obviously the "no-communication" rule was not rigidly enforceable.
7. That is, the players were allowed to say things such as, "That move would hurt me a lot," but never, "That would reduce my payoff from \$20 to only \$5." The restriction to qualitative communication was important, for the reason discussed in note 9.

8. Fiorina and Plott, "Committee Decision," p. 594.

9. Differences in the payoff schedules were such that the total payoff to the group of players was actually maximized at a point somewhat northwest of the zone defined by the payoff breaks in Figures 9.1 and 9.2. But special pains were taken to prevent the players from ever learning of this (see note 7). So it is puzzling why the authors should interpret the results as inconsistent with altruistic choice. If we imagine an observer trying only to be fair, who knew only what the players themselves were permitted to know, then it is obvious that he would choose an outcome inside the payoff breaks.

10. Phillip Wicksteed, *The Common Sense of Political Economy* (1910; reprint, Routledge and Kegan Paul, 1933).

11. Recall, as discussed in Chapter 5 and in Appendix E that "non-subversiveness" leads us to expect that taxes are allocated between G- and S-spending, not all allocated to G-Smith.

12. This is certainly an oversimplified remark; we do not expect the scheme of Chapter 5 to be exactly applicable. In the world we do not have the neat arrangement of programs and associated tax prices of the formal analysis. But it is as much as can be said here.

13. This sketch, even more than other material in this chapter, is subject to the cautionary remarks about far-reaching inferences made earlier. On the other hand, inferences of this kind, although necessarily speculative and not (foreseeably) amenable to convincing empirical test, nevertheless often turn out to be important. For more conventional views of this topic in terms of rational choice and detailed citations to the literature, see Richard Auster and Morris Cohen, *The State as Firm* (Martinus Nijhoff, 1979); James Buchanan, Robert Tollison, and Gordon Tullock, *Towards a Theory of the Rent-Seeking Society* (Texas A&M University Press, 1980).

14. I take for granted the existence of human aggregates (canonically, tribes of five hundred, consisting of twenty or so living groups of twenty-five or so individuals) up to just short of the scale at which at least part-time specialists in government of the society emerge. We want to consider here the evolution of larger aggregates (loosely speaking, the evolution of the state). If the recent and controversial work of Lumsden and Wilson discussed at the conclusion of Chapter 3 should hold up, it would be highly significant for this topic. My own hunch is that their work will, in fact, prove to be significant. But it is too early to say anything more specific, and their ideas on "co-evolution" (of genes and culture) are not used here.

15. A more conventional view (in terms of rational choice) – see Buchanan, Tollison, and Tullock, *Towards a Theory of the Rent-Seeking Society* – stresses the role of sheer exploitation. Essentially, some people get together to exploit the rest (or to exploit their neighbors). Acquiesence is obtained by the combination of carrots (sufficient provision of public goods, including protection from other exploiters) and sticks (coercion). Historically, it would be naive to deny the significance of these effects. However, an account limited to exploitation does not explain how the exploiters are able to organize themselves well enough to do their exploiting; nor does it account in a way that seems realistic for much in the way of state

building, where exploitation seems only a side issue, if a serious issue at all (to be cynical is no guarantee against being naive in a perverse instead of soft-hearted way). Nor, finally, does it account for the long-term stability of many aspects of societies, the rate at which they are often reestablished after some natural or man-made disasters, the loyalties they command.

16. *Rationalize* here means three things, only the last of which would yield a direct G-contribution to a powerful individual's personal well-being. Private spending may be rationalized in a manipulative way to make it more palatable to the general public. It may be rationalized in a self-deceptive way, to the extent that the individual feels committed to principles that are inconsistent with private enrichment, yet feels out of equilibrium without the enrichment ($W > G'/S'$). The first concerns what the public is told, the second what the individual tells himself. Neither directly affects the individual's allocation, although indirect effects need not be wholly insignificant. However, the individual will also have some judgment about the best distribution of income – in particular the share to the well-off – and, even on Rawls's argument, this does not rule out private enrichment of leading individuals. Opinions naturally will differ on the optimal distribution of income, even among individuals with a common sense of social values. Further, these differences are not merely self-serving. (It is certainly empirically false that all economists in modest circumstances are skeptical of President Reagan's economic views and that all prosperous economists accept them.) However, we would all expect some tendency for those who will prosper under a view to be readier to believe that view than those who benefit only indirectly at best. In this (weakest) sense of *rationalize*, where an individual's belief might even be objectively correct although his degree of belief exceeds what he should objectively feel, the G- versus S-allocation could be directly affected.

17. That is, in terms of FS there is no reason to take seriously such notions as "noble blood." "Noble" propensities turn on more than wealth alone, the sub-culture in which an individual is raised and in which he lives certainly being significant. But there is nothing inherently genetic about such propensities.

18. See, for example, Michael Taylor, *Anarchy and Cooperation* (Wiley, 1976). But it seems to me that Taylor's optimistic conclusions depend on a tacit assumption with respect to the neatness with which it would be possible to distinguish cooperative from free-rider behavior. The problem is not merely what happens when someone behaves in a way that unambiguously identifies them (if observed) as a lout, but that there are many in-between situations ("I meant to cooperate, but I forgot"; "I had a headache"; "I honestly don't think that task is worth-while"; "I was working as hard as I could"; and so on. The nearest child will be able to provide details.) Taking account of ambiguity limits (severely, I would agree) the feasible scale of anarchic societies.

19. In a small community a larger component of voluntary contributions would commonly be chargeable to S-spending (because the "other people will notice" effect will be more important) and to jointly optimal gs spending (see p. 139). Hence an individual spending a given fraction of resources in the form of voluntary contributions would tend to have a lower participation ratio (g/s; hence W, will be

smaller) than similar behavior would produce in a large society. In other words, it will be less nearly true in a small than in a large community that voluntary contributions will ordinarily consist almost entirely of G-spending.

Aside from the "others may be watching" effect, we should not assume that the value ratio will be more favorable to socially useful behavior in small rather than large societies. However, taking account of the "others may be watching" effect, we expect S' to be lower for conspicuously selfish uses of resources. In sum, then, other things being equal, we expect in a small society that (for a given set of resource choices) W will be smaller, G'/S' larger, so that the equilibrium allocation (from the result on p. 40 or P3, Appendix C) will be larger in the small society.

Appendix A. Goods versus participation altruism

1. Gary Becker, *The Economic Approach to Human Behavior* (University of Chicago Press, 1976), pp. 253–94, esp. pp. 273–5.
2. Jack Hirshleifer, "Shakespeare vs. Becker on Altruism: The Importance of Having the Last Word," *Journal of Economic Literature* (June 1977).
3. Harold Hochman and James Rogers, "Pareto Optimal Redistribution," *American Economic Review* (September 1969).
4. If we interpret Figure A.1 in the large charity context, with the shift from I to $I+$ representing a fractionally tiny shift in Charity's income, Smith's donation would drop from a substantial fraction of his income (the vertical distance between X and P) to zero, because Smith would now actually prefer that Charity donate to Smith ($P+$ being slightly higher on the vertical axis than is X, which still gives Smith's income).
5. Jerry Rothenberg suggested a figure of this sort, replacing a much clumsier one I had worked out.

B. The FS Model

1. James Buchanan, *What Should Economists Do?* (Liberty Press, 1979).

C. Properties of the FS model

1. G. C. Archibald and Donald Donaldson, "Notes on Economic Equality," *Journal of Public Economics* 12 (1979).
2. I was hardly immune to this temptation. The following is from the early draft mentioned in the Preface:

> A slightly theological interpretation: man has some instinct for following the Golden Rule. As long as the utility of spending on himself exceeds that of spending on private goods for others or public goods for everyone, this is an easy enough guide. Doing unto others what he would like to be done unto him turns out to be nothing more onerous than providing himself with the basic necessities of life. Having provided these necessities, he is

led to contribute to the welfare of others. However, the Golden Rule, like everything else, seems to yield diminishing marginal utility. Spending something for the well-being of others diminishes the appetite for more of the same. W (the weight given to pure self-interest) increases monotonically with income. Although both our model and observation indicate that it is the rich who shell out more substantial fractions of income for good works, nevertheless it is the poor who are purest in heart.

This sort of thing is harmless only if you treat it as a manner of speaking (like a physicist speaking of a particle wanting to minimize its potential energy, or a biologist speaking of a tree wanting to maximize the sunshine collected by its leaves). But if you take it literally, and start to worry about specifying the total utility which yields these diminishing marginals, then the remarks of the text come into play.

E. Coerced and voluntary spending

1. It is easy to imagine situations in which G-Smith, as well as S-Smith, may be motivated in part by the effect of his behavior on others' opinion of him, because a person's reputation, credibility, and so on influence the effectiveness with which he is able to use G-resources.
2. That is, an individual's conventional "Lindahl price" (S-wtp^* here) is the price at which he could "buy" (pretending that he could do so) Q units of the public good at issue. S-wtp or S-$wtp+$, on the other hand is wtp for units in addition to Q. In the Lindahl context, Smith's wtp for the $Q+$1st unit will be affected by what he pays for the first Q units (or, put a little more precisely, by what Samuelson's demon divines he would pay, supposing he actually could make such a choice); but in the voluntary purchase context he already has the first Q units, and his ability to spend for further units is exactly the same, whether S-wtp^* at Q is zero or enormous.
3. For a public good, S-wtp will ordinarily be negligibly small compared with the cost, and FS-$wtp \approx G$-wtp. For a private consumer good the reverse will ordinarily hold, and FS-$wtp \approx S$-wtp, but not so for G-wtp^* and S-wtp^*.

F. Interaction of FS and Schelling's "inner struggle"

1. See especially the work of Amos Tversky and his collaborators, much of which bears on this set of issues.
2. For a discussion, see Robert Luce and Howard Raiffa, *Games and Decisions* (Wiley, 1957). A fairly large literature has developed on this theme.

G. Notes on further psychological issues

1. See, for example, his "Economics, Sociology, and the Best of All Possible Worlds," *Public Interest* (Summer 1968).

2. Harvey Liebenstein, *Beyond Economic Man* (Harvard University Press, 1970); Tibor Scitovsky, *The Joyless Economy* (Oxford University Press, 1976); Thomas Schelling, "The Intimate Context for Self-Command," *Public Interest* (Summer 1980); and the discussion in Chapter 5 and Appendix F.

Literature cited

Archibald, G. C., and Donaldson, Donald. "Notes on Economic Equality." *Journal of Public Economics* 12 (1979): 202–13.

Arrow, Kenneth J. *Social Choice and Individual Values.* Rev. ed. Wiley, 1963.

Barry, Brian. *Sociologists, Economists and Democracy.* 1970. Reprint. University of Chicago Press, 1978.

Becker, Gary. *The Economic Approach to Human Behavior.* University of Chicago Press, 1976. *p 26 ↙altruism*

Boorman, Scott, and Leavitt, Paul. *The Genetics of Altruism.* Academic Press, 1980.

Buchanan, James. *The Demand and Supply of Public Goods.* Rand McNally, 1968.

———. "Individual Choice in Voting and the Market." *Journal of Political Economy* (August 1954): 334–43.

———, Tollison, Robert, and Tullock, Gordon. *Towards a Theory of the Rent-Seeking Society.* Texax A&M University Press, 1980.

———, and Tullock, Gordon. *The Calculus of Consent.* University of Michigan Press, 1962.

Chamberlin, John. "Provision of Public Goods as a Function of Group Size." *APSR* (June 1974).

Clarke, E. *Demand Revelation and the Provision of Public Goods.* Ballinger, 1980.

Collard, David. *Altruism and the Economy: A Study in Non-Selfish Economics.* Oxford University Press, 1978.

Daly, John, and Giertz, Fred. "Welfare Economics and Welfare Reform." *American Economic Review* 62 (1972).

Dawkins, Richard. *The Selfish Gene.* Oxford University Press, 1976.

Downs, Anthony. *An Economic Theory of Democracy.* Harper & Row, 1957.

———. "An Economic Theory of Political Action in a Democracy." *Journal of Political Economy* (1957).

Eldredge, Roy, and Gould, Stephen J. "Punctuated Equilibria: An Alternative to Phyletic Gradualism." In *Models in Paleobiology,* edited by Thomas Schopf. Freeman, Cooper, 1972.

Fiorina, Morris, and Plott, Charles. "Committee Decision Under Majority Rule: An Experimental Study." *APSR* (June 1978).

Freud, Sigmund. *The Ego and the Id.* Translated by Joan Riviere. Norton, 1963.

Frohlick, Norman, and Oppenheimer, Joe. "I Get by with a Little Help from My Friends." *World Politics* (October 1970).

Gould, Stephen J. "Evolutionary Biology of Constraints." *Daedalus* (Spring 1980).

Groves, Theodore, and Ledyard, John. "Optimal Allocation of Public Goods: A Solution to the 'Free Rider' Problem." *Econometrica* (May 1977).

Hardin, Russell. *Collective Action.* Johns Hopkins University Press, 1982.

Harsanyi, John. "Cardinal Welfare, Individualistic Ethics, and Interpersonal Comparisons of Utility." *Journal of Political Economy* (August 1955): 309–21. *p 66 ↙altruism*

———. "Rational Choice Models of Political Behavior vs. Functional and Conformist Theories." *World Politics* (July 1969).

Hirschleifer, Jack. "Natural Economy vs. Political Economy." Department of Economics Working Paper, no. 114, University of California at Los Angeles, 1979.

——— "Shakespeare vs. Becker on Altruism: The Importance of Having the Last Word." *Journal of Economic Literature* (June 1977).

Hirschman, Albert. *Exit, Voice and Loyalty.* Harvard University Press, 1970.

Hochman, Harold, and Rogers, James. "Pareto Optimal Redistribution." *American Economic Review* (September 1969): 542–57.

Kuhn, Thomas. *The Structure of Scientific Revolutions.* 2d ed. University of Chicago Press, 1970.

Layzer, David. "Altruism and Natural Selection." *Journal of Social and Biological Structures* (1978).

Leibenstein, Harvey. *Beyond Economic Man.* Harvard University Press, 1970.

Luce, Robert D., and Raiffa, Howard. *Games and Decisions.* Wiley, 1957.

Lumsden, Charles, and E. O. Wilson. *Genes, Mind, and Culture.* Harvard University Press, 1982.

McGuire, Martin. "Group Size, Group Homogeneity, and the Aggregate Provision of a Pure Public Good Under Cournot Behavior." *Public Choice* (Summer 1974).

McKelvey, Richard, Ordeshook, Peter, and Winer, Mark. "The Competitive Solution for N-Person Games Without Transferable Utility, with an Application to Committee Games," *APSR* (June 1978).

Margolis, Howard. "A 'Demand-Revealing' Thought Experiment." *Public Choice* 37 (1982).

———. "Politics of Auto Emissions." *Public Interest* (Fall 1977).

———. "Probability of a Tie Vote." *Public Choice* (Winter 1977).

———. "Public Goods and Group Size." Unpublished paper. September 1974.

Marschak, Jacob. "Decision-Making: Economic Aspects." In *International Encyclopedia of the Social Sciences.* Free Press, 1968.

Masters, Roger. "The Value – and Limits – of Sociobiology." In *Sociobiology and Human Values,* edited by Eliot White. Lexington Books, 1981.

Maynard-Smith, John, "The Limitations of Evolutionary Theory," In *The Encyclopedia of Ignorance,* edited by R. Duncan and M. Weston-Smith. Pergamon, 1977.

———. *On Evolution.* Edinburgh University Press, 1973.

Mueller, Dennis. *Public Choice.* Cambridge, 1979.

Niskanen, William. *Bureaucracy and Representative Government.* Aldine-Atherton, 1971.

Olson, Mancur. "Economics, Sociology, and the Best of All Possible Worlds." *Public Interest* (Summer 1968).

———. *The Logic of Collective Action.* Harvard University Press, 1965.

Pareto, Vilfredo. "Mathematical Economics." In *Economic Theory: A Historical Anthology,* edited by J. Gerrity. Random House, 1965.

Quirk, J., and Saposnik, R., *Introduction to General Equilibrium and Welfare Economics.* McGraw-Hill, 1968, p. 16.

Rapoport, Anatol, and Chammah, Abraham. *Prisoner's Dilemma.* University of Michigan Press, 1965.

Riker, William, and Ordeshook, Peter. "A Theory of the Calculus of Voting." *APSR* (March 1968): 25–42.

Robbins, Lionel. *On the Nature and Significance of Economic Science.* 1935; reprint St. Martins, 1962.

Rothenberg, Jerome. *The Measurement of Social Welfare.* Prentice-Hall, 1961.

Salkever, Stephen. "Who Knows Whether It's Rational to Vote?" *Ethics* (1980).

Samuelson, Paul. "Pure Theory of Public Expenditure and Taxation." In *Collected Scientific Papers.* Vol. 3. MIT Press, 1972.

———— "Social Indifference Curves." In *Collected Scientific Papers.* Vol. 2. MIT Press, 1972.

Schelling, Thomas. "The Intimate Contest for Self-Command." *Public Interest* (Summer 1980).

————. *Micromotives and Macrobehavior.* Norton, 1978.

Schneider, Friedrich, and Pommerehns, Werner. "Free-Riding and Collective Action." *Quarterly Journal of Economics* (in press).

Scitovsky, Tibor. *The Joyless Economy.* Oxford University Press, 1976.

Sen, Amartya. *Collective Choice and Social Welfare.* Holden-Day, 1970.

————. "Rational Fools." *Philosophy and Public Affairs* (1977).

Smith, Vernon. "Experiments with a Decentralized Mechanism for Public Good Decisions." *American Economic Review* (September 1980).

Taylor, Michael. *Anarchy and Cooperation.* Wiley, 1976.

Tideman, T. Nicolaus, and Tullock, Gordon. "A New and Superior Process for Making Social Choices." *Journal of Political Economics* (December 1976): 1145–59.

Tullock, Gordon. *Toward a Mathematics of Politics.* University of Michigan Press, 1967.

Wicksteed, Phillip. *The Common Sense of Political Economy.* 1910; reprint Kelley, 1962.

Williams, George. *Sex and Evolution.* Princeton University Press, 1975.

Wilson, E. O., *Sociobiology.* Harvard University Press, 1975.

Wilson, J. Q., *Political Organizations.* Basic Books, 1973.

Index

academic work, 132
Allais paradox, 165
altruism: and Downs, 97; and social choice, 11; as a technical term, 15; *see also* egoistic altruism; goods vs. participation altruism; self-interest
anarchy, 130, 185n18
Arrow, K. J., 15, 16, 44, 66, 172n3

Barry, B., 7, 59, 172n3, 179n1
Becker, G., 66, 174n7, 177n9
Beer, S., 15, 48
bifurcated man, paradox of, 105
Boorman, S., 34
Brahe analogy, 43
Buchanan, J., 44, 96, 105, 172n2,3

Carter-Reagan debate, 94
Chamberlin, J., 171n1, 174n6
Chammah, A., 173n4
charity, 11-12, 122-5, 133-6
Clarke, E. C., 177n3, 178n16
coerced spending, 52, 124, 160-4
cognition, 43, 49, 51, 58, 165, 167, 168
cognitive dissonance, 8
Coleman, J., 1, 12, 121
Collard, D., 172n10
compatibility of G- and S-preferences, 46, 163, 180n11
conspicuous consumption, 59, 131
correspondence between FS and conventional model, 61, 76-8, 81, 120-2
criminal behavior, 130, 140
culture and individual preferences, 50-1, 125

Darwinian argument, x, 2, 4, 44, 111; and allocations "inside Smith," 52, 55; and coerced spending, 163-4; and dual utilities, 46; and economic analog of FS, 42-3; and goods vs. participation altruism, 26-30; and group-loyalties, 47-8, 129; and intuitive argument for FS, 36; and mathematical specification of FS, 30, 138, 139, 140, 142-3; and

sense of "fair share," 59-60; *see also* nonsubversiveness; selfish gene
Dawkins, R., 33, 174n3; 175n8, 11
demand-revealing: *see* DR
Downs, A., 13, 95, 172n3, 173n12, 181n1
DR: defined 62-4; interpretation under FS, 80-1; and Lindahl-Samuelson, 63, 73-7; practical aspects ignored, 177-8n10; thought experiment, 71-3; and *wtp* schedule, 178n10-14
dual significance of g and s; *see* FS
dual utilities: and economic analog to FS, 41-3; and formal FS specification, 140-1; and Freudian structure, 54; and G-Smith, S-Smith, 2; and rationality, 15-16; relation to Schelling's "inner struggle," 57-8; *see also* compatibility of G- and S-preferences; Harsanyi; U-function; tacit commitments.
duty, *see* psychic income

economic man; *see* self-interest
economics: contrasted to politics, 9-13; as a paradigm, 7-8, 61-2, 70-1, 73-4; and sociology, 7-8, 168
egoistic altruism, 98, 103, 173n2, 175n13
Eldredge, R., 34, 175n13
equilibrium: G-Nash and S-Lindahl, 80, 122, 157-8; *see also* extended Lindahl-Samuelson; FS; Lindahl-Samuelson
ESS (evolutionarily stable strategy), 27, 30, 139
experiments, *see* DR; self-interest
extended Lindahl-Samuelson equilibrium, 76-80, 122, 156-9
externalities, 9; *see also* public goods

fair share: intuitive argument for FS, ix, 36; role in formal model, 59-60
free-rider arguments, 6, 124, 127, 181n4; and anarchy, 185n18; and DR, 62-5; and FS, 121-2; G-analog